GREAT MOTHERS

BY

REV. HUGH FRANCIS BLUNT

For the Best
Wife and Mother
and Grandmother
Ever.
I love You, P!

Jeff

12-24-2006

Catholic Authors Press
Hartford, 2006

Great Wives and Mothers.
Copyright © 1927 Devin-Adair
New elements
copyright 2006 Catholic Authors Press

ISBN: 0-9776168-8-6

Library of Congress Control Number: 2006921474

Printed in the United States of America

Catholic Authors Press
www.CatholicAuthors.org

CLEAN literature and clean woman-hood are the keystones of civilization. This aphoristically defines the ideals of the Devin-Adair imprint.

TO

THE GREAT MOTHER OF US ALL

MARY

THE MOTHER OF GOD

PREFACE

The following popular biographies were prepared originally for various societies of women. It has been the experience of the author that it is difficult year after year to get fresh topics for addresses to sodalities. In offering these papers to the public he has in mind first of all his brother clergy, hoping that they will find herein some suggestions for a series of interesting talks. More than that, he desires that the life of each of these great wives and mothers be known to all. One of the greatest glories of the Church is her noble womanhood. And to-day especially, when the world in many different ways is seeking to turn our women from the pursuit of the Christian ideal in wifehood and motherhood, there is need surely of recalling the inspiriting stories of these women who sought first of all the kingdom of God.

HUGH FRANCIS BLUNT.

CONTENTS

		PAGE
MOTHERS AND MARTYRS		1
MATRONS OF THE EARLY CHURCH		25
ST. MONICA		44
THE QUEEN SAINTS		69
ST. ELIZABETH OF HUNGARY		98
ST. RITA		123
ROYAL LADIES		148
ISABELLA THE CATHOLIC		176
MARGARET ROPER		197
MARGARET CLITHEROW		224
ANNA MARIA TAIGI		250
ELIZABETH SETON		272
JERUSHA BARBER		294
MARY O'CONNELL		320
LADY GEORGIANA FULLERTON		341
MARGARET HAUGHERY		367
PAULINE CRAVEN		380
SOME LITERARY WIVES AND MOTHERS		396

GREAT WIVES AND MOTHERS

MOTHERS AND MARTYRS

(126–313)

FOR us that live in peace, with freedom to practise our religion, the story of days when men and women, and even little children, were persecuted and tortured, and suffered death for their faith, seems like the product of some wild imagination. Could men of flesh and blood like ourselves, to whom the very thought of murder is so repulsive, be so diabolical as to destroy the lives of their fellow-creatures merely because of the manner in which they worshiped God? Strange, that of all hatreds, religious hatred is the most unrelenting. And of what crimes against humanity and God has that hatred been the cause!

Christ Himself was a martyr for the truth. He went the way of the Cross. Most of His apostles went the same way, laying down their lives for the Gospel they preached. As Christ had foretold, the day came when the enemies of His religion thought that they did a service to God when they put to death His followers. So down through the ages love for Christ and His Church has exacted its toll of lives.

Even in days when all has seemed peaceful for the Church, suddenly the persecution has come, and men have had to choose between God and man, between truth and falsehood, between life and death. And it has been to the glory of the Church that countless numbers have died on the Cross rather than deny the Master, knowing that so to die was the sure way to eternal life.

The Church has grown from the beginning by martyrdom. The blood of the martyrs is the seed of Christians. Its first saints were those who had been drenched in their own life-blood. And it is not strange that in that multitude, which numbered the old men, like St. Polycarp, the little maidens, like St. Lucy, there were also the mothers of men, mothers with the tender babe at their breast, mothers that loved their little ones, yet allowed themselves to be torn from them for the love of God and the salvation of their soul; mothers, too, that even urged their children on to suffering and death, because they knew that the true glory of their children was not in worldly preferment, but in the way in which they served their Creator.

What an example for the mothers of to-day! How many a mother devotes herself through all manner of trial and suffering in order that her children may be healthy, may be educated, may have a good place in the world, yet neglects the thing that is of supreme

[2]

importance—the sanctification of the souls of these same children. We may wonder at the heroism of St. Rita as she prayed that God would take her two sons rather than have them commit the crime of murder, yet is not that the true spirit of the Christian mother, who knows that it is the soul that counts, and that it would be better for those children never to have been born than to be false to their God?

And so, as we hear the story of the heroic women, wives and mothers, who suffered in the persecutions that afflicted the early Church, it is not merely to marvel at the strength which God gave to their weakness, but to be inspired by their example, to know that the better part is to seek and do the will of God for ourselves and our families, no matter through what trial the way leads.

In the history of the Mother of the Machabees the Christian mother of the early Church had an example of loyalty to God in the midst of pain. King Antiochus IV of Syria had sought to paganize the Jews. He attempted to abolish the Jewish religion, and forbade, under pain of death, the observance of Jewish rites. Altars were set up, and the people were commanded to offer up sacrifice to the pagan gods. The majority of the Jews, however, remained faithful, and many of them laid down their lives rather than be unfaithful to their religion. This was 168 B. C.

Among those who suffered death were a mother and her seven sons. They all had been apprehended, and ordered to eat swine's flesh, which was contrary to the Jewish law. But they refused, even though they were scourged for their refusal; for as the eldest son said, "We are ready to die rather than to transgress the laws of God, received from our fathers." Then the angry King ordered that the frying-pans and brazen caldrons should be heated. He commanded then that the tongue of the oldest boy be cut out, and the skin of his head drawn off, and his hands and his feet cut off, while his mother and his brothers looked on, helpless, at the awful brutality. Still alive, he was thrown on the frying-pan to suffer long, agonizing torments.

But the brothers and the heart-broken mother did not weaken, but rather urged one another to be as brave as the dying one. The second oldest was then put through the same suffering, and the third and fourth, and so till the youngest of all was reached. All the while the mother had watched her noble, strong sons going to their death, but she bravely exhorted all of them to suffer for their religion, as the Bible says, "joining a man's heart to a woman's thought."

"I know not how you were formed in my womb," she said, "for I neither gave you breath, nor soul, nor life, neither did I frame the limbs of every one of you. But the Creator of the world that formed the nativity of man, and that found out the origin of all, He will restore to you again in His mercy both breath and life, as now you despise yourselves for the sake of His laws."

[4]

The King, angry at his inability to break down the courage of the six sons, sought to weaken the youngest lad by swearing to make him rich and happy and bring him to court if only he would give up his religion. But the boy was steadfast in his faith. Then he begged the mother to reason with her son and save his life. She promised to advise the boy, and then bending towards him, said:

"My son, have pity upon me that bore thee nine months in my womb, and gave thee suck three years, and nourished thee, and brought thee up unto this age. I beseech thee, my son, look upon heaven and earth and all that is in them, and consider that God made them out of nothing, and mankind also. So thou shalt not fear this tormentor, but being made a worthy partner with thy brethren, receive death, that in thy mercy I may receive thee again with thy brethren."

And so the last of the sons went to his death, and the mother, who a short time before had seven fine sons, was now childless. But she did not moan. She was happy that her sons had died for God. God had given them to her, and now she had given them back to Him. And God blessed her by making her endure the same sufferings. Last of all she was put to death, and so went to be united to her loved ones. It is a sad, yet a thrilling story, a glorious tribute to the heights to which mother-love may ascend.

With such heroism among the Jews, it is not surprising to find it also among Christian mothers. Every age and condition of life has its patrons among the martyrs of the early Church. It is in this way God would teach us that all may aspire to sanctity. He has given the blessed boon of martyrdom to those of every rank; He did not forget the mothers. Somehow it is hard to think of a mother being obliged to lay down her life. How much good, we say, she could do with her family, if she were allowed to remain with them. Yet we see women like Margaret Clitherow, in the persecutions of the Reformationtime, praying to God for martyrdom, even though it would take her from her small children. She had faith enough to believe that God could look after her children even better than she, their own mother. And through the persecutions of the early Church we note this same confident carelessness on the part of the suffering mothers to their children. It was God that counted, even more than their children. And what a glorious heritage it was to hand down to the motherless child, the knowledge that she who gave him birth was a martyr and a saint!

So we choose from the long line of martyrs those holy women who were wives and mothers, in order that their example of steadfastness in the faith, and of seeking the spiritual welfare of their children more than all else in the world, may be a source of strength to others in the married state.

From the time of the reign of the Emperor Hadrian, perhaps even from the time of Nero, a Christian was regarded as an outlaw. Christians had

suffered death in the time of Nero, and in that of
Domitian, too. But the earliest clear enactment
against the Christians is found in the law of Trajan
(98–117). He had sent Pliny to one of the provinces
of the empire to restore order there, and one of the
great difficulties met by Pliny was how to deal with
the Christians, whose "superstition" was fast menac-
ing the empire, one result being that, so many were
they, it was hard to sell the meat that had been sacrificed to the gods. For a long time Christians had been
considered by the Romans the same as Jews, and were
allowed the same privileges. When the difference became evident it meant persecution, for whereas the
Jews were freed of the obligation of sacrificing to the
Roman gods, since they had a national God of their
own, the Christians had no legal right to worship their
God, and hence when they refused to worship the
Roman gods they were regarded as atheists. But up
to Trajan's time there had been no special law of
proscription against them. Trajan answered Pliny
that no steps should be taken by the magistrates to
find out who were Christians, but if they were denounced, and admitted that they were Christians, they
were to be punished with death. The Christians
thereby became outlaws.

So during the reign of Hadrian (117–138) we find
the first Christian matron of whom we have record
among the martyrs. This was St. Sabina, who suffered death in the year 126. No doubt there had been
other noble defenders of the faith before her. Thus

we find St. Symphorosa, who, though not a martyr, was a true Christian heroine. She was a very wealthy woman, and lived on a great estate. Her husband and her brother had been tribunes, or colonels, in the Roman army, and both had been put to death for the faith. Symphorosa had them buried on her own farm, and gave herself to a life of sanctity. But Sabina was called to lay down her own life. She had been married to a man named Valentine, and was now a widow. She lived at Rome, and was converted to the faith by the example of her slave Serapia. Serapia met her death by being beaten with clubs, and in that same year, 126, Sabina also suffered martyrdom, and so was enrolled among the saints of the Church.

Towards the end of this same reign there is related to us the story of a martyrdom which is very similar to the history of the Machabees. It is the story of another Symphorosa and her seven sons. She was the widow of the tribune, Getulius, who had been martyred some time before. The story goes that when the Emperor Hadrian had completed his magnificent palace at Tibur and began to dedicate it by offering sacrifice to the gods, these same gods complained and said:

"The widow Symphorosa and her sons torment us daily by invoking their god. If she and her sons offer sacrifice, we promise to give you all that you ask for."

The Emperor immediately had the widow and her sons arrested, and sought to induce them to offer sacrifice to the gods. But they refused. Symphorosa had been brought to the Temple of Hercules and commanded to offer sacrifice. When she refused she was made to suffer many tortures, among others being hung up by the hair of the head, and at last was thrown into the river Anio with a heavy rock fastened to her neck. Her brother Eugenius buried her in the outskirts of the city. The following day the Emperor summoned her seven sons, and when they refused to offer sacrifice he ordered them to be tied to seven stakes which had been erected around the temple for that purpose. Every one of them suffered a different kind of martyrdom, and then the bodies of them all were thrown into a ditch.

During the reign of the Emperor Antoninus, a few years later (138–161), we find a similar story regarding St. Felicitas and her seven sons. She was a noble Christian widow, who was given over to a life of prayer and fasting and charity. By her great zeal for Christ she had converted many idolaters, so that the pagan priests hated her. They had her arrested and tried to make her and her sons offer sacrifice to the gods. But she refused.

"Unhappy woman," said the Prefect to her, "is it possible you should think death so desirable as not to permit even your children to live, but force me to destroy them by the most cruel torments?"

"My children," she answered, "will live eternally with Christ if they are faithful to Him; but must expect eternal death if they sacrifice to idols."

Again the Prefect exhorted her: "Take pity of

your children, Felicitas; they are in the bloom of youth, and may aspire to the greatest honors and preferments."

"Your pity is really impiety," she answered, "and the compassion to which you exhort me would make me the most cruel of mothers."

All the sons refused to offer sacrifice, and they were martyred in different ways. St. Gregory the Great delivered a discourse on her festival in which he said that she, "having seven children, was as much afraid of leaving them behind her on earth, as other mothers are of surviving theirs. She was more than a martyr; for seeing her seven children martyred before her eyes, she was in some sort a martyr in each of them." In these great women who urged their sons to die rather than be false to God we see mother-love in its most glorious light.

Under the proscription of Trajan the Church existed from the year 112 to the reign of Septimius Severus (193–211), during which time the Christians were ever in danger of being denounced for their religion and made to suffer as enemies of the state. With Septimius there was the aim to check the growth of the Church by stopping conversions, and so he added to the former law of Trajan a clause forbidding any one to become a convert to the Christians.

In the persecution of the early Church one can distinguish three different stages. At first the Christians were let alone. They were to be ignored as harmless fanatics, and were not to be molested unless they

were denounced as practising an illegal religion.   In
the second stage there is an advance.   It was thought
that they were growing too fast, that by their increasing numbers they were threatening to become a men-
ace to the state.   And so the authorities tried to make
the new sect die out by forbidding any new converts.
But at last it was realized that the Christians were become too strong, that too many conversions were being
made, and this led to the attempt to settle the question by annihilating all Christians.

One sees a similar policy in the Elizabethan persecutions.   The persecution of the Catholics became active
as soon as it was realized that it was vain to expect
that the Church would die out from lack of the per-
petuation of the priesthood, seeing that the missionary
priests were keeping the faith alive.

So this new law of Septimius Severus forbidding
a pagan to become a Christian produced many martyrs,
among them the noble woman Perpetua and her slave
Felicitas, both of whom are commemorated in the
Church on the same day.   Their story has always been
a popular one in the Church from that day to this.
It is as follows:

There were certain young catechumens, Revocatus,
Saturninus, and Secundulus, waiting their time to be
fully admitted into the faith.   They were arrested,
and with them Felicitas, who was a fellow-slave with
Revocatus.   Among the catechumens, too, was Vivia
Perpetua, a woman of fine family, well educated, and
married.   Her father and mother were living, also

two brothers, one of whom was a catechumen like herself. She was about twenty-two years of age, and had an infant son still at her breast. It is she herself that tells the story of her sufferings quite up to the end.

When she was arrested, her father, through the great love he had for her, sought to reclaim her to paganism. But as she would not be persuaded by him, he threw his arms about her, as if, said she, he would tear her eyes out. But she adds: "He only distressed me, and went away overcome by the devil's arguments. Then in a few days after I had been without my father, I gave thanks to the Lord; and his absence was a source of consolation to me." She and the other catechumens were then baptized. After a few days they were taken to the dungeon, and Perpetua was very much afraid, because she had never before felt such darkness. "O terrible day!" she writes. "O the fierce heat of the shock of the soldiery because of the crowds! I was unusually distressed by my anxiety for my infant. There were present Tertius and Pomponius, the blessed deacons who ministered unto us, and had arranged by means of a gratuity that we might be refreshed by being sent out for a few hours into a pleasant part of the prison. Then going out of the dungeon, all attended to their own wants. I suckled my child, which was now enfeebled with hunger. In my anxiety for it, I addressed my mother and comforted my brother, and commended to their care my son. I was languishing because I had seen them languishing on my account. Such solicitude I suffered for many days. I obtained leave for my infant to remain in the dungeon with me; and forthwith I grew strong, and was relieved from distress and anxiety about my infant; and the dungeon became to me as it were a palace, so that I preferred being there to being elsewhere."

Her brother urged her to ask for a vision in order that she might know whether she was to die or escape. And Perpetua tells us simply: "And I, who knew that I was privileged to converse with the Lord, whose kindness I had found to be so great, boldly promised him and said, 'To-morrow I will tell you.'"

She asked for the vision, and God heard her prayer. She saw a golden ladder of marvelous height, reaching up even to heaven, and very narrow so that persons could ascend it only one by one. On the sides of the ladder was fixed every kind of weapon, swords, lances, hooks, daggers. Under the ladder was a dragon of wonderful size, who lay in wait for those who ascended, and frightened them from the ascent. Secundulus, who had delivered himself over to the authorities after the others, was the first to ascend. When he got to the top of the ladder, he turned and said:

"Perpetua, I am waiting for you; but be careful that the dragon do not bite you."

And Perpetua answered: "In the name of the Lord Jesus Christ, he shall not hurt me."

She trod upon the dragon's head, and ascended the ladder. As she went up, she saw an immense garden, and in the midst of it a white-haired man, sitting in the dress of a shepherd, of large stature, milking sheep, and standing around were many thousand white-robed ones. He raised his head and said to Perpetua, "Thou art welcome, daughter." He called her, and from the cheese as he was milking gave her as it were a little cake, and Perpetua received it with folded hands. She ate it, and all who stood around said, "Amen." At the sound of the voices she awoke from her vision. She told the vision to her brother, and they both understood that it was to be martyrdom, and she says, "We ceased henceforth to have any hope in this world."

A few days afterwards the report went out that the prisoners were to have their trial. Perpetua's father came to her from the city, worn out with anxiety.

"Have pity, my daughter," he pleaded, "on my gray hairs. Have pity on your father, if I am worthy to be called your father by you. If with these hands I have brought you up to this flower of your age, if I have preferred you to all your brothers, do not deliver me up to the scorn of men. Have regard to your brothers, have regard to your mother and your aunt, and have regard to your son, who will not be able to live after you. Lay aside your courage, and do not bring us all to destruction; for none of us will speak in freedom if you should suffer anything."

Greatly her father loved her. He kissed her hands, and threw himself at her feet, and called her, not

Daughter, but Lady. Perpetua grieved over his **gray** hairs, sorrowful that he alone of all the family would not rejoice at her coming martyrdom. She comforted him, saying, "On that scaffold whatever God wills shall happen. For know that we are not placed in our own power, but in that of God." The father departed in sorrow.

One day, while the prisoners were at dinner, they were suddenly taken away to the town-hall to be heard. An immense crowd had congregated. The accused ones mounted the platform. All the others were examined, and confessed that they were Christians. "Then they came to me," says Perpetua, "and my father immediately appeared with my boy, and withdrew me from the step, and said in a supplicating tone, 'Have pity on your babe!' And Hilarianus, the Procurator, said, 'Spare the gray hairs of your father, spare the infancy of your boy, offer sacrifice for the well-being of the Emperors.' And I replied, 'I will not do so.' Hilarianus said, 'Are you a Christian?' and I replied, 'I am a Christian.' And as my father stood there to cast me down from the faith, he was ordered by Hilarianus to be thrown down, and was beaten with rods. And my father's misfortune grieved me as if I myself had been beaten, I so grieved for his wretched old age. The Procurator then delivered judgment on all of us, and condemned us to the wild beasts, and we went down cheerfully to the dungeon. Then, because my child had been used to receive suck from me and to stay with me in prison,

I sent Pomponius the deacon to my father to ask for the infant, but my father would not give it to him. And even as God willed it, the child no longer desired the breast lest I should be tormented by care for my babe and by the pains of my breasts at once."

One day she had a vision of her little brother, Dinocrates, who at the age of seven had died of cancer of the face. She saw him in his sufferings, and prayed God for him. Again she had a vision, and by it she knew that his soul was happy.

As the day of the exhibition and the games drew near, her father came to her again. He was worn out with suffering. He began to tear out his beard, and to throw himself on the ground, and to cast himself down on his face, and to reproach his years, and to utter such words as might move all creation, and Perpetua grieved for his unhappy old age. She had a vision in which it was shown to her what she would endure in the amphitheatre. She perceived that she was to fight not with beasts, but against the devil. "Still," she adds, "I knew that victory was awaiting me." Many visions they had to comfort them and strengthen them in the prison.

Meanwhile the slave Felicitas was in great grief. She was eight months with child, and as the day of martyrdom was nearing, she feared she would not be suffered to die, since pregnant women were not allowed to be publicly punished. The others, too, grieved that she was to be left behind. Hence they all prayed for her, and immediately after the prayer she gave birth to her little girl, who was adopted by a fellow-Christian.

In her pains one of the servants said to her, "You who are in such suffering now, what will you do when you are thrown to the beasts, which you despised when you refused to sacrifice?" And she replied: "Now it is I that suffer what I suffer; but then there will be another in me, who will suffer for me, because I also am about to suffer for Him."

On the day before the exhibition, as they enjoyed their last meal together, they were happy, talking of the joy of the coming martyrdom, and even laughing at the curiosity of the people that came to watch them. Many, seeing such a strange thing as men and women laughing at the approach of death, were converted to the faith.

The day at last arrived. The martyrs were led into the amphitheatre, joyous and of brilliant countenance. Perpetua came with a placid look, and "with step and gait as a matron of Christ, beloved of God, casting down the lustre of her eyes from the gaze of all"; and with her Felicitas, "rejoicing that she had safely brought forth so that she might fight with the wild beasts." The persecutors tried to make them put on pagan priestly garments, but they refused.

Perpetua sang psalms, while the men, Revocatus, Saturninus, and Secundulus, uttered threatenings against the gazing people about this martyrdom. "Thou judgest us," they said, as they passed the Procurator, "but God will judge Thee."

At this, the people, exasperated, demanded that they should be scourged as they passed along. The men were set on by a wild leopard, a bear, and a boar; the women by a wild cow, provided especially for that occasion, and contrary to the custom. They were stripped, and clothed with nets, and brought into the arena, while the populace shuddered at the sight of the delicate women, one of them but three days since a mother. They were then unbound.

Perpetua was first led in. She was tossed by the cow, and fell on her loins, and when she saw her tunic torn from her side she drew it over her as a veil, "rather mindful of her modesty than her suffering." Again she was called for, and bound up her disheveled hair. So she rose up; and when she saw Felicitas crushed, she approached and gave her her hand, and lifted her up. And both of them stood together; and the brutality of the populace being appeased, they were recalled to the Sanavivarian gate.

Perpetua seemed to have been in an ecstasy, for she did not believe what she had been through until she saw the injuries to her dress and body. Then she said to one of the catechumens and to her brother, "Stand fast in the faith, and love one another, all of you, and be not offended at my sufferings."

All the martyrs then gave one another the kiss of peace. The men and Felicitas were pierced with a sword. But, the story says, "Perpetua, that she might taste some pain, being pierced between the ribs, cried out loudly, and she herself placed the wavering right hand of the youthful gladiator to her throat." And so she died, the young mother, a brave and blessed martyr for the faith of Christ.

But still the persecutions did not destroy the Church. In spite of prohibitions, in spite of persecutions, men and women embraced the Cross. For a while the Church enjoyed peace, and then with the Emperor Decius (250–253) a new era of persecution began. He wished to restore the empire to the prestige it was losing, and he felt that the great obstacle was Christianity. So he issued an edict, prescribing that on a certain day all Christians of the empire should offer sacrifice to the gods. There was no more peace for the Christians. Now they were to be sought out by the magistrates, and to be persecuted if they would not apostatize. Christianity was to be annihilated. Sad to relate, many Christians fell away, and offered sacrifice, denying their faith for fear of persecution; others apostatized under torture, but there was a multitude ready to endure anything rather than offend their conscience. This persecution lasted eighteen months, and did incalculable harm. A few years' respite, and persecution broke out afresh. The Church was never safe, but always the Christian was ready to lay down his life.

Under the reign of Aurelian (270–275) we have another wife and mother as martyr. This was St. Martha, who was put to death in 270. She and her husband, St. Maris, belonged to the Persian nobility, and had come to live at Rome. They were zealous

Christians and sympathized with the persecuted faithful, and buried the bodies of the martyrs. This enraged the Emperor, and they were seized and condemned to tortures. When they did not flinch under the persecution, Maris and his sons, Audifax and Abachum, were beheaded and their bodies burnt. Martha was cast into a well. A Roman lady named Felicitas had the remains of them all buried in one of the Catacombs. The feast of all these martyrs is observed on the same day. What a glorious family! What a happy mother to know that her husband and children had gone before her into eternal happiness!

The last persecution against the Church was begun in the reign of the Emperor Diocletian (284–305). Christian assemblies were forbidden, churches and sacred books were ordered to be destroyed, and all Christians were commanded to abjure their religion at once. The penalties were death and degradation for the higher classes, reduction to slavery for freemen of the humbler sort, and for slaves incapacity to receive the gift of freedom. Later on a new edict ordered the imprisonment of ecclesiastics of all grades. A third edict imposed the death penalty for refusal to abjure, and granted freedom to those who would sacrifice, while a fourth enactment commanded everybody, without exception, to offer sacrifice. This was the last effort to destroy Christianity. It failed, but it gave the Church countless martyrs. Among them were many wives and mothers.

Of these was St. Julitta. She was very rich. One

of her neighbors, abetted by the new law, seized her property and denounced her as being a Christian. She was arrested and commanded to offer incense to the gods. But she refused.

"May my estates perish," she said, "or be disposed of to strangers; may I also lose my life; and may this body be cut in pieces, rather than that by the least impious word I should offend God that made me. If you take from me a little portion of the earth, I shall gain heaven for it."

They threw her on the fire, but she died immediately and the flames did not harm her body.

During these same days of persecution we find a striking story in that of Hilaria, the mother of St. Affra. Affra had led the life of a prostitute, but had been converted, as was Magdalen. She was put to death for the faith, and during the night her mother came and carried away the body to bury it. She also was seized and put to death. A happy mother to know that her daughter, who had gone the road of wickedness, had been reclaimed to God! Not all the suffering in the world could take away her joy.

So also St. Domnina and St. Theonilla. Domnina had been scourged to death, even though she had a little child. But her love for the child would not let her seek to save her life through the denial of her God. So she died bravely. On that same day died her friend, Theonilla. She was a widow, and was accused of being a Christian, in which accusation she gloried.

"Shave her head," ordered the brutal Proconsul, "that she may undergo greater confusion. Gird her about with thorns; extend her body, and tie it to four stakes; scourge her with thongs not only upon the back, but over all her body; lay live coals upon her belly, and so let her die!"

And so she endured all these torments and went to God.

There is also St. Lucy, a widow, of whose death no details have been handed down.

Another mother-martyr was St. Crispina. She was of high birth, was very rich, and the mother of several children. She was a refined, delicate lady, but a woman of great heroism. Her children wept piteously at the thought of her being taken from them, but their tears did not move her. She even gave thanks to God for choosing her for one of his blessed martyrs. She was brought before the Proconsul in Africa, where she lived, and ordered to sacrifice to the gods. She declared that she honored only one God. Her head was shaved at the command of the judge, and then she was exposed to the public to be mocked. But nothing moved her from her loyalty to Christ. And so she was beheaded.

In those days it was no strange thing for whole families to die together, as in the case of St. Martha and her family. United on earth, their desire was to be united in heaven.

In one of the persecutions at this time we find another husband and wife dying for the faith. These were St. Chrysanthus and St. Daria. According to the legend, Chrysanthus was the son of a nobleman, Polemius of Alexandria. He had come to Rome with his father and had been converted to Christianity. Every inducement was offered to make him apostatize. Daria was a beautiful and intelligent vestal virgin who sought to pervert him. But instead of being perverted by him, he succeeded in winning her over to the faith. Then they married, but made a vow of virginity. Many Romans and Roman ladies were converted by them, among these being the tribune Claudius, his wife, Hilaria, and their two sons, Maurus and Jason. All of this family except the mother suffered the death of martyrs. Chrysanthus and Daria were at last condemned, and were thrown into a sand-pit and there stoned to death.

Finally there was the woman whose name was considered worthy of special remembrance in the Canon of the Mass, St. Anastasia, the noble Roman matron who gave all she had to the Christians in prison, and was rewarded for her charity with the crown of martyrdom.

So ended the persecutions. Of the two hundred and forty-nine years from the persecution under Nero (64) to the year 313, when Constantine established lasting peace, the Christians suffered persecution for about one hundred and twenty-nine years, and enjoyed a certain degree of peace for one hundred and twenty years. Yet even in the times of peace they were always in danger. St. Justin tells us of one wife who was denounced by her husband, and put to death, because she had given up the evil life she used to lead in his society. St. Justin himself was converted largely by the example of the fortitude of those who suffered for the faith. No one was spared. Dionysius states that "men and women, young and old, maidens and mothers, soldiers and civilians, of every age and race, some by scourging and fire, others by the sword, have conquered in the struggle and won their crowns."

These were our ancestors in the faith. What heroines were these wives and mothers to suffer such martyrdom! What an example to the mothers of to-day! You wives and mothers are not called upon to lay down your life for your religion. But if these women may not serve you as examples of how to die for your faith, surely they are examples of how to live for it. They have shown that the true glory of motherhood is first of all to build up in the hearts of children the Kingdom of God. Blessed, surely, is the child who has a mother that first of all seeks the Kingdom of God and His justice!

MATRONS OF THE EARLY CHURCH

(90-592)

DURING the ages of faith there was nothing re-markable in the fact that women of royal birth lived a life that was patterned after the cloister. In times when kings and queens patronized the re-ligious houses, when the monastery was at the gate of the palace, it was not strange that the children who were educated by the religious received a training they never forgot. No wonder that many of them, seeing the peace, the charm of a life hidden with Christ in God, left the court and followed My Lady Poverty as their queen. And many there were who, while their duty kept them in the royal halls, made the life of regal splendor compatible with the simplicity of the Gospel.

We are apt to think that sanctity and nobility of birth do not go together. But sanctity is possible everywhere. The millionaire can be poor in spirit. How evident that is as we read the lives of many noble women! They had all that this world can give of wealth and glory, yet amid it all they preserved sim-plicity of soul. They did not presume on their worldly position, for they knew that the greatest empress might be the lowest in the Kingdom of God—yea, not even fit to enter that kingdom. There have been great queens who have become great saints. But besides these there have been other great women of noble family who, in spite of their dwelling in the houses of kings, living the busy life of the court, found time to do much for God. Some of them have been canonized; others have not. But all are worthy to be remembered inasmuch as they are shining examples of virtue.

We hear continually the plea to us to advance in virtue, to aspire even to holiness, yet so often our answer is, How expect us to be saints when we have so much to do, so little time for church and prayer, so little opportunity to do charity? The answer to that argument—which is no argument at all—is the life of every one of these noble women who might more justly have advanced that reason for a cold, indifferent life in the service of God. They were wives and mothers, with all that that means of labor and sacrifice, yet their earthly duties never stood in the way of their duty to God.

So has it been through all the ages of the Church. The Christian motherhood of the first century is the same as that of the twentieth. The same Gospel governs all our lives. The same Mother of God is the never-changing example of motherhood. The good St. Ann is still a pattern. So, too, St. Elizabeth, "just before God, walking in all the commandments and justifications of the Lord without blame" (St. Luke i, 6). With true motherhood, God is always first.

We see that in the life of a wife and mother of the very first years of the Church, Flavia Domitilla. She was of the highest station; she belonged even to the imperial family of Rome. Her grandfather was the Emperor Vespasian, and her mother's two brothers, Titus and Domitian, also wore the purple. She was married to a nephew of Vespasian, Titus Flavius Clemens, and they had two sons who were chosen by Domitian to be his successors. It was a great honor for the young mother to be able to look forward to the day when her children would be the Emperors of Rome, even though, as events turned out, they never attained to that honor.

But she had given them a greater honor even than the royal purple, inasmuch as she had made them Christians, and that, too, at a time when the new religion was a despised thing in cultured Rome. Both she and her husband had become Christians. He had been a consul under the Emperor, but he resigned the honor, perhaps because it interfered with the practice of his faith. After his resignation he was put to death on the most trivial charges, and may almost be considered a martyr for the faith.

Flavia was then banished from the empire because of her religion, and retired to the island of Pandataria. Her property at Rome was used by the Christians as a place of burial, and was known as the Cemetery of Domitilla. We know very little of the life of this woman, save these few facts. And yet they are enough to enable us to picture her as a great wife and mother, a woman who gave up all rather than deny her God, preferring banishment to a life of ease and luxury, even in the imperial household, when that life meant a denial of her faith. What was even the throne itself compared with the dignity of Christian matron?

A striking example to husbands and wives is the life of St. Melania and her husband, Pinianus. She was the second famous woman of that name, her grandmother Melania, though not a canonized saint, being worthy of mention in the history of the early Church. Melania the elder, as she is known, was very rich and belonged to a noble Spanish family. She had been left a widow at the age of twenty-three, with one son, Publicola. After she had placed him in the care of good tutors, she went to Palestine, where she built a monastery, and there lived a life of penance, wearing a coarse habit and sleeping on the floor. She led this kind of life for twenty-seven years. Meanwhile her son had married a woman named Albina, of which union a son and daughter were born. The daughter was the younger Melania, known now as St. Melania, born in Rome about 383.

We know very little of her childhood; in fact, she was scarcely more than a child when, at the age of thirteen, she was married to one of her relatives, Pinianus, who also belonged to a noble family. She lived with him as his wife for seven years and was the mother of two children. But the children died young, and then Melania got her husband's consent to live a life of chastity. He, too, was a man of great sanctity, for we find him taking part in all the efforts of his wife towards sanctity. When the elder Melania heard of this, she returned from Palestine after an absence of thirty-seven years, and was welcomed by all the nobility of Rome. She advised her granddaughter and husband to give their goods to the poor and retire to a life of solitude. They took the advice of one who herself had led such a holy life for so many years. Gradually they gave away their wealth, and at the time that the Visigoths invaded the country they left Rome and for two years lived at Messina in Sicily, where, in company with some of their former slaves, they led a monastic life.

In the year 410 the elder Melania returned to her monastery in Palestine and died there that same year at the age of sixty-eight. The young husband and wife, together with Melania's mother, Albina, and many of their relatives who had been converted by them, went to Africa, where they lived seven years, and where Melania came to know St. Augustine. Here she gave herself to a life of prayer, and founded a nunnery of which she became superior, and also a monastery which was presided over by her husband. Later on, in 417, she and her husband and her mother went to Palestine and lived in a hospice, where they became friends of St. Jerome. They had freed some eight thousand of their slaves, had given away or sold their property in Spain, and what money they now had was used in furthering works of religion. Melania traveled in Egypt, visiting the various monastic houses, and then retired to Jerusalem, where she lived twelve years in a hermitage near the Mount of Olives. She built a new series of monasteries, which she supported.

This was the way she used her wealth. In her own life there was absolute poverty. She lived on bread and water. One would never guess that she and Pinianus were of noble families, so humbly did they live. Their occupation was to copy good books, and Pinianus could also be seen tilling his little garden—he that at one time had thousands of slaves under him. After his death she built a cloister for men and a fine church, and then went to Constantinople, where she succeeded in converting her pagan uncle, ambassador at the court of Theodosius II. She also helped in the conflict of the Church against the heresy of Nestorius. She died in 439, at the age of fifty-seven.

St. Melania was an active woman, a builder, a founder of convents, a traveler; yet always was she animated with the love of God. She might have lived in luxury and worldly happiness, but in her contempt of these things she showed that the greatest happiness in life comes from the despising of all that keeps the soul from God. She, her mother, and her grandmother were a noble line of Christian women.

One finds at this same time another group of noble women, also grandmother, mother, and daughter, in the famous Proba family. Anicia Faltonia Proba belonged to one of the noblest families in Rome, a family unbounded in its wealth and influence, and in which the consulate seemed hereditary. The family had been Christian from the time of Constantine, and perhaps longer, even from the time of the persecutions. She was married to Sextus Petronius Probus, who was Prefect of Italy from 368 to 375. His riches were so abundant that some Persian noblemen who had come to Milan to see St. Ambrose continued on to Rome to witness the grandeur of Probus. Proba was a learned woman, a poet of no mean ability, besides belonging to the highest aristocracy. But religion was more to her than wealth and position. She succeeded in converting her husband to Christianity.

In the life of St. Melania we have seen that the Visigoths plundered Rome in 410. Proba and her house suffered. Her home had always been a centre of Christianity. Many of the holy virgins had taken refuge there, but all fell into the hands of the barbarians. At last they all obtained their liberty, and Faltonia, her daughter-in-law Juliana, and her granddaughter Demetrias, with a number of widows and virgins, went to Africa, then the centre of so much fervent faith. It was the time of the great St. Augustine, and Proba, seeking to sanctify her soul, wrote to him, asking for instructions as to how she should pray. We have his answer to her, in which he wrote that she must despise the world and its pleasures, and strive for the true happiness of divine grace and charity, which is to be the object of all our prayers; to pray without ceasing; to have regular hours for devotions; and to raise her heart to God in all her actions. It is a practical, common-sense letter, such as we would expect to find from the practical St. Augustine to a practical woman like Proba.

The exiles lived some time at Carthage and later on they returned to Rome. The granddaughter, Demetrias, gave all her great wealth to the Church and entered a life of religion. We know little, after all, about Proba except the poetry she wrote on sacred subjects, but we may well believe that she followed the advice of St. Augustine and devoted herself to a life of prayer. And her influence was felt in the other members of her family. She was a great wife and mother.

Those were days in which we find more than one saint in a family. Particularly evident is this in the life of St. Macrina, who may be called the founder of a long line of saints. She was born at Neocæsarea in Pontus in the middle of the third century. St. Gregory Thaumaturgus was the first bishop of her native town, and in her childhood she knew him, and had received from him, no doubt, her first inclination to a holy life through his example. He was a great man and had converted almost all of Neocæsarea to Christianity.

Macrina had to suffer for the faith. At the time of the persecution under Diocletian she had to flee, together with her husband, from her native town and endure many privations for professing Christianity.

It was the last storm that broke over the Church, and she may be regarded as a confessor for the faith. She was the mother of St. Basil the elder.

Basil was a professor of rhetoric, and wealthy. He married Emmelia, afterwards St. Emmelia, who was also of fine family. On both sides there were high functionaries, both civil and military. Both had reason to be loyal to the faith. Emmelia's father was a martyr, and Basil's parents had lived seven years in the woods and mountains during the persecution; and the faith they had received in so full a measure they handed down to their children. The family has well been called a "nursery of bishops and saints." They had ten children, of whom three were bishops, and of whom four became saints—St. Basil, St. Gregory of Nyssa, St. Peter, and St. Macrina. The younger St. Macrina was the eldest, and she exerted a wonderful influence on the other members of the family. She was an intellectual woman, and besides had been well trained by her mother and her grandmother. When she was twelve years of age a marriage had been arranged by her father with a young lawyer of fine family. But he died suddenly, and she resolved to devote herself to a life of virginity.

On the death of the father, Basil took Macrina and his mother to the family estate in Pontus, where they led a life of retirement, penance, and prayer, consecrating themselves to God. Macrina induced her mother to help her in founding two monasteries on the estate, one for men and one for women. Here were gathered to them other saints, and St. Emmelia presided over the community till her death, when Macrina took her place. What a blessed mother was Emmelia to raise up four children to be canonized saints! A mother of ten children—how much that means of hard work; how easily such a mother could excuse herself for a life of coldness in the service of God; yet Emmelia, with all her cares, found time to develop in the hearts of her children the love, above all else, for the things of the soul. She surely deserves to be remembered as a great wife and mother.

Another remarkable woman of the early ages was St. Fabiola. She belonged to the patrician Roman family of the Fabia. She had made an unfortunate marriage, for her husband led such a wicked life that she became disgusted with him and got a divorce. So little inclination did she have then towards sanctity, that we soon find her marrying another man even while her first husband was living. It was, of course, a serious sin on her part; but soon grace touched her heart.

On the day before Easter, following the death of the second husband, she dressed herself in penitential garments and appeared before the gates of the Lateran basilica, and there did public penance for her offence. Considering the high social position of Fabiola, this act of penance made a great impression on the Christians of Rome. The Pope received her back into the Church. To show the sincerity of her repentance, she renounced the world and devoted her immense wealth to the needs of the sick and the poor. She built a fine hospital in Rome and tended the patients herself, even when their diseases were most repulsive. Besides that, she gave a great deal to the churches and religious houses all over Italy. In 395 she went to Bethlehem, and lived there in the hospice directed by Paula, the friend of St. Jerome. She studied the Scriptures under him and interested herself in works of piety and charity.

Fabiola returned to Rome some time afterwards and kept up a correspondence with him. At Rome she joined with the former senator, Pammachius, in erecting at Porto a large hospital for the pilgrims who used to come to the Eternal City even in those days. In a word, she was a woman whose whole life was filled with charity, and when she died (400) there was universal sorrow, and her great funeral showed the love and veneration in which she was held by the people of the city where once she had given scandal.

St. Jerome, while at Rome, was universally loved and esteemed on account of his piety and learning. Many among the chief nobility, clergy, and monks came to him for instruction. Besides these, there were many devout women who looked to him for advice in regard to the duties of their state in life. Among them we find such women as St. Marcella, her sister Asella, and their mother Albina, also Melania the elder, Marcellina, Felicitas, Lea, Fabiola, Laeta, Paula, her daughters, and many others.

St. Marcella was styled by St. Jerome as "the glory

of the Roman ladies." Her husband had died seven months after their marriage. Cerealis, the ex-consul, had sought her hand then, but she refused him and then retired to a country-house near Rome. She had heard of the life that St. Anthony was then living in the desert, and she decided to embrace the monastic life. She was a charitable woman, and directed a great many of the Roman ladies in the higher life. being looked up to by them on account of her own holy life. So also St. Lea, also a wealthy Roman lady, who gave up her social position to lead a life of mortification, often spending whole nights in prayer.

But the most illustrious of these women was St. Paula. She was born in 347, and was the leader of all the Roman ladies of her time, because of her riches, her noble blood, and her fine intellect. At the age of thirty-two she lost her husband. Her heart was broken, but her friend St. Marcella encouraged her to devote the rest of her life to God. At once she began to lead a life of penance, sleeping on the ground, mortifying herself in other ways, and giving all her property to the poor. When St. Jerome came to Rome she induced him to accept a lodging in her house, so that she and her family might consult him as their spiritual director. At the request of Marcella, St. Jerome used to give readings in the Scriptures to a group of patrician women. Paula studied hard. St. Jerome tells us that Marcella and Paula and her two daughters, Blesilla and Eustochium, spoke, wrote and recited the Psalter in Hebrew as perfectly as in Greek

and Latin.   They all sought Christian perfection.
After three years of residence in Rome, St. Jerome
returned to the East.

But, learned as she was, Paula did not neglect her
home.   She married her daughter Pauline to the senator Pammachius.   Her daughter Blesilla had also
married, but her husband died soon after and she
wished to enter religion.   But she died before she was
able to accomplish her purpose.   Another daughter,
Rufina, died a couple of years later.   And there was
still another daughter, Eustochium, who later became
her mother's companion in the East.

After the death of Blesilla and the departure of St.
Jerome, Paula also determined to go to the East where
she longed to lead the monastic life.   So with Eustochium she made a pilgrimage to the holy places, and
finally came to settle at Bethlehem.

It was not an easy task.   It broke her heart to leave
her other children.   When she was sailing her little
son came to the shore and pleaded with her not to
go.   But the call of God was even stronger than the
call of her children.   In Bethlehem she helped in the
founding of two monasteries, one for men and one
for women, and besides that work, she and her daughter helped St. Jerome in his exegetical studies.

It was a holy life, yet not without its trials.   One
of these trials was her need of money, since she had
ruined herself by her generosity.   In the midst of
these cares she died in 404, at the age of fifty-six.
After her death, her granddaughter, Paula the

younger, the daughter of her son Toxotius, came to Bethlehem. It was she that had the honor of closing the eyes of St. Jerome in 420.

Just as Appia, the wife of Philemon, must have been a consolation to St. Paul, who called her his "sister," so were these noble women to the early bishops of the Church, helping them in their works of charity, building churches, monasteries, and hospitals, content to be the humble servants of the servants of God.

So do we find it in the case of St. Olympias (360–408), a disciple of the great St. John Chrysostom. She has been called the glory of the widows in the Eastern Church. She came from an illustrious family of Constantinople, her father being a Count of the Empire. Her parents died when she was very young, leaving her an immense fortune, and she was brought up by a great woman, Theodosia, sister of St. Amphilochius. She married Nebridius, treasurer for the Emperor Theodosius. St. Gregory Nazianzen was invited to the wedding, but he wrote a letter excusing his absence, and also wrote a poem in honor of the occasion, both being still in existence.

But the happiness of the marriage did not last long. Nebridius died twenty days after the wedding. The Emperor tried to induce her to marry a relative of his, but she refused, and then the Emperor took her great fortune to put in trust until she should be thirty. She thanked him, and asked him to give it to the Church and to the poor. He was so struck by her life that he gave her back her estate. But she received it only to give it to religion and to charity. She had herself consecrated a deaconess, and built with her own money the chief church of Constantinople, and besides that a convent into which she, with some of her relatives and a great number of young ladies, withdrew to lead the religious life. When St. John Chrysostom became Bishop of Constantinople in 398, he acted as her spiritual guide and advised her as to the distribution of her property. She always had the greatest confidence in him, and put at his disposal great sums of money for the use of the Church and for charity. Everywhere her charity extended. Then, when Chrysostom was driven into exile, she remained faithful to him, refusing to have anything to do with his successor, who had been unlawfully appointed. She gave herself up to a life of poverty, penance, and prayer. Her dress was mean, her furniture poor, and yet she was a woman of vast wealth. More than that, she suffered from sickness, and was even slandered and persecuted. Concerning these sufferings St. Chrysostom wrote to her:

"As you are well acquainted with the advantages and merit of sufferings, you have reason to rejoice, inasmuch as by having lived constantly in tribulation you have walked in the road of crowns and laurels. All manner of corporal distempers have been your portion, often more cruel and harder to be endured than ten thousand deaths; nor have you ever been free from sickness. You have been perpetually overwhelmed with slanders, insults, and injuries. Never have you been free from some new tribulation; torrents of tears have always been familiar to you. Among all these, one single affliction is enough to fill your soul with spiritual riches."

Her virtue was the admiration of the whole Church. Great saints corresponded with her. After Chrysostom's banishment, she, too, was persecuted. Her goods were sold at auction, she was dragged before tribunals, her clothes torn and herself insulted, and the community of nuns which she had governed dispersed. In a word, she endured a living martyrdom.

St. Olympias died in exile, and after her death was venerated as a saint. She was, indeed, a great woman. The world held out many attractions to one of her wealth and position, but she preferred to put all aside, or rather to use it all, in order to extend the glory of God.

In the lives of the women who are noted in the history of the Church one finds many a romance. But none is stranger than that of the poor little girl who became an empress. It is similar to the romance of the Empress Helena, who from being the humble keeper of an inn became the mother of the great Constantine and the first woman of the world. The poor little girl mentioned above was Eudocia. Her original name was Athenais, and she was the daughter of Leontius, a pagan, who taught rhetoric at Athens. When he was dying he left nearly all his property to his two sons. To his daughter Athenais he left only a hundred pieces of gold, saying that "her luck was greater than that of all women." Athenais, however, was not content with that kind of inheritance, and so she went to Constantinople to contest the will. She was very beautiful. In Constantinople she was seen by Pulcheria, the elder sister of Theodosius II. Theodosius was still under age, and Pulcheria was ruling as regent. He was twenty years of age and wished to be married. As soon as he saw Athenais it was a case of love at first sight, and Pulcheria, too, had the greatest admiration for the girl. So she was instructed in the Christian faith, as she was a pagan; was baptized by the Patriarch Atticus; and took the new name of Eudocia. In 421 she was married to Theodosius. Pulcheria was still devoted to her, and instructed her in her duties as empress. Eudocia had one daughter, Eudoxia by name, who later on married the Emperor of the West, Valentinian III.

But at length there was a falling out between Pulcheria and the new Empress. Pulcheria was jealous of her whom she had virtually made. It was the beginning of trouble. Eudocia made a pilgrimage to Jerusalem, and on the way stopped at Antioch, where she made a speech that so delighted the citizens that they erected a golden statue in her honor. From this first pilgrimage she brought back St. Peter's chains, and sent half of them to her daughter in the West, who gave the relic to the Pope. Twenty years after her marriage she suffered a terrible trial, being unjustly suspected of infidelity with one of the officers of the court. He was murdered and Eudocia was banished. She went back to Jerusalem and remained there till her death, nearly twenty years after.

Eudocia fell away from the faith into heresy for a time, but was finally brought back through the efforts of Pope St. Leo I, who wrote to her. Her husband and Pulcheria died, and Eudocia was forgotten by the great world in which she had once been a leader. But she did not mind that. She spent her last years in the holy places of Jerusalem, devoting herself to piety and charity and to the writing of religious poetry. She built the Church of St. Stephen, and there she was buried after having for some years lived the life of a mystic.

The next great woman among the matrons of the early Church was St. Galla, who lived in the sixth century. Her father had been a learned and virtuous patrician of Rome and had been unjustly put to death. She was made a widow before the end of the first year of her married life, and then, refusing to marry again, she gave up the world and chose for her dwelling a little cell near the tomb of the apostles, where she prayed and did charity. There is a tradition that the Blessed Virgin appeared to her. For two years she suffered from cancer of the breast and led a life of extreme suffering by which she sanctified her soul.

The last woman of this period is St. Silvia, the mother of Pope St. Gregory the Great. We know very little about her. But she belonged to a distinguished family, as did her husband, and they had two sons, to whom she gave an excellent education. When her husband died she left the world and devoted herself entirely to religion. But little as we do know of her, she deserves mention as having raised up a son who was a great Pope and a great Saint; and yet a greater honor even than that is hers in that she obtained the crown of personal sanctity.

They were a noble line of women. They had all the cares of the world; they had wealth and family position, yet counted all but little in comparison with the service they gave to God. Truly the matrons of to-day may well look to them as the models of what constitutes true womanhood.

ST. MONICA

(333–387)

"THE child of such prayers will never be lost." In
these words is summed up the life-story of St.
Monica. When she came, a broken-hearted mother,
almost despairing of her son Augustine, who was careless of her tears as he continued his life of iniquity,
and begged a certain bishop to take pity on her desolation and pray for him for whom her own prayers
seemed powerless, her heart received the consolation
of what was in reality a prophecy of the power of
mother-love to conquer even the plots of hell. The
words, too, sum up the story of all true mother-love,
of the mother-love that pursues relentlessly its children, that looks not merely for their worldly prosperity and fame—who so prosperous and famous as the
young Augustine when his mother wept over him and
considered him the most unfortunate of beings?—but
knows that all these things are valueless so long as
the soul is an enemy of God and in danger of eternal
suffering. So, through all the history of Christianity
since then, Monica ever shines forth as the great
patroness of grieving mothers, a consolation, an in-
centive to them to continue their prayers for erring

[44]

loved ones even when all seems hopeless. There would be more Augustines in heaven if there were more Monicas. Augustine became a saint, even through the vilest degradation, because his mother was a saint.

We know but little of the early days of Monica. She was born at Tagaste, in the northern part of Africa, in the year 333. Those were the early days of the Church, which had not been long out of the Catacombs, out of the furnace of persecution. We know nothing of her parents, only that they were Christians, pious, and careful to bring up their children religiously. The family was, no doubt, fairly well to do and kept servants. It was to an old servant in this Christian home that Monica attributed her good training in mortification. The old servant had long been in the family. Augustine tells us in his *Confessions* that she had been servant to his grandfather, and had carried himself when he was a child. So long had she been in the family, a very part of it, that Monica's parents had the utmost confidence in her, and respected her for her age and her excellent character. To her was confided the care of the daughters, and well did she perform the task. She did not pamper her charges. She felt that she had the care of their souls as well as their bodies, and Monica told Augustine how she trained them even in their young days to mortification. She never would let them take a drink of water except at their meals.

We can fancy that good old soul as she gave her reason to the little girls, parched with thirst. "You

drink water now," she said, "because you have not
wine in your power; but when you are married and
are made mistresses of cellars and cupboards, you will
scorn water, but the custom of drinking will last."
It is but a sample of the restraint the old servant exercised. How little she knew that in her wise simplicity
she was laying in the little Monica's heart the foundations of sanctity!

Yet, as Monica herself told the story, the little girl
did not always follow the advice of the old governess.
When she was sent by her parents to draw wine out
of the hogshead, she used to sip a little of it, until
gradually in the exuberance of youth she got so that
she could drink off "her little cup, brimful almost, of
wine." She was but a little girl at the time; and one
day when she had a dispute with one of the servants,
the latter taunted her with what she had done, and
called her a wine-bibber. It was enough for Monica;
she saw her fault and never again committed it. St.
Augustine gives us only a glimpse of these childhood
days of his mother. But so human is that glimpse
that one wishes he had given more details of the life
in what he calls "a Christian home."

The society of northern Africa in those days was a
peculiar mixture. The Church was growing strong,
but there were still many remnants of idolatry. Christians lived side by side with pagans, did business with
them, and mingled with them socially. There was
even intermarriage, and so it is not surprising to find
that when Monica reached marriageable age she was

betrothed to a pagan. His name was Patricius. Evidently he was a man of good family, and in the eyes of the world a man of honor. But the young wife was not overhappy with him. Being a pagan, without religion, he had little sense of morality. He was, indeed, no better than his times, and Monica knew that he was often unfaithful to her. Yet she never complained, never reproached him for his infidelity, even though the knowledge of it must have been a bitterness to the young wife that so loved him. She simply prayed for him, and begged God to make him a Christian, knowing that when he became a Christian he would also become chaste.

But besides being unfaithful, Patricius was also a man of high temper—"fervid as in his affections, so in anger," says Augustine. But there never was any cause for him to quarrel with Monica. "She had learned," says Augustine, "not to resist an angry husband—not in deed only, but not even in word." When he would flare up about something, she would keep her temper, and it was only when he was cool again that she would answer him and explain. Even the neighbors remarked that while their husbands, who were so much more mild-tempered than Patricius, beat them, Monica was never beaten, and never had any domestic difference with her husband, even for a day. They asked Monica how she so managed affairs, and she told them that she kept a civil tongue in her head, and did not argue with her husband; and she advised them to do the same. "Those wives who observed it," says

Augustine, "found the good and returned thanks; those who observed it not, found no relief and suffered."

In a word, Monica regarded her husband as her lord and master, and when other women complained of the infidelities of their husbands, she would answer them, half joke, whole earnest, that from the time they were married they should consider themselves servants, and so remembering their condition, should not set themselves up against their lords. Even in those days Monica, in patiently bearing the disgrace which her husband by his loose life heaped upon her, and in suffering his anger, showed that she was of that strong womanhood of which saints are made. Even if Augustine had never lived, Monica would still be worthy of perpetual remembrance as an example of the ideal wife, calm and prayerful in the midst of difficulties that tried her soul.

Besides the trials she had to endure from her husband, she also suffered at the hands of his mother. Through the ill-will of the servants, who perhaps sought to gain favor with the older woman by carrying stories to her, Monica was disliked by her mother-in-law. But in this, too, even while she knew that she was treated unjustly, she never complained, but was ever meek and respectful to the woman who showed so great a dislike for her.

Monica's gentle disposition finally won over the heart of her mother-in-law. The old lady found that the servants were mischief-makers, and immediately she went to her son and told him all, asking him to punish the meddlers. Patricius, with his usual anger, soon set matters right by using the whip on the servants, and his mother clinched the matter by telling them that they would get the same treatment the next time they sought to please her by telling stories about Monica. After that the two women were all kindness and sweetness to each other.

Monica must have been a woman of wonderfully gentle disposition. Not only was she a peacemaker at home, but also among her neighbors. She had the great gift—as her son calls it—of never carrying stories. Whenever she heard one neighbor say bitter things about another, she did not hurry off to bring the news and so increase the enmity, but she hid the disagreeable things and repeated only what would help to a reconciliation.

It is these little touches that make the life of St. Monica so interesting, and at the same time show her genuine holiness. It was not that she was a cold individual. We know how she must have felt when she knew that her husband was unfaithful. In her heart she must have mourned over it. Yet she did not give him up. She set out to win him back by her gentleness, by her love, and above all by her prayer. It was a long struggle, and many a woman would have given it up as hopeless. But not so Monica. Year after year she continued her life of patience, and it was only towards the end of his life that her husband was finally won back. She had prayed for his conversion

from paganism, and at last he expressed the wish to
become a Christian. He was baptized, and from that
time to his death, which took place within a year, he
gave up the sins which had disgraced his life and was
a model Christian. Monica had won, and one can
imagine that even the death of her beloved husband
lost some of its sting as she realized that she had
brought him back to God. If Patricius saved his soul,
who can doubt that it was through the prayers of his
good wife? What an example to many wives who
complain and cry about the defection of their husbands, yet never seek to win them back by prayer and
by the holiness of their own lives!

For Monica was above all a practical Christian.
Kind in word, she was also kind in deed. Like all
saints, she had a special affection for the poor, and
always sought opportunities to come to their aid.
Every morning she assisted at Mass, and made other
visits to the church and to the tombs of the martyrs
who had died for the faith but a few years before. In
a word, she lived chiefly for God, and, living for God,
imitating the examples of the saints, it is no wonder
that her prayers had such power in the conversion of
her husband, and later on in that which has made her
the model for grieving mothers—the conversion of
her son Augustine.

The chief interest of Monica's life is in her relation-
ship with the great St. Augustine. When one thinks
of what he accomplished for the Church, of his great
sanctity, and then contrasts that with what he was, a

very cesspool of iniquity, one realizes a little the work which his mother accomplished in making Augustine the saint out of Augustine the sinner.

If Augustine went wrong, it was not from lack of care on the part of his mother to bring him up right. One who was so particular about her own life could not but be so in regard to her children. Her whole desire was to serve God, and, intelligent woman that she was, she knew that she could not serve God well unless she looked after the spiritual interests of her children, for whose souls she was responsible to God.

But the curse in Monica's home, after all, was her marriage to a man that had no religion. Even though he was in time converted, his bad example, his irreligion, his immorality, no doubt had their influence upon Augustine. Like father, like son.

Augustine was sixteen, almost a man, when his father became a Christian. If Augustine himself had been a Christian, he would have had the strength to keep his soul clean. But he was not. Monica herself wished to have him baptized in his infancy, but her husband opposed it. Once, when the boy was ill, he granted the permission, but as soon as he recovered the permission was withdrawn, and so the baptism was again deferred. In those days Patricius did not know any better. Perhaps he fancied that Augustine would advance more rapidly in the world if he remained a pagan. For it is evident that the father had great ambitions for his son. He wanted him to be a learned man, because it was an age in which learning was

[51]

highly regarded. Monica, too, wanted to see the boy excel in learning, though on her part she desired this chiefly in order that he might one day use his talents for the glory of God. In those days, as she sought to instil piety into him, no doubt she often had the desire to see him one day consecrated to the priesthood. She little knew the thorny road that was to lead him to the altar.

Monica began well with Augustine. She was a thoroughly Christian mother. She saw that he received a good Christian education, and had him enrolled among the catechumens. As we have said, it was not her fault that he was not baptized. Any one who knows the character of Monica knows that she must have saturated the soul of her boy with religion. As Augustine himself says in his *Confessions*, "From my tenderest infancy, I had in a manner sucked with my mother's milk that name of my Saviour, Thy Son; I kept it in the recesses of my heart; and all that presented itself to me without that Divine Name, though it might be elegant, well written, and even replete with truth, did not altogether carry me away." Not altogether; but very far—so far that only the continual tears and prayers of a saintly mother could bring him back.

Augustine paid the price for deferring his baptism, which he was eager enough to receive when he was ill, but which he disregarded in the fullness of his strength. It was a deplorable custom of the times, that of deferring baptism for fear of falling into sin after it. And the youth, deprived of this grace, went the way of his father.

Patricius was proud of his son's great talent. But the opportunities of Tagaste, where they lived, were limited, and so he longed to have him go to the great city of Carthage in order to become a lawyer. But Patricius, while comfortable, was not rich. He did not have the money at hand necessary to educate Augustine at Carthage, and while he was busy getting it together the boy spent his sixteenth year at home with nothing to do. As Augustine said, "Who did not extol my father, for that beyond the ability of his means he would furnish his son with all necessaries for a journey for his studies' sake? For many far abler citizens did no such thing for their children. But yet this same father had no concern how I grew towards Thee, or how chaste I were; so that I were but copious in speech, however barren I were to Thy culture, O God, who art the only true and good Lord of Thy field, my heart."

So through this idleness, and in spite of the warnings of his good mother, he fell into impurity. He even boasted of it when his companions bragged of their iniquity, and he made himself out even worse than he was so that he might be considered their superior in vice. He tells us that he used to steal just for the pleasure of stealing and because it was wrong. He knew how wicked he was; perhaps the sight of his holy mother reproached him for doing things which he would blush to have her know. He even prayed to be delivered from the temptations, but, as he tells us himself, without a sincere wish to be heard.

So we find him ready to go to Carthage to begin his studies, a youth already corrupt. But it was only the beginning of his wickedness. At home there was some little restraint in the presence of his mother; at Carthage, away from home, there was none.

There was a great deal of wickedness in Carthage. It was a city half pagan, and consequently a licentious city. The theatres were bad, and the students with whom Augustine mingled were for the greater part without any moral restraint. They made the young Augustine as wicked as themselves. He was by his talent the leader of the school, and he wanted to be leader in everything else—even vice. He formed an immoral liaison with a woman in Carthage, who bore him a son. One can imagine the grief of Monica, who had done so much and prayed so hard for her son, now to learn of his guilt. But it was she alone that wept. She bore her grief in solitude. Her husband had died the year before, and had died in the faith. Her loneliness now made it all the harder for her to know that this son, to whom she and her husband had looked to be their consolation, was now but a youth for whom she had to blush. It was all the worse because Augustine was not ashamed. He had no notion of breaking off the sinful life; he continued it for fifteen years—fifteen years of sorrow for the mother, who prayed all that time that he might not die in his sins.

But Monica was obliged to see her son fall lower still. Long ago he had lost his virtue—lost it even as a boy. Now he lost whatever faith he had.

Augustine everywhere received applause for his remarkable talent—so much so that he grew conceited in his learning. The faith which he had learned from his mother now came to be questioned. His mind felt superior to it. He was an easy victim, therefore, for the chief heretics of the day, the Manicheans, with their promise of a free philosophy unbridled by faith. It was an easy doctrine, as it endeavored to remove moral responsibility since it denied liberty. It was something to justify Augustine's wicked life, and he grasped at it. He went at the new religion as he went at everything else, with great earnestness. He read all its books and adopted all its opinions, becoming a Manichean through and through, and even was apparently so sincere in it that he made converts to it.

Sometime after this loss of faith he returned to his native city of Tagaste to teach rhetoric there. He was brazen in his heresy. His talents, his manner, captivated his pupils, and some of them followed him into the new religion.

Monica's heart was broken. To think that a child of hers could turn his back on the faith which she regarded as her dearest possession! It was worse than death. And in her unflinching loyalty to the faith she beheld her son as an enemy of the Church, a heretic, and therefore as one dead. He was, indeed, spiritually dead—dead to God, hence dead to her. She loved him as a mother must love her children, but she would not allow sentiment to interfere with what she considered her duty as a Christian and as a mother; for it was, no doubt, the desire to bring Augustine to his senses that made Monica turn her back on him. She put him out of the house, and would not even let him eat at the same table with her. It must have torn her heart to do this, but the thing that counted most for her was the welfare of his soul. As Augustine writes: "And Thou sentest Thy hand from above, and drewest my soul out of that profound darkness, my mother, Thy faithful one, weeping to Thee for me, more than mothers weep the bodily deaths of their children. For she, by that faith and spirit which she had from Thee, discerned the death wherein I lay, and Thou heardest her, O Lord; Thou heardest her, and despisedst not the tears when, streaming down, they watered the ground under her eyes in every place where she prayed. Yea, Thou heardest her."

Monica had a dream in which she saw herself standing on a wooden rule, and a shining youth coming towards her, cheerful and smiling upon her, herself overwhelmed with grief. He inquired why she wept daily, and she answered that she was bewailing the perdition of her son. The youth told her to be contented and to look and see that where she was, there also was Augustine. She looked and saw Augustine standing at her side.

When she told this dream to Augustine, he told
her it meant that one day she would follow him into
Manicheanism, but Monica answered quickly that she
had been told, not that she would be where Augustine
was, but that Augustine would be where she was. But
still Augustine remained in his error and his vice.
For almost nine years he continued in the false religion—"all of which time," he says, "that chaste,
godly, and sober widow (such as Thou lovest), now
more cheered with hope, yet no while relaxing in
her weeping and mourning, ceased not at all hours of
her devotions to bewail my case unto Thee."

What a wonderful example of perseverance in
prayer! All these years of daily weeping and prayer
—yet how many a mother gives up the fight if her
first prayer is not answered! There would be more
conversions of sons if more mothers prayed like
Monica. So unceasing, so earnest were her prayers,
that they made a deep impression on those who beheld
her struggle for the soul of her son. One day she
came to a certain bishop, and begged him to have a
talk with Augustine and seek to convince him of his
errors. But the bishop, knowing the condition of
Augustine's mind at the time, refused. He knew that
Augustine would not listen to argument, "being puffed
up with the novelty of that heresy." "Let him alone
awhile," said he; "only pray God for him; he will of
himself, by reading, find what that error is, and how
great its impiety."

But this answer did not satisfy the broken-hearted

mother. All the more she urged him to see Augustine, and have a talk with him. And the good bishop, a little displeased at her importunity, said to her: "Go thy ways, and God bless thee, for it is not possible that the son of these tears shall perish." It was a prophecy, but more than all it was an encouragement to Monica to continue to pray.

Soon after this, Monica had a fresh heart-ache in seeing Augustine leave home again. She had taken the advice of the bishop and let her son come to live with her, where she would have some hold on him. But now he was breaking the bonds again. A better opportunity was offered him to teach at Carthage, and thither he went to seek greater fame—"here proud, there superstitious, everywhere vain." Vanity was a besetting sin with him. Surely he had not learned it from his humble mother. And everything contributed to increase that vanity. He was learned, he had a great audience before which to display his ability. He entered the poetry contest, carried off the great prize, and was publicly honored for it. He was, in a word, intoxicated with the praise of the world. What chance had his poor mother to win him away from what was the breath of his life?

But her prayers even then were beginning to have effect. His mind now was fully developed. He was thinking for himself. He saw the foolishness of the heresy into which he had fallen; he saw that it was a depraved philosophy, that it encouraged immorality in spite of all its fine pretence; and he saw, too, that the

Manicheans could not hold their own against the arguments of the Catholics. They did not even know anything about the things the knowledge of which they had promised him, namely, the natural sciences in which he was so interested. He lost faith in Manicheanism, yet he did not have the courage to return to the Catholic faith.

Dissatisfied with things at Carthage, Augustine determined to go to Rome. He had always longed to go there. So when he was twenty-nine years of age he made up his mind to make the voyage, confident that at Rome he would do better work as a teacher. But as soon as Monica heard of his intention, she bitterly opposed his going, fearing that it might lead to other dangers and so delay his conversion. She did not waste any time lamenting. She followed him to the sea. She was determined to keep him from sailing, and if he insisted on that, she was bound she would sail with him. And so she held to him by force.

Augustine was displeased at this. He would go, and he did not want her with him. So he made believe to her that he was not sailing just then, that he had a friend whom he could not leave till he had a fair wind to sail. "And I lied to my mother," he writes, "and such a mother, and escaped."

But Monica must have had her suspicions. She refused to return home without him, but was at last persuaded by him to spend the night in a near-by chapel dedicated to St. Cyprian. That night he quietly departed, even while she was asking God not to let

him depart. What was her surprise in the morning
to find that Augustine had lied to her, and was now far
away on the sea! She came out of the chapel. The
vessel was gone, and there on the sands she stood
wringing her hands and bemoaning the son that was
gone; "for," as Augustine says, "she loved my being
with her, as mothers do, but much more than they."
The deception almost broke her heart. She little knew
that her prayers were being answered in the departure
of Augustine for Italy. But in spite of her grief she
was not discouraged; for, as Augustine writes, "And
yet, after accusing my treachery and hardheartedness,
she betook herself again to intercede to Thee for me,
went to her wonted place, and I to Rome."

No sooner was he arrived at Rome than he fell
dangerously ill with a fever. He tells us later on that
he knew that had he died then he would have gone
to hell for all his sins; for during the illness he had
no desire even to be baptized. But he recovered, and
attributed that recovery to the prayers of his mother,
who while she was praying did not guess the terrible
sickness he was suffering. "Couldst Thou," he asks,
"despise and reject from Thy aid the tears of such a
one, wherewith she begged of Thee not gold or silver,
nor any mutable or passing good, but the salvation of
her son's soul? Thou, by whose gift she was such?
Never, Lord."

As soon as he was sufficiently recovered, he opened
a school at Rome, but he did not conduct it long; for
some of the scholars left without paying their tuition,

and this so revolted him that he was glad to get away from the city. Some people of Milan had written to the Prefect of Rome, asking him to send them a professor of rhetoric, and Augustine applied for and received the appointment. Among the first persons he met at Milan was the famous Bishop Ambrose, now the immortal St. Ambrose, whom he had heard preach. The great Ambrose was kind to him, and this was the way to the heart of Augustine. The confidence of Augustine, on the other hand, won its way to the heart of Ambrose, and he took advantage of the friendship to seek to convince Augustine of the errors of the sect to which he belonged. But while Augustine was soon convinced that he had been in error, he would not accept the Catholic faith. He tried everything rather than that, perhaps because he had the consciousness that if he became a Catholic he would have to renounce his sinful pleasures, for he was still a prey to impurity. He sought peace in several systems of philosophy, but to no avail. The true remedy was at his hand, but he did not have the courage to take it.

Meanwhile Monica, as soon as she heard that Augustine was at Milan, followed him thither, after a stormy voyage, in which she had comforted the sailors and encouraged them, assuring them of a safe arrival. She did not sulk over Augustine's running away from her. She would follow him to the end, eager for his soul's salvation.

The grace was beginning to work. She saw the

influence which Ambrose was having upon him, and she redoubled her prayers that it might be effective. Finally she had the satisfaction of seeing Augustine separate from the woman that had enslaved him for so many years. This woman left Augustine of her own accord, and retired to a life of penance; but her place was soon filled by another mistress. Augustine had convinced himself that it was impossible to be pure. Monica, knowing in her heart how his passions were keeping him from being converted to the faith, arranged a marriage for him, but the girl was too young, and so Augustine did not marry her. He continued in sin, though all the time he had a fear of death and judgment.

When the schools closed that year, Augustine, with some of his friends, retired to a country house in order to carry on their studies. Monica accompanied them. She was always the good angel. She took part in their conversations, and many a time lifted their hearts to God by the wisdom she had learned in prayer.

Augustine during these days was worried in soul. He longed to embrace the truth, but his passions held him back. One day, as he wept over his iniquities and the slavery that held him, he heard a child in a neighboring house singing as if playing some game, "Take up and read, take up and read." He was in the garden at the time and had been reading the Epistle of St. Paul to the Romans. He opened it again at random, and his eyes fell on these words: "Not in rioting and drunkenness, not in chambering and impurities, not in contention and envy; but put ye on the Lord Jesus Christ, and make not provision for the flesh" (Romans xiii, 13, 14).

He read no further. The light had come. Monica's prayers were heard. Then he and his friend Alypius went into the house to Monica. They told her the story, and Monica leaped with very joy and thanked God. Her sorrow had been turned into joy. Augustine resigned his professorship, and in the year 387, at Easter, he was baptized by St. Ambrose in Milan.

After this Augustine and his friends decided to retire into the solitude of Africa. But he remained at Milan, finishing certain books he had begun to write, until the fall, when they began their journey. After much travel they arrived at Ostia, and there it was that Monica died, while they were resting preparatory to the new voyage. It is Augustine that tells us the story of her end. One day the mother and the son were alone, sitting at a window overlooking the garden. They were talking of the things of God, wondering what the life of the saints in heaven might be. They were both almost in ecstasy. At length she said: "Son, for mine own part, I have no further delight in anything in this life. What I do here any longer, and to what end I am here, I know not, now that my hopes in this world are accomplished. One thing there was for which I desired to linger for a while in this life—that I might see thee a Catholic Christian before I died. My God hath done this for me more

abundantly, that I should now see thee, withal, despising earthly happiness, become his servant.   What do
I here?"

Augustine could not remember what answer he had
made her.   Five days later she became sick of a
fever.   One day she fell into a swoon.   All hastened
to gather about her.   She recovered, and looking at
Augustine and her other son, Navigius, she asked,
"Where was I?"   And then she said: "Here shall
you bury your mother."

Augustine said nothing, but Navigius spoke, telling
her he hoped she would die in her native land.   But
she checked him, giving him another look.   "Behold
what he says," she remarked to Augustine; and then
she said to them both: "Lay this body anywhere; let
not the care for that anyway disquiet you; this only
I request, that you would remember me at the Lord's
altar, wherever you be."   And then she was still.

Augustine, however, wondered, for he had known
how anxious she had always been to be buried beside
her husband.   Later he had heard from one of his
friends, who had asked her if she were not afraid to
leave her body so far away from her native city, that
she had replied: "Nothing is far to God; nor is
it to be feared lest at the end of the world He should
not recognize whence He were to raise me up."

And so on the ninth day of her illness, in her fifty-
sixth year, she passed to God.

"I closed her eyes," said Augustine, "and there
flowed withal a mighty sorrow into my heart, which

was overflowing into tears; mine eyes at the same time, by the violent command of my mind, drank up their fountain wholly dry; and woe was me in such a strife! But when she breathed her last, the boy Adeodatus [his son] burst out into a loud lament; then, checked by us all, held his peace. In like manner, also, a childish feeling in me, which was, through my heart's youthful voice, finding its vent in weeping, was checked and silenced. For we thought it not fitting to solemnize that funeral with tearful lament and groanings; for thereby do they for the most part express grief for the departed, as though unhappy, or altogether dead. Of this we were assured on good grounds, the testimony of her good conversation and her faith unfeigned.

"What, then, was it," he continues, "which did grievously pain me within, but a fresh wound wrought through the sudden wrench of that most sweet and dear custom of living together? I joyed, indeed, in her testimony, when, in that her last sickness, mingling her endearments with my acts of duty, she called me 'dutiful,' and mentioned, with great affection of love, that she never had heard any harsh or reproachful sound uttered by my mouth against her. But yet, O God, who madest us, what comparison is there betwixt that honor that I paid to her, and her slavery for me? Being, then, forsaken of so great comfort in her, my soul was wounded, and that life rent asunder, as it were, which of hers and mine together had been made but one."

The friends then joined in singing a psalm. And while good neighbors prepared the body for burial, Augustine talked with his friends and neighbors upon "something fitting the time." It was hard work keeping back the tears; and he tells us that those who listened to him thought that he had no sense of sorrow. But his whole soul within shook with grief.

The saintly woman was carried to burial. But neither at the Mass nor at the grave was there weeping. It did not seem to be a time for tears. Augustine struggled with his grief, and tried to shake it off. And then, he says, "by little and little I recovered my former thoughts of Thy handmaid, her holy conversation towards Thee, her holy tenderness and observance towards us, whereof I was suddenly deprived; and I was minded to weep in Thy sight, for her and for myself, in her behalf and in my own. And I gave way to the tears which I before restrained, to overflow as much as they desired; reposing my heart upon them; and it found rest in them, for it was in Thy ears, not in those of man, who would have scornfully interpreted my weeping. And now, Lord, in writing I confess it unto Thee. Read it who will, and interpret it how he will; and if he find sin therein, that I wept my mother for a small portion of an hour (the mother who for the time was dead to mine eyes, who had for many years wept for me that I might live in Thine eyes), let him not deride me; but rather, if he be one of large charity, let him weep himself for my sins unto Thee, the Father of all the brethren of Thy Christ."

But now, after he had written that, Augustine tells us that he poured forth a different kind of tears—tears for her soul. Holy as he knew her to be, he would not say that she did not need prayers. He beseeches God for the sins of his mother. And then he concludes: "May she rest, then, in peace with the husband before and after whom she had never any; whom she obeyed, with patience bringing forth fruit to Thee, that she might win him also unto Thee." He begs then that all who read his *Confessions* shall remember at the altar Monica and her husband, "that so my mother's last request of me may through my *Confessions* more than through my prayers be, through the prayers of many, more abundantly fulfilled to her."

St. Monica does not need our prayers. During all these centuries she has enjoyed the vision of God. Rather do we pray to her, while we marvel at her wonderful holiness. She had trials enough to daunt even a fervid soul. But God allowed all these trials, both from her husband and her son, those she loved the most, as if He had the purpose through her example of encouraging other wives and other mothers. What more helpless case than that of Augustine—a man without morals, without faith? Who would dare to prophesy that this worldling would become a great bishop, a great doctor of the Church, a great saint? Who? Nobody but Monica. With her mother-love sanctified by penance and prayer, she braved everything, knowing that faith can move mountains. She is one of the most human characters in history, the tender mother who knew that the greatest glory she could obtain for her son was that of being converted to God. Never will the world forget her, for she has shown to what heights true motherhood can reach.

THE QUEEN SAINTS

ONE thing that stands out in the history of the Church is that sanctity is possible to all. The Litany of the Saints is the most cosmopolitan catalogue in existence. It is the census-book of the "great multitude, which no man could number, of all nations and tribes and peoples and tongues, standing before the throne, and in the sight of the Lamb, clothed with white robes, and palms in their hands." The young and the old, the rich and the poor, the learned and the ignorant, the king and the peasant, the queen and her slave, from every walk of life they advance to the throne of God. What a consolation there is in that! It is for us an act of hope.

Sometimes the possibility of sanctity seems so remote. We fancy that if our lot in life were different, we would serve God better. But that is generally a delusion. The chances are that if we are cold and careless to God in our present circumstances, we would be just the same in any other walk of life. If we but lived in the time of Christ, we say, how blessed were we to follow him! Perhaps we would have followed Him; perhaps, on the other hand, we would have been of the mob that demanded His blood. For if we earnestly desire sanctity, have we not at our disposal the same graces which the friends of the Master had? And with that thought we should make the most of our state in life.

Most of us are just where God wants us to be. All are not called to the cloister. There is God's work to be done in the world as in the nunnery; and while we know that they are specially blessed who have a vocation to the religious life, we also know, as St. Augustine showed in his book *On the Advantages of Matrimony,* that there have been many married women who have surpassed many virgins in sanctity. Whatever the condition of life, God can sanctify it. It is easy for the poor to be good, say the rich; it is easy for the rich to be good, say the poor. Anything for an excuse, when all in their heart know that God will come to dwell in their cottage or in their palace, if they but invite Him.

Yet there is something especially striking in the lives of those who, living in the midst of wealth, have chosen poverty; who, when they might be flattered and fawned upon, have made themselves humble. It requires a great deal of heroism for a queen to be humble; rather, it requires a great grace from God. There are so many temptations for queens to consider themselves as little less than God Himself. Surely, it is hard for the rich man to enter the Kingdom of Heaven; hard for the man that wears a crown; hard, but not impossible. How many kings have been raised to the altars of God! How many queens, too! And through what difficulties! It is not an easy thing.

The consciousness of power, of superiority, is a sweet morsel. St. Augustine would have been converted long before he was, if he had not been so conceited about his talents. Men and women, from being worshipped, get to worship themselves. Somehow it is in the nature of things, and we who find fault with the dignity assumed by the great would be, perhaps, overbearingly proud if the tables were turned. The notorious Madame Roland, when she was a poor, unnoticed woman, used to protest against the worldly glory of the regal Marie Antoinette. But as soon as Madame Roland got a little power with the Girondists she was overbearing. It was harder to see her than the Queen. A little power made her lose her head in more senses than one.

So that it gives our Catholic souls a thrill when we see women, having all that the world can give, living amid the temptations inseparable from the court, yet becoming poor in spirit, humble maid-servants of the Lord, their greatest glory to doff their crown and cry out, "Behold the handmaid of the Lord!" There have been many of these noble women in all ages of the Church. During the middle ages there were many queens who, though on their thrones, lived the life of the cloister. Such were the wife of Charlemagne; Cunegonde, wife of Henry I, King of England; Agnes, wife of Henry III; Elizabeth, wife of the Emperor Albert, first Archduke of Austria; Radegonde, wife of Clotaire; Adoere, wife of Chilperic; Bathilde, wife of Clovis II; and Agnes of Bohemia, betrothed to the

Emperor Frederick II. To relate all the great Catholic queens who have, amid their worldly glory, edified civilization would be but to give a catalogue of names. From the vast number we have chosen those of special sanctity—those who stepped from their throne in the world to a throne in heaven, raised to the altars of God as canonized saints.

The first queen-saint that we have memory of is the great St. Helena, who, according to the old tradition that persists from the fifth century, discovered the true Cross in the place where it had been buried in Jerusalem. Helena was one of the women who did not lose their heads by being lifted from lowliness to a throne. In the wildest dreams of her girlhood she never fancied anything approaching the reality of her later life. She was born in humble circumstances, far removed from royalty. St. Ambrose tells us that she was an innkeeper. It was while she was doing this humble work in her native city of Drepanum on the Nicomedian Gulf that she met the Roman general Constantius Chlorus. He fell in love with her and married her. Perhaps if he had foreseen that one day he would be the great Roman Emperor, he would not have condescended to wed the poor innkeeper. Anyway, when, in the year 292, he became co-regent of the West, he began to think of making a marriage that would mean more to him politically. So without any scruple he put aside the wife that was good enough for him when he was a mere Roman officer, and married Theodora, the stepdaughter of the Emperor Maximianus Herculius, who had been his patron. Helena had then been his wife nearly twenty years, and it is easy to picture her grief at being put aside for another woman. This was especially so from the fact that in 274 she had borne to him a son, the boy who was afterwards to be so glorious as Constantine the Great.

There is nothing in all history more affecting than the love of Constantine for his mother. He must have deeply resented the action of his father in setting her aside. At the time of his mother's rejection he was about eighteen. He was loyal to her, and no doubt longed for the time when he could restore her to the position from which his father had dethroned her. When he did succeed to the throne in 306, his first thought was for her. He summoned her to the court, gave her the title of Augusta, and ordered that all honor should be paid to her as the mother of the sovereign. He even had coins struck bearing her image. She was rewarded for her days of humiliation. Up to this time she was not a Christian, but after Constantine had won his immortal victory, when the miraculous cross was seen in the sky, she became a Christian through his influence, and, as Eusebius says, "such a devout servant of God, that one might believe her to have been from her childhood a disciple of the Redeemer of mankind." It was in the great design of God that the poor pagan innkeeper was now a great Christian empress, for from the very moment of her conversion she used her influence and her wealth to spread Christianity. She built many churches all over the empire, and especially in the Holy Land. She was an old woman when she undertook to make a pilgrimage to Palestine. That was the land she loved above all others, and in spite of her years she gave herself untiringly to the work of exploration. There is an old tradition that she discovered the Holy Sepulchre and near it the instruments of Our Lord's Passion, and built a temple as a shrine for the true Cross, part of which she brought home to her son Constantine, and part of which she sent to Rome.

Helena helped everybody. She remembered the day when she was poor herself, and so the poor were especially dear to her. And everywhere she went over the vast empire, she always brought her generosity, delighting in devoting her wealth to the building and decorating of churches and the helping of religious communities. Constantine loved her devotedly. He delighted to honor her, and as one proof of this he rebuilt her native town, where she had been so lowly, and decreed that it should be called, after her, Helenopolis, the city of Helen. And then, when she was an old woman of eighty years and had returned from the Holy Land, she had the great happiness of dying in the arms of the son who, though occupying the greatest position in the world, found his greatest joy in honoring the humble mother that bore him. If Constantine was great, cannot we attribute much of his greatness to the fact that he had a great mother, whose joy was not to queen it and to show her importance in the world, but even as empress to live humbly, to help the poor, and to bring glory to the Church of God?

As a contrast to the life of this woman who was so loved by her son, we have another great empress who lived in after years (she died in 876)—the Empress Theodora, who is ranked by the Greeks among the saints. Her husband was a brute and delighted in persecuting those who defended the use of images during the Iconoclast heresy. By her mildness and gentleness she softened his temper, and on his death she became regent during the minority of her son. She put an end to the Iconoclast heresy, which had endured for one hundred and twenty years; and she governed the empire with the greatest glory for twelve years. But she got no thanks for it. She was banished by her son and his uncle, and after that devoted herself to preparation for death in the monastery where she lived for eight years.

The next great queen-saint after St. Helena is St. Clotilda, Queen of the Franks. She was the daughter of a king, Chilperic, King of the Burgundians, and his wife Caretena. Both the King and his wife were Catholics, and Clotilda received a religious education from her mother, a remarkable woman who lived to a great age. It was a religious family, and we find one of Clotilda's sisters, Chrona, founding the Church of St. Victor at Geneva and taking the religious habit. Soon after the death of her father, Clotilda was married to Clovis, King of the Franks. It was a happy marriage. They loved each other, and Clotilda made use of that love to persuade her husband to become a Catholic. The King, however, at first would not listen to her appeals.

Clovis had allowed their first child to be baptized; but, as he died in infancy, the grieving father used that as an argument against the God of Clotilda and refused to serve such a God. Nevertheless, when the second son was born he allowed him to be baptized, even though he refused himself to be baptized. But the good Queen was not disheartened. She prayed continually for his conversion, and finally had the happiness of seeing her prayers answered. The occasion of his conversion was the battle against the Alemanni. He saw his army about to yield, and then in his fear of defeat called upon the God of Clotilda, promising that if he were victorious he would become a Catholic. He won the victory, and then, true to his promise, was baptized at Christmas, 496, his sister and three thousand of his warriors embracing the faith at the same time. It was a great victory for Christianity, meaning as it did by the conversion of Clovis the establishment of the Church among a great people. And that fact, with all that it has meant to civilization, was due to the piety of one woman, to whom religion meant more than everything else in the world.

Clotilda had four sons and one daughter. Her life was wrapt up in them, as became a pious Christian mother. Queen though she was, her life was one of retirement, for during the lifetime of her husband we search in vain for any account of her. Clovis died in the year 511, and Clotilda had him buried in the Church of the Apostles, later called the Church of St. Genevieve, which she and he had built as a mausoleum.

Clotilda had known great happiness with Clovis, but as soon as he was gone her sorrows began. Her widowhood was a cross. She saw one of her sons, Clodomir, make war against his cousin Sigismund and put him to death with his wife and children. Later on Clodomir was killed in war by the brother of Sigismund, and Clotilda had the new task of caring for his three little boys. Added to that misery, her two other sons, Childebert and Clotaire, who had divided between them the inheritance of their dead brother, set about the murder of the little ones in order that later in life they might not demand their father's possessions. They got the children away from the care of Clotilda and murdered the two elder. The third escaped and entered a monastery. Clotilda, pious woman that she was, was heart-broken at these terrible crimes against her own and by her own. She could stay in Paris no longer, and withdrew to Tours, where, by the tomb of St. Martin, to whom she had great devotion, she spent the rest of her life in prayer and works of charity.

But even then she was not allowed to be at peace. Her daughter Clotilda had been cruelly treated by her husband, Almaric, King of the Visigoths, and had appealed for help to her brother Childebert, who waged

a war against Almaric in which Almaric was killed.
The young queen Clotilda died on the way home from
the hardships she had to endure. Finally the two
brothers Childebert and Clotaire began to quarrel, and
engaged in war against each other. Clotilda threw
herself on her knees and begged St. Martin not to
permit the shedding of any more blood in her family. All night long she remained on her knees, weeping and praying.

Her prayers were heard. A sudden tempest arose
and dispersed the two armies. The poor mother's
time of trial was over. She died in the year 545, at
the age of seventy-one, after a widowhood of thirty-four years, and was buried beside her husband and
children in Paris.

Clotilda lived rather the life of a nun than a queen.
And yet hers was not the quiet life of the cloister.
She lived in times little removed from barbarism.
That is evident from the crimes of her own children.
They were crimes that tore her heart, not only on
account of her great mother-love, but because they
were terrible sins against God. It was through these
trials, however, that her soul was sanctified. They
were her road of the Cross. And surely every grieving mother must find comfort and strength in thinking of the holy motherhood of the great St. Clotilda.

From the France of St. Clotilda we pass to the
England of St. Etheldreda, Queen of Northumbria.
She was born about the year 630, the daughter of
Anna, the King of East Anglia. When she was still

very young her father gave her in marriage to Tonbert, a subordinate prince, from whom she received the Isle of Ely, where she afterwards lived and died. She never lived in wedlock with him. He died soon after the marriage, and the young widow gave herself over to the religious life. Her father, however, was unwilling that she should enter the cloister, and so he had her married to Egfrid, a mere boy fourteen years old, who was heir to the throne of Northumbria. From her young husband she received more property, but she gave it to St. Wilfrid to found the minster of St. Andrew. The young husband appealed to St. Wilfrid to make her come and live with him rather than lead the life of a religious. But the Saint persuaded him to let her remain awhile in the nunnery. At last, fearing that Egfrid would come and carry her off by force, she left there and came with two attendants to her possessions at Ely, and there began the foundation of the minster of Ely. Her relatives gave her the necessary means to continue the work, and it was there that, soon after, she died from the plague. At Ely, in the church founded by her, she was buried, and for many centuries her body was the object of devout veneration.

"Happy as a queen," sometimes we say. We are so apt to think that a queen, with her power and her wealth, must be happy. Yet there have been queens that sacrificed all this, eager for the quiet life of religion, wherein they might serve God and sanctify their souls, which they considered as of so much greater value than all the kingdoms of the world. Little do we know of St. Etheldreda, yet that little is enough for us to learn from her the truth that the great thing in life is the friendship of God, even though it may lead away from thrones.

St. Etheldreda recalls another English queen that became a saint. This was St. Sexburga. She was also the daughter of a king. It was a saintly family, for St. Hilda was a sister of her mother. Sexburga married the King of Kent, and they were a happy, devoted couple. When he died she entered the religious life, and succeeded her sister, St. Etheldreda, as abbess. Sexburga's daughter, Ermenilda, was also a saint, and was married to the King of Mercia; likewise her sister, St. Withburg. Surely sanctity flourished in those days, when we find so many women of royal blood following the way of the Cross.

The life of St. Etheldreda reminds us of another woman who might have been an empress, yet refused the dignity, that would almost turn any woman's head, in order to hide herself in the cloister. This was the Blessed Agnes of Bohemia, herself the daughter of a king and a relative of the great St. Elizabeth of Hungary. She was betrothed to Frederick II, Emperor of Germany, but fled from him and became a nun. The Emperor was, of course, disappointed, but said he: "If she had left me for a mortal man, I would have taken vengeance with the sword, but I cannot take offence because in preference to me she has chosen the King of Heaven." Yet what sublime cour-

age it takes to choose the King of Heaven in preference to the glitter of an earthly crown!

History is filled with examples of this Christian
courage in the women who have set aside crowns in
order to serve God more faithfully. Ghisla, the sister of Charlemagne, refused to marry the son of the
Eastern Emperor and withdrew into a monastery;
Catherine of Lorraine refused to be the wife of the
Emperor Maximilian, became a Benedictine nun, and
gave to the Benedictine monastery which she founded
at Nancy all the jewels which various princes had
given her.

There was, not so far from our own times, Christine
of Sweden, who renounced her crown in order to become a Catholic. There was the Empress Agnes who
governed Bavaria for seven years in peace, and then,
when she saw disturbances and dissensions arising,
gave up her high place in the world and entered a
monastery for the love of Christ. St. Cuthburge,
too, a sister to King Ina and married to another king,
Alfred of Northumbria, left all the glory of the world
and went into a monastery, where she led a life of
the greatest sacrifice. There was St. Kyneburge, the
daughter of the pagan King of Mercia. She was
married to Alcfrid, King of Bernicia. They lived a
life of perpetual continence, and when she was left
a widow in the bloom of her youth she renounced the
world and entered a nunnery which was built by her
and her brother. She was a woman of great sanctity
and of great charity. Her sister also entered the same

monastery and died a saint. St. Kinga, another queen, was the daughter of the King of Hungary and the granddaughter of the Emperor of Constantinople. She was married to another king, Boleslas of Poland, and lived with him in chastity. Her life was one of prayer, mortification, and charity; she waited upon the poor in the hospitals; and finally, when the King died, she became a nun.

Another example of sanctity is St. Rodegunde. The daughter of a king, she was carried off at the age of twelve by King Clotaire as part of the spoils of war. He educated her and made her his wife. But he was not overpleased at her great virtue. He used to say that he had married a nun and not a queen. She was bitterly persecuted, but was patient under it all. Finally, when her brother was assassinated at the instigation of her husband, she ran away from the court and gave herself up to a life of hardship, sleeping on a bed of sackcloth and ashes.

All this sounds like a mere catalogue of names. The lives of all these royal women are all according to the same formula. But it is according to the formula that tells us the wisdom of seeking first the Kingdom of God.

One of the most interesting and charming characters in all history is St. Bathilde, who from slavery became Queen of France. Her career is more like fiction than history. She was a slave in the house of the Mayor of Neustria, being a servant of his wife. She attracted notice by her unusual qualities of mind and by her piety, so much so that the Mayor had the utmost confidence in her and gave into her care the management of many of the affairs of his household. So great was his admiration for the slave, that after his wife died he wanted to marry her. But Bathilde would not listen to him, fled from the palace, and did not return there until she heard that he had married again. But a greater dignity was in store for her.

One day King Clovis II met her in the Mayor's palace, and he was so struck by her beauty and by the fine things said in her praise that he freed her and then married her in 649. Bathilde was too sensible a woman to lose her head at the new honor. She was always humble as queen—humble as when she had been a slave. Her new dignity only gave her more time to pray and a better chance to do the works of charity which she always loved. Seven years after the marriage, Clovis died, leaving three sons, Clothaire, Childeric and Thierry. The oldest was proclaimed king by the assembly of the nobles as Clothaire III; and as he was but five years of age, his mother was made regent, ruling a kingdom where but a few years before she had been a poor slave!

Bathilde applied herself to the work of governing the kingdom, and, aided by good advice, she made many reforms, among other things abolishing the custom of trading in Christian slaves. She founded many charitable and religious institutions; she even desired to become a religious, but her duties kept her at court.

Finally, when her children were well established in their respective territories, she was able to carry out her wish. She retired from the world and went to live in the Abbey of Chelles near Paris. She put aside all her royal insignia, and wished to be considered the lowliest in the convent, even taking her position after the novices and serving the sick and the poor with her own hands. It was now a life of prayer and toil, and she would allow no one to refer to her past dignity as queen.

So she lived the life of religion for fifteen years, edifying all by her holiness and humility. She was a simple handmaid of the Lord. From slavery she had come to a throne, and now from the throne back to slavery—the slavery of a follower of Christ—another wonderful lesson that there is more real happiness in humbly serving God than in queening it over a great kingdom.

God has raised up His saints in every nation. From France we pass to Germany and behold another great queen-saint in St. Matilda. She was born in Westphalia about the year 895, and was brought up in the monastery of Erfurt. The German king, Henry I, called "the Fowler," married her in 909 at Wahlhausen, which he gave to her as her dowry.

Matilda was a great mother even in a worldly sense. She was the mother of Otto I, Emperor of Germany; of Henry, Duke of Bavaria; of St. Bruno, Archbishop of Cologne; of Gerberga, wife of Louis IV of France; and of Hedwig, wife of Hugh Capet. In 918 her husband became King of Germany, where he reigned for seventeen years. She had wonderful influence over him, and when he died he bequeathed her great possessions. She was deserving of it all, for as queen she was always humble, full of piety and charity to the poor.

Yet she had her troubles. The King wanted his oldest son to succeed him, but Matilda's choice was her favorite son, Henry; and on the plea that he was the first-born after her husband became king, she induced some of the nobles to vote for him. But she was not successful. Otto was elected king. Three years later the defeated Henry revolted against his brother, but was unsuccessful and submitted, finally being made Duke of Bavaria by Otto at the wish of Matilda.

Henry was ungrateful to the mother that did so much for him. He and Otto joined in persecuting her because they said she had impoverished the crown by her too great charity. To satisfy them she renounced the property her husband had given her and returned to her villa in Westphalia. Later on, when misfortunes befell the sons, they begged her pardon and implored her to return to the palace.

Matilda's days were filled with good works. She built many churches and monasteries and supported them. All her zeal was for the glory of God, and at last, in 968, at the age of seventy-three, she died in one of the convents she had founded and was buried there by the side of her husband. So great was her piety that immediately after her death she was venerated as a saint. A great mother, a great queen, because she was a great saint!

After all, the lives of all these queens tell the same story. The epitaph of all could be the same—she was pious, she was charitable, she loved God more than she loved her crown.

The same story is true of St. Adelaide. She was the daughter of a king, Rudolph II of Burgundy. He had been at war with Hugh of Provence for the crown of Italy. Finally they made peace, and one of the conditions was that Adelaide, then only two years of age, should marry Hugh's son, Lothaire. The marriage took place fourteen years later, when Adelaide was sixteen. Her father had died in the meantime, and her mother had married Hugh. Then it was that Berengarius claimed the crown of Italy for himself, and forced Hugh to abdicate in favor of Lothaire. Berengarius is supposed to have poisoned Lothaire in prison. He tried then to persuade Adelaide to marry his son Adalbert. She refused and was thrown into prison.

A priest named Martin rescued her through an underground passage, and concealed her in the woods, where he supported her by the fish he caught. From there the Duke of Canossa carried her off to his castle. Meanwhile the Italian nobles were tired of the rule of Berengarius, and prevailed on Otho the Great to invade Italy. After doing this he married Adelaide at Christmas, 951.

So much did the people of Italy love her that it

was easy for Otho to subjugate them. And not only in Italy was she loved. She was idolized by the German people as well while her husband lived. But when he died her troubles began. When her son Otho II ruled, she had to suffer from the jealousy of his wife; moreover, she was made to suffer because they blamed her for being too charitable. It was the same charge that was made against St. Matilda and St. Elizabeth of Hungary. At any rate, she left the court for the sake of peace and went to live at Pavia. For a time she was reconciled to her son's family, but again the same troubles broke out in the reign of her grandson, owing to the enmity of her daughter-in-law, who was still jealous of the popularity of Adelaide. At length, after the death of the daughter-in-law, Adelaide was summoned from her seclusion to be regent. It was a time to show the true character of the woman. She showed no spirit of revenge to those who had been against her. She was a big-hearted woman who could not stoop to pettiness. Her rule was one of great wisdom. Her court was said to be more like a religious house than a worldly palace. Everywhere she built churches and monasteries and labored hard for the conversion of the pagans of the North.

Her last act was one of devotion. She left home to go to Burgundy to reconcile her nephew with his subjects, and on the journey died at Seltz in Alsace in 1015, at the age of eighty-four—a woman who had spent her best days in serving God.

Sometimes we find two saints sitting on the same throne, as in the case of St. Cunegonde and her husband St. Henry. Both her father and mother were very pious and so trained her. Henry was Duke of Bavaria when she married him, but he was afterwards chosen King of the Romans, and then she was crowned queen, on which occasion she made great presents to the churches of Paderborn, where the coronation took place. They then went to Rome and there received the imperial crown.

Before her marriage she had with Henry's consent made a vow of virginity. But in spite of that she was calumniated to him, and to prove her innocence of the charges walked over red-hot ploughshares without being hurt.

They were a loving couple. When he died in 1024 she gave away all her property, put off her royal robes, and donned a poor habit. She became the lowliest of women, and did not wish even to be reminded that once she had been an empress. She led a life of hard labor, and gave most of her time to the sick and the poor. In this manner of life she spent fifteen years; and finally, worn out by these mortifications, she died a poor woman, to receive an eternal crown for the one which she had sacrificed in order to sanctify her soul.

How much a queen can accomplish for the good of her people and for the spread of religion is evident in the lives of all these holy women, and is especially evident in the life of her who, during the ages of faith, was such an inspiration to her subjects—St. Margaret of Scotland. She belonged to a royal family, being granddaughter of Edmund Ironside and a niece of St. Edward the Confessor. When Canute was declared King of England he was made guardian of the sons of Edmund Ironside, Edward and Edmund. But he secretly had designs on their life, and sent them to the King of Sweden to have them murdered, so that they might not claim the possessions that belonged to them. There is a tradition that the King of Sweden, to save them, sent them to the King of Hungary, by whom they were protected and educated. Edmund died, but Edward married Agatha, a sister of the Queen and a splendid woman, and had by her three children, Edgar, Christina, and Margaret.

When Edward the Confessor succeeded to the throne of England, he invited Edward with his children to return from Hungary to England, where Edward died three years later. When William the Conqueror became king after the battle of Hastings, many Englishmen wanted to make Edgar, the brother of St. Margaret, king, since he was the lawful Saxon heir. But he was not strong enough, and so, fearing the tyranny of William, he left the country, taking his sister Margaret with him, and sailed for the Continent. But a storm drove the vessel to Scotland, and there the two exiles were kindly received by King Malcolm, who himself had once been an exile when he fled after Macbeth had murdered his father Duncan and usurped the throne. But later he had defeated Macbeth and was now King of Scotland.

William the Conqueror demanded that he should return Margaret and her brother, but he refused, and war ensued, in which Malcolm was victorious. Soon he fell in love with Margaret. It is said that her beauty was extraordinary, and this, added to her wit and her great piety and virtue, won over the whole court to her. It was a great honor to be asked to marry the King, but she was not eager for the union. All her life was taken up with meditation and prayer and in helping the poor, so that she had thoughts of devoting herself to God in the religious life. But finally, after serious thought, she decided to marry Malcolm, and was crowned Queen of Scotland in 1070, when she was twenty-four.

She brought a great fortune to the King; but her greatest fortune was her own heart. The King loved her devotedly. He was rough and unpolished, but upright and free from wickedness. Margaret had great influence over him. She softened his temper, cultivated his mind, polished his manners, and in- stilled deep piety into his soul. So great was her in- fluence over him that he even followed her advice in ruling the kingdom. By her influence he became one of the most virtuous of kings that ever sat on the throne of Scotland. And while she was interested in all these things that looked to the welfare of the king- dom, she was more than all devoted to the things of

God. It was her prayers, her charity, that brought in those days so much happiness to Scotland.

They had a large family—six sons, three of whom ruled as kings of Scotland, and two daughters—Maud, who married Henry I, King of England, and Mary, who married the Count of Boulogne. Needless to say, all these children received a good Christian training. Not only did the Queen see that good masters were provided for them, but she herself instructed them. Her first care was that they should be good Catholics. That to her was more important than their royal blood. In that court the only recommendation to the royal favor was virtue, and to want devotion was the most certain disgrace. With her the whole kingdom appeared as one large family of which she had to take care. Hence it was her first aim to correct all abuses, and to make the people love religion. Not only did she attend to the religious education of her people, but she aimed also at teaching them the useful and polite arts, and had her husband make many good laws for this purpose. And with all this work she had plenty of time for the poor. Wherever she went, she was surrounded by the widows and the orphans and the other poor ones, who regarded her as their mother. She would even wash the feet of the poor, and before sitting down to her own meals would serve nine little orphans and twenty-four grown-up poor. Often, especially in Lent and Advent, the King and Queen brought in three hundred poor people, and on their knees served them with the dishes from the royal

table. She visited the hospitals, and personally looked
after the sick. In a word, there was nothing that she
considered foreign to her, so long as it helped her
neighbor. And the King came to be of the same mind.

"He learned from her," says one writer, "often to
watch the night in prayer. I could not sufficiently
admire to see the fervor of this prince at prayer and
to discover so much compunction of heart and such
tears of devotion in a secular man." And another
writer remarks: "She excited the King to the works
of justice, mercy, alms-deeds and other virtues; in all
which by divine grace she brought him to be most
ready to comply with her pious inclinations. For he,
seeing that Christ dwelt in the heart of his queen, was
always willing to follow her counsels." All her
history is contained in those words—that Christ dwelt
in her heart.

She gave little time to sleep; she gave none to
amusement: so that most of her time was spent in
the service of God. In Lent and Advent she rose at
midnight and went to church to Matins. After that
she began the day by giving alms and tending the poor.
She then slept for an hour or two, after which she
rose again and heard four or five low Masses and
then a High Mass. And every day, besides her other
prayers, she recited several of the short offices. And
this in a mother of eight children, and a queen besides!

At last a great sorrow came to her in the death
of her husband while he was defending his country
against the English. After his death his son Edward

carried on the siege, and he, too, was slain. Margaret at this time was lying on her death-bed, where she had been for six months, during which time she suffered excruciating pain. Her death happened four days after that of the King.

When she heard of his death she exclaimed: "I thank Thee, Almighty God, that in sending me so great an affliction in the last hour of my life, Thou wouldst purify me from my sins, as I hope by Thy mercy." She died in 1093, aged forty-seven years. At the time of the Reformation her remains, with those of her husband, were saved from plunder, and the principal parts carried into Spain. St. Margaret's head, which was brought to Mary Queen of Scots, was later given to the Scots Jesuits at Douai, where it disappeared at the time of the French Revolution.

St. Margaret sanctified the kingdom by her prayers. A great queen, she considered her highest privilege that of serving God. This she did by sanctifying herself and all those about her. She was a great wife, a great mother, a great queen, but above all a great saint.

Another great queen-saint was St. Elizabeth, or Isabel, of Portugal so named after her great-aunt, St. Elizabeth of Hungary. She was born in 1271, daughter of Pedro III of Aragon. She was brought up very piously, said the Divine Office every day, and led a life of penance—such a life, indeed, as seemed to destine her for the cloister. But God had other designs. She was very young when she married

Diniz, King of Portugal, a very able and devoted king, a poet, but as immoral as his court. It was not a pleasant place for a virtuous young queen, but Isabel continued her life of devotion there, interested other ladies of the court in her charities, and even though she aroused ill-will on account of her piety, which was a reproach to an evil court, she finally succeeded in winning her husband back to a virtuous life, though that did not happen until near the end of his life and after many deeds of wickedness that must have well-nigh broken her heart.

They had a son and daughter. The son, Alfonso, so resented the favor shown by his father to illegitimate sons, that he declared war against him. We can imagine the feelings of the wife and mother who loved them both. But she was a woman of action, and, mounting a horse, rode between the contending armies, and so made peace. On the death of the King, she entered a convent of the Poor Clares which she had founded and took the habit of the Third Order, anxious to give the rest of her days to penance, prayer, and charity.

But she was not allowed to remain there in peace. Her son Alfonso, now king, made war against the King of Castile, who had married his daughter and was now ill-treating her. Isabel was now an old woman, but again she mounted her horse and rode between the contending armies. She made peace, but the exertion killed her. She contracted a fever and died in 1336, leaving behind her the memory of a great sanctity. Isabel was queen, but her life was not a bed of roses. She knew the suffering that comes from the knowledge of a husband's infidelity. It was to her a crown of thorns, yet it helped to sanctify her soul in drawing her nearer to God.

One of the unhappiest queens in the eyes of the world, yet happiest in the eyes of God, was Blessed Jeanne de Valois, popularly known as St. Jeanne de Valois. She was the daughter of Louis XI, King of France, by his second wife, Charlotte of Savoy, and was born in 1464. Her father hated her not only because he had desired a son, but also because Jeanne was deformed and sickly. His hatred was so bitter that he would not keep her at court, but had her brought up by guardians in a lonely country château. There she was ill-used, being often without the necessities of life; but the hardships served to bring her closer to God. So great was her love for the Blessed Virgin that it is said she had a vision in which she was promised that one day she would found a religious community in her honor. But that was only after many and long trials.

Her father, for political reasons, married her to Louis, Duke of Orleans, his second cousin, who was afterwards Louis XII of France. The husband insulted her, even publicly, at every opportunity. She loved him, however, and when he was in disgrace and in prison she came to his aid and had him freed. But he was ungrateful. When he became king he put her away and had the marriage annulled on the ground that he had never consented to it and that it had never been consummated. She fought for her rights as long as possible, but when the case was decided against her she took it all in deep humility, and thanked God that it left her free to found the Order she had wished. She was made Duchess of Berry, and governed that province ably. In 1500 she founded the Order of the Annonciades in honor of the Blessed Virgin. It was her consolation in sorrow, and towards the end of her life she took the vows, gave up her wedding ring, and wore the habit under her rich garments. Her health was always poor, but to her sufferings she added voluntary penance. She never ceased to love the husband who had repudiated her, and when she was dying begged her Order always to pray for him. So dear was she to her people that when she died in 1505 she was universally mourned. Many miracles were wrought through her intercession. It had been a life of trial, a way of the Cross, yet by that way she came to sanctity. Surely she is a patron for afflicted wives.

The last of the queen-saints is one who lived almost in our own times—Blessed Marie Christine of Savoy. She was the daughter of Victor Emmanuel I, King of Sardinia, and of Maria Theresa of Austria, niece of Emperor Joseph II, and was born in 1812. She was married to Ferdinand II, King of the Two Sicilies, and died after the birth of her first son, at the age of twenty-three. It was a short, uneventful life; but even during her few years the young queen was noted for her great piety, and so many graces were obtained through her intercession that as early as 1859 the process of her canonization was introduced, and in 1872 her name was placed in the list of the blessed.

It is a glorious list, that of these queens of earth who became queens in heaven. They might have had life easy, might have lived in power and luxury, yet they put aside all things in order to serve God. It is not easy for a queen to be a saint—it is not easy for anybody. It is only the way of the Cross that leads to sanctity. But the example of these noble women who overcame so many temptations towards a life of frivolity, a life of the world, is but another proof that sanctity is possible to all. And surely wives and mothers can go to these holy queens who were wives and mothers, too, knowing that they will understand their cares and show them the way to bear them.

ST. ELIZABETH OF HUNGARY

(1207–1231)

"THE dear St. Elizabeth!" What a charming
name has been given to her, the young wife and
mother! She was dear to those of her age, dear to
those of every age, a wonderful saint that so impressed her personality on the world that she is still as
vital to-day as she was more than seven hundred years
ago when she spent her few years of existence in this
world. But she is especially redolent of her age. She
may be regarded as the personification of the wonderful thirteenth century, which, as Montalembert says,
was perhaps "the most important, the most complete,
and the most resplendent in the history of Catholic society."

One of the greatest princes that reigned in Germany at the beginning of the thirteenth century was
Hermann, Landgrave (or Duke) of Thuringia. He
was the nephew of the Emperor Frederick Barbarossa,
was the owner of vast estates in the centre of Germany, and had so much power that he virtually determined the choice of emperor, since it was his influence that decided the seven electors of the Holy
Roman Empire. Besides being so powerful as to take

and give crowns, he was noted for his generosity, learning and piety. He was an ardent lover of poetry and a good patron of the Minnesingers, who always found a welcome at his castle.

In the year 1206, when he was at his castle at Wartburg, there were assembled at that place six of the most renowned poets of Germany. They engaged in a contest of song, five of them nobles and one a poor burgess. So wonderful was the poetry sung on that occasion that the Duke could not choose the winner, and sent the simple burgess, Heinrich, to Transylvania to induce Klingsohr, renowned for his wisdom, to come to Eisenach and decide the contest. At the end of the year Heinrich returned with the great Klingsohr. When Klingsohr entered the garden of his host there was a great crowd to greet him. They asked him to tell them something new, and Klingsohr, after contemplating the stars for some time, said: "I will tell you something both new and joyous. I see a beautiful star rising in Hungary, the rays of which extend to Marburg, and from Marburg over all the world. Know even that on this night there is born to my lord, the King of Hungary, a daughter who shall be named Elizabeth. She shall be given in marriage to the son of your prince, she shall become a saint, and her sanctity shall rejoice and console all Christendom."

At once the news of this was brought to the Duke at his castle, and immediately he rode with a great escort to visit Klingsohr, and to bring him to the castle, where he was treated with the highest honor. He answered all the questions of the Duke in regard to the King of Hungary, presided at the new poetical contest, in which he upheld the poor Heinrich, and then returned to his home.

The King of Hungary of whom he had spoken, the father of the dear St. Elizabeth, was Andrew II. He was a noble ruler, noted for his piety and charity, building churches and convents and giving alms to the poor. His wife was Gertrude of Merania, a member of one of the most illustrious houses of the empire in the thirteenth century, and a direct descendant of Charlemagne. Her brother had refused the imperial crown; one of her sisters was Hedwige, Duchess of Silesia and Poland, afterwards St. Hedwige; while another sister, Agnes, was wife of the King of France. Gertrude was as pious as her husband and withal a courageous woman; and she and her husband loved each other devotedly.

Into this royal house was born, in 1207, Elizabeth. As the royal babe was carried under a canopy of the richest stuffs to be baptized, no one guessed that she was to give to her native land undying fame.

It is said that even in her cradle the little Elizabeth gave signs of her future greatness and holiness. The first words uttered by her were the sacred names. Even at the age of three she expressed her compassion for the poor, and sought to alleviate their misery by gifts. How well her biographer expresses the history of those baby days: "Her first act was an almsdeed, her first word a prayer."

It is related that immediately after her birth the wars in which Hungary was engaged ceased. Peace and prosperity reigned throughout the kingdom. The people used to say that Elizabeth had brought these blessings with her.

Meanwhile the Duke of Thuringia, as soon as he had verified the predictions of Klingsohr as to the birth of the child, and had learned of the peace and happiness that had come with her, eagerly desired the fulfilment of the rest of the prophecy—that his son should be espoused to her. Travelers who came from Hungary always had something wonderful to relate about her. Once there came to the court a monk who declared that he had been blind from the age of four years and was cured by the touch of the little princess. "All Hungary," said he, "rejoices in this child, for she has brought peace with her."

And so the Duke sent an embassy of lords and ladies to the King of Hungary to ask, in the name of his young son Louis, the hand of Elizabeth, and, if possible to bring her back with them. It was a lordly embassy of at least thirty horses in the train, received with the greatest respect by all the princes and prelates through whose estates they passed. When they announced to the King of Hungary the purpose of their coming, he assembled his council to decide the matter. Klingsohr made an address, in which he told how desirable the match would be, both on account of Hermann's wealth and power and his fine personal character. The King was impressed, and yielded to the influence of his wife Gertrude, who was in favor of the marriage. They both agreed to give up their child to be trained by Hermann as the future wife of his son Louis. A great feast lasting three days, with games, dances, music, and poetry, was then given in honor of the little Elizabeth, after which the ambassadors took leave, bringing with them the little girl, four years of age, whom the attendants laid in a cradle of massive silver and covered with a silken robe embroidered with gold.

The King and Queen wept at losing their dear child; but it was the custom of the times, and they felt that they were making the sacrifice for the benefit of Elizabeth herself. It was a glorious dowry they sent with her, presents such as never before had been seen in Thuringia. With the little girl went thirteen noble Hungarian maidens as companions, all of whom Duke Hermann dowered and married in Thuringia. Elizabeth was received with great outbursts of joy. The Duke pressed her to his heart, and thanked God, who had sent her. The Princess was then solemnly affianced to the Duke Louis, then aged eleven, and the castle resounded with jubilation.

The profound piety which Elizabeth seems to have inherited from her good parents became intensified when to her, a little maiden in a foreign land, the news was brought that her mother Gertrude had been assassinated by her husband's subjects, whether from revenge at a crime of her brother or through accident from the plot against the life of her husband is not now certain. But it must have been a heavy blow to the precocious, serious little Elizabeth.

On her arrival in Thuringia, the Duke had selected seven maidens of the noblest houses to be her companions, amongst them his own daughter, Agnes. One of these companions was Guta, five years old, who remained with Elizabeth, her constant companion up to a short time before Elizabeth's death. From her we get the details about the girlhood of Elizabeth. All the child's thoughts seemed centred in God. Even before she knew how to read she would take a large Psalter, go to the chapel, open the book and kneel and give up her soul to prayer and meditation. In the games she would lead the other little girls to the chapel. If it were shut she would kiss the door as a mark of love to her dear Lord. Even in her games she thought of God. Fancy her leading her playmates to the cemetery and saying to them, "Remember that one day we shall be nothing but dust!" And then she would make them kneel and pray with her. Every moment she had was given to prayer. And even in those days of childhood, when most little girls think of dolls, she was beginning the life of charity for which later on she was to be so noted. All the money she could get she gave to the poor, and she would even go into the kitchen of the castle to gather the remains of victuals to carry to the needy. A precocious child? Rather a child to whom had come in the infant days the wisdom of God.

When she was nine years old, in the year 1216,

the Duke Hermann died, and his eldest son, Louis, then sixteen, succeeded him. The death of the Duke was a blow to Elizabeth, for he had loved her as his own child, especially so on account of her great piety. Louis was still too young to rule, and his mother governed in his stead. She cared little for Elizabeth. The great piety of the child provoked her, as it did also Agnes and the other companions, who felt that Elizabeth's devotion was a reproach to them. Agnes used to tell Elizabeth that she was fit only to be a servant. To none of them did she appear as a real princess. And so even in those young days she had to suffer insult.

Elizabeth cared little for society. She was happiest when among the poor children, giving alms to them. It bothered her little that the others made fun of her. A story is told that once, when she went with the Duchess and the Princess Agnes to church on the Feast of the Assumption, Elizabeth, as soon as she saw the crucifix, took off her crown and laid it on a bench, and then prostrated herself. The Duchess reproached her for lack of dignity in "behaving like an ill-reared child." But Elizabeth replied, "My coronet would be a mockery of His thorny wreath"; and then she wept at the sufferings of Our Lord.

Already Elizabeth was being made to bear the Cross. When the time of her marriage approached all the relatives of Louis and all the councilors tried to prevent the union, saying that she ought to be sent back to her father, that she had too much of the peasant in her manners, and was not worthy to be the wife of the great Duke of Thuringia. The Duchess even tried to prevail upon her to enter a convent, and Agnes continued to insult her; but the persecution brought her nearer to God and she trusted in Him. She would do His will, whatever it was.

The only real friend she had at court was Louis himself. He rejoiced in what others condemned in his future wife, and his love for her increased day by day. In her moments of sadness he came to console her, and every time he returned from a journey he would bring her a gift. When one of the courtiers asked him if he intended to marry her, he exclaimed: "I love her, and love nothing better in this world. I will have my Elizabeth; she is dearer to me for her virtue and piety than all the kingdoms and riches of the earth."

So in 1220 the marriage was celebrated with great pomp at the castle of Wartburg. The tongues of the slanderers were silenced; Elizabeth was exonerated before the world. Louis was twenty, she was thirteen; two young hearts united in love, united in faith and virtue. The old biographers tell us that they loved with an inconceivable love. It was one of the happiest marriages in the history of the world, a romance of holiness.

The young Duke Louis was a man of whom any woman would be proud. He was celebrated for his beauty, having a perfect figure, fresh complexion, long fair hair, and a gentle expression, with a smile that was irresistible. No one could see him without loving him. And withal he was modest and bashful as a girl, so great was his unaffected purity, a great tribute to a youth who at the age of sixteen had become master of one of the richest principalities of Germany, and who was surrounded by insidious flatterers who would have been delighted to see him overcome, and who in fact did seek to entrap him in sins of lust.

Every morning he assisted at Mass. Religion was to him a practical matter, and the Church and the monasteries found in him an able defender. He enjoyed the society of religious men, and often came to the Benedictine Abbey where he had chosen his burial-place. On arriving there, his first visit was to the sick and poor, whom he would console, bestowing upon them alms, and sometimes leaving with them part of his rich costume. And in the midst of all his wealth he practised mortification, a true knight without fear and without stain. Yet he was no weakling. He was noted for his courage and for his physical strength and agility; a big man, big in strength and big in virtue. No wonder the young wife loved him dearly. It was a happy home, full of gaiety and good cheer, a truly royal house. And above all was the Duke's sense of justice. He banished from the court all who were haughty to the poor, all who did violence to others, and all bearers of slander. If a subject blasphemed or used an impure word, he was made to wear publicly for a certain time a mark of ignominy. He worked for the good of his people. Once he made war against Franconia in order to exact retribution for an injustice committed against a poor peddler. It was a happy reign, all too short, and all was due to the splendid, manly virtue of Duke Louis and the prayers of his noble lady, the dear St. Elizabeth.

And dearer than his kingdom to Louis was the possession of Elizabeth. What a handsome couple they must have been! She is represented as a perfect beauty, with a complexion clear brown, black hair, elegant figure, and wonderful eyes of tenderness. And more beautiful than all else was her lovely soul. Her love for Louis was almost childlike. She looked to him as her head, as a wonderful being whom she should respect as well as love. Her consideration was ever for him, and she answered his least sign or word. He was her king, and she his loving slave. She loved him all the more because she loved God so much. Piety was no obstacle to their affection; rather did it encourage her in her devotions and her works of charity. Together they advanced in virtue, just as they had grown together in life as "Brother" and "Sister," the loving names they called each other even after their marriage.

Louis and Elizabeth were inseparable. They could not endure being absent from each other. On his hunting excursions she went with him, even though it were over rugged roads and through storms. But when he went on long journeys and she had to remain at home she would lay aside her royal robes and dress as a widow and spend the time of his absence in prayer and mortification. But as soon as word came that he was returning, she would array herself in all her magnificence and go forth in simple, childlike joy to meet him. She sought to please him alone.

The only fear of the young wife was that she was too happy. Hence she sought to mortify herself. Sometimes, when her husband was away, she would spend the whole night in prayer. Under her royal robes she always wore the hair shirt. Every Friday, in memory of the Passion, and every day during Lent she had herself scourged, after which, joyful and serene, she would return to court. They were heavy penances that she endured, yet she was never gloomy. She was as merry as anybody at court and would take her part in the dance and play. She was a joyful saint, indeed. She used to say of those who prayed with long faces: "They seem as if they wished to frighten our good God; can they not say to Him all they please with cheerful hearts?" Yet she chastised her body, mortified her appetite by fasting, even at the royal table, without drawing attention to herself, and without making those who ate with her uncomfortable. Some days her only food was a bit of black bread. And all this from a girl who was only fifteen!

No wonder that Elizabeth was reproved by the whole court for these "extravagances," which were a reproach to the lives of those who were less spiritual. But she cared not so long as she pleased her God and her husband.

One day, when she entered the church, a crown on

her head, and dressed in regal splendor, her gown covered with precious stones, she glanced at the Crucifix, and seeing her Saviour naked and crowned with thorns, she fell fainting to the ground. From that moment she resolved to renounce all pomp of dress, save when the duties of her rank or the will of her husband required it. But even when she dressed in robes of state she would wear under them her simple robes and her hair shirt. She was a reformer in dress, and induced others of the noble ladies at court to imitate her simplicity, even making patterns of dresses for them.

Strict with herself, she was generous to the poor, so much so that she merited to be known as the "Patroness of the Poor." We have seen that even as a little girl she loved to help the poor; and now, with her husband encouraging her in this holy work, it became one of the dominating thoughts of her life. Rich as she was, it often happened that she would despoil herself of her clothes rather than see any poor person unaided, so great was her generosity to the poor.

But she gave them more than money and food and clothes: she gave them love, her personal care, visited them in their homes, tended their sick-beds, and always with that matter-of-fact simplicity that put them at their ease. Poor women about to become mothers were her special care. She would take the new-born babe and dress it with garments she herself had made, and many a time would hold it at its baptism. When one of her poor died she would come and watch the body, and cover it with her own hands, often with sheets from her own bed, and many a time she would take part in the funeral procession as the humblest mourner.

And with all that charity to others, she was not idle at home. She spun wool with her maids, and made it into garments for the poor. She was, in fact, always solicitous for the poor, and when she discovered that any one of them had been treated unjustly she would denounce the injustice to her husband and seek redress for him.

There is a beautiful legend that one day, as she left the castle carrying under her mantle food for some of her poor people, she was suddenly met by her husband as he was returning from the hunt. Astonished at seeing her carrying a burden, he said, "Let us see what you carry," and at the same time lifted her mantle. But beneath it he saw only red and white roses, the most beautiful he had ever seen, and this, too, when it was not the season of flowers. Seeing that she was troubled, he sought to caress her, and then he beheld over her head a luminous crucifix. He told her to continue on her way, and he went on to the castle, carrying one of the roses, which he always preserved. At the spot where this meeting took place he had a pillar erected surmounted by a cross to consecrate the place of the vision.

The more repulsive the sickness, the more eager was Elizabeth to tend the sufferer. Lepers especially touched her heart. While others drew away from them, she drew near. On Holy Thursday she would gather a great number of lepers, wash their hands and feet, and kiss their sores. There was one poor little leper whose condition was so deplorable that no one would come near him. Elizabeth, however, tended him and then laid him in her own bed. The Duke's mother, who was still unfriendly to her, came to her son and told him what had happened, leading him to the room where the leper lay. The Duke was irritated that a leper had been put in his bed, but as he raised the covering he saw in the place of the leper the figure of Jesus Christ crucified, and he burst into tears. Shortly after that Elizabeth got his permission to build an almshouse, and there she kept twenty-eight sick and poor, whom she daily visited, feeding and tending them. She loved the poor and she loved poverty. "O my God," exclaimed St. Francis de Sales, "how poor was the Princess in her riches and how rich in her poverty!" Sometimes she would remove her royal robes and put on a mantle like those worn by the poor, and, walking before her companions, would feign to beg her bread. "Thus will I walk," she said, "when I shall be poor and in misery for the love of my God." She little knew that the day would come when these words would prove true. She loved the poor, but she loved God more. Her greatest happiness was to be in church. She received Holy Communion frequently. Holy Thursday night she would remain in the church. "All her glory," said one of her contemporaries, "was in the cross and passion of Christ; the world was crucified to her and she to the world." She wept over her simple faults, seeing how they withdrew her from God, but often as she was in tears, the beauty of her countenance was never harmed.

The spirit of St. Francis of Assisi was then in the air. His abandonment of the world took place the year Elizabeth was born. He had established his Third Order for those whose duties kept them in the world, an Order that required special sacrifices from those who joined it. The Order spread rapidly everywhere. No one encouraged it more than Elizabeth. She founded a convent of Franciscans in the capital city, and was the first person in Germany to be associated with the Third Order. Francis, at the request of the Cardinal Protector of the Order, afterwards Gregory IX, who canonized her, sent her his poor old mantle, which she cherished until her death. And all the while, under the direction of Conrad, a learned and holy priest, she was making remarkable progress in sanctity.

In 1223, at the age of sixteen, Elizabeth gave birth to her first child, a son who was called Hermann. A year later she gave birth to a daughter, Sophia. She had two other daughters, one also called Sophia— though her existence is denied by some biographers— and Gertrude, who later on took the veil. After each of her confinements, as soon as she was able, she went secretly from the castle, barefoot, clothed in plain woolen robes, to the Church of St. Catherine outside the city, and laid the infant on the altar, offering it to Christ and His Blessed Mother.

When the Duke joined the Emperor in the war against the Bolognese a frightful famine overspread all Germany, and especially Thuringia. The poor were reduced to the extremity of eating roots and stuff such as only animals eat. They even ate dead horses and unclean beasts. Many died, so that the roads were covered with dead bodies. It may be easily imagined that the Duchess Elizabeth had no other thought than the alleviation of this distress. She spared nothing. She emptied the ducal treasury, sold its lands, opened the granaries of her husband, and gave all the grain to the poor. She had bread baked at the castle and with her own hands served the needy. She gave the poor her personal attention, and even built two almshouses in the city, visiting them morning and night, and going from bed to bed to console the afflicted, making their beds, washing their faces, and all with a kindness and gaiety that made them regard her as an angel from God. In one of the hospitals she established an orphanage, and there she found her delight sitting in the midst of the little ones, who called her "Mamma." She was everywhere, in the hospitals, in the huts of the poor, in the prisons, wherever there was suffering to be alleviated. She even sold her jewels and other precious articles in order to get money to carry on her charities.

When the Duke returned from the wars the officers

of his household went out to meet him, and told him of what they considered the reckless extravagance of the Duchess in giving his possessions to the poor. "Is my dear wife well?" he asked. "That is all I care to know; the rest matters not. I wish that you would allow my good little Elizabeth to give as much alms as she pleases, and that you would rather assist than contradict her. We shall never be impoverished by almsdeeds."

The joy of Elizabeth at the return of the Duke was boundless; she kissed him a thousand times, happy to be reunited with him. But the joy of the reunion did not last long. They were soon again separated, and this time forever. The occasion of the separation was the new Crusade to rescue the tomb of Christ, a desire that animated the whole thirteenth century. To none did it appeal more than to Louis when he was summoned by Emperor Frederick II in 1227, and at once he was eager to go, as his ancestors had gone. When Elizabeth heard of it—she was then pregnant with her fourth child—she swooned at the thought of losing her dear husband and at the thought of her unborn child. But when he told her of the vow he had made she overcame her grief, and bade him go in the name of God. But it wrenched her heart. With sobs they parted, and as he went she put on widow's mourning which never again would she lay aside. For scarcely had Louis set sail than he was stricken with fever and died at Otranto, a man in the vigor of youth

—he was only twenty-seven—one of the noblest men that ever lived.

When the news reached home Elizabeth had just given birth to her daughter Gertrude. It was the Duke's mother that broke to her the bad news. The young wife cried out in her grief, "O Lord my God, my God, now indeed is the whole world dead to me; the world and all it contains of happiness!" Then she rose from her bed and ran distractedly through the castle, crying out, "He is dead! He is dead!" The young widow of twenty was heart-broken, for after God she worshipped her husband. So ended one of the happiest marriages history records, a union not only of love, but sanctified by piety of heroic degree on the part of both husband and wife.

But God, who had sent her the years of happiness, now sent her the years of pain. Scarcely had the nine days' wonder of the Duke's death on foreign shores passed away than there was plotting against his widow. The Duke's brothers, Henry and Conrad, taking advantage of the powerlessness of Elizabeth and her children, assumed control of the government and ordered them to leave the castle. She pleaded with them for delay, but they were inexorable. Their mother also pleaded with them, for she pitied deeply the misery of her daughter-in-law and her grandchildren. But they would not relent in their course of injustice. Out of the castle they turned her, penniless, and the gates were closed on her and her helpless little ones. On foot, carrying her infant and with her other children following, accompanied by her two faithful companions, she descended the rugged road, not knowing where she was to find shelter. She came into the city of Eisenach, where so often she had befriended the poor, but no one would give her a helping hand. The Duke Henry had issued a proclamation that whosoever received the Duchess Elizabeth and her children would incur his displeasure. Door after door they came to, only to be turned away, until finally they found a lodging in the miserable outhouse of a tavern, where the owner kept his swine.

Elizabeth, however, for her own sake rejoiced in the humiliation, happy to suffer for the love of God; and, going to the Franciscan convent to assist at the office, she begged the monks to sing a Te Deum in thanks to God for the trials He had sent her. She remained in the church that night and part of the next day, until the cold and hunger drove her forth to beg for her children. A poor priest took her and her children in and gave them shelter and food. But as her misery soon increased, she found it necessary to give up her children to the care of friends, and they were taken away and concealed in different places. Now that they were provided for, she cared not for her own destitution, and tried to earn her living by spinning. Yet even in those days of poverty she divided what she earned with the poor. Some later biographers have questioned this story of her persecutions, and say that she left the castle voluntarily in order the better to serve God. But whatever the case, she endured great trials, and they served only to bring her nearer to God. She suffered for Him, and, as a reward for those trials, it is related that she had many ecstasies and visions to console her.

Word was soon brought to her aunt, Matilda, abbess of Kitzingen, the sister of her mother, of the deplorable condition of the young widow. Immediately she sent carriages for her and her children to bring them to the abbey. Elizabeth, glad to be with her children once more, accepted the invitation, and there in the monastery found peace for her soul. She even expressed the desire, if she were free from the care of her children, to become a nun.

Meanwhile her uncle, the Bishop of Bamberg, desired her to marry again, and invited her to his dominions, assigning to her the castle of Botenstein as her residence, where she lived with her children and servants. It is said that he wished her to wed the Emperor Frederick, who had lost his wife. But she would not listen to the proposal. "Sire," said she, "I had for my lord a husband who most tenderly loved me, and who was always my loyal friend. I shared in his honor and his power; I had much of the riches, jewels, and pleasures of the world; I had all these, but I always thought, what you, my lord, know full well, that the joys of this earth are worthless." During her husband's life, even, she had made a vow never to marry again if he died.

When the Crusade was ended the body of the Duke was brought home by his companions to be buried in his own country. Elizabeth was summoned to take part in the final service. Her grief was heart-rending. She threw herself upon the coffin and wept out her love · and her misery. "You know, O my God," she exclaimed, "how I loved this husband who loved you so much; you know that I would prefer him to all the delights of the world, if your goodness permitted it. You know that with him I would be willing to spend my life in misery, and beg my bread from door to door, throughout the whole world, solely to have the happiness of being by his side, if you willed it, O my God. Now I resign myself and him to your divine pleasure, and I would not, even if I could, purchase him back again at the price of a single hair of my head, unless it were agreeable to you, my good God!"

The procession then set out for Thuringia, and the noble Louis was laid to rest in the place he himself had chosen. As soon as this was done, the knights who had been his friends, having heard of the woes endured by Elizabeth and her children, demanded redress and obtained it. The usurping brothers expressed their repentance, and Elizabeth and her children were restored to their rights. Elizabeth resumed her place in the castle, and was given all the honors due her rank, as also the privilege to continue her works of piety and charity. She founded the hospital of St. Mary Magdalen, and again devoted herself to the sick and poor. But the courtiers did not relish such heroic virtue. They again called her a mad woman and a*fool, and some of them refused to speak to her. Finally she prevailed upon her brother-in-law, the Duke Henry, who was regent for her oldest son, to set aside a residence where she might dwell by herself.

Elizabeth was granted the city of Marburg with all its revenues. She had constructed near the convent of the Friars Minor a small house, like a poor cabin, and there she dwelt with her children and her faithful servants. She yearned for poverty, and even sought permission from her confessor to embrace the Franciscan rule in all its severity and beg her bread like the Poor Clares. But he refused to allow her to do this, thinking that for one in her position and with her responsibilities it was better to continue as a member of the Third Order. But in her heart she renounced all wealth, sought to draw herself away from the world, even trying to curb the excessive love she bore her children. And so on Good Friday, in the presence of her children and friends, she laid her hands on the altar-stone and vowed to renounce her will, her children, her relations, her companions, and all the pomps and pleasures of the world. Her hair was cut off, and she was clothed with the gray robe and girded with the cord. Ever after she went barefooted. She separated from her children, though it must have broken her heart to do so, Hermann and Sophia being sent to the castle of Creutzburg, and the other two girls placed in convents. She had made the supreme sacrifice for the Cross of Christ. She was criticized for this, called heartless, a fool, but she did not heed the insults. God had called her, and she had answered the call; that was all.

It was a life of poverty. The revenues from her property she gave to the poor, and then supported herself by her own work, living in a poor cottage and spinning wool. What a life for a duchess, slaving day by day, dividing her food, poor as it was, with the needy, wearing clothes that even the poor would have despised! No wonder her former friends regarded her as insane. But, like all saints, amid her trials she never lost the sweetness of her disposition.

When her father, the King of Hungary, heard of her poverty, he was displeased, and sent an ambassador to find out the reason. Her brother-in-law, the Duke, said to the ambassador: "My sister has become quite mad; every one knows it; you will see it yourself." And then he told of Elizabeth's voluntary poverty, and her predilection for the poor and the lepers. The ambassador wept when he saw her poverty, and asked: "When did any one ever see a king's daughter spinning wool?" He begged her to return to her father, but she refused, saying that she was happiest in her poverty, serving the King of kings.

So she served her King in lowliness and charity, till at last He called her home. She was but twenty-four when she died, just beginning life, one would say, but how much she had crowded into those few years! One day she was stricken with a fever. For twelve or fourteen days she suffered under it, always joyous, however, and always praying. She knew that she was going to die and her heart was glad. She wished to see none of her friends; the time was all too short to give herself wholly to the preparation for death. Humbly she made her confession, received the last sacraments, and then during the night of November 19, 1231, passed to her God.

When the news of her death was made known there was universal sorrow. It was known then what a loss the world had suffered in her who in her life had been despised and calumniated as a fool because she had chosen to be a humble follower of the Lord rather than a proud duchess. On the night before her obsequies in the Franciscan church in which she was buried, it was said that on the roof of the church an immense number of birds congregated to sing such music as never had been heard before. "These little birds," said St. Bonaventure, "rendered testimony to her purity by speaking of her in their language at her burial, and singing with such wondrous sweetness over her tomb."

As Elizabeth had herself worked miracles during her life, so when she was dead great wonders were wrought through her intercession. Scarcely was she buried when there was a movement toward her canonization, which took place at Pentecost, May 26, 1235. And thus, within five years after her death, Elizabeth was raised to the altars of God amid the universal acclaim of the people who through all the generations since have loved her.

What an example she was! A woman, daughter of

a king, a duchess, with all that the world holds dear, a woman who loved her husband and children, a woman blessed with wonderful affection, yet eager to sacrifice all for the service of God. To us who complain of hardship, who set our hearts on worldly treasures, what an example she is of the truth, that, after all, the only thing that really counts is to love God. The dear St. Elizabeth!

ST. RITA

[(1381–1457).

IT is related in the life of St. Jane Frances de Chantal that when, after the death of her husband and after having provided for the education and maintenance of her four children, she decided to leave the world and retire to Annecy, where she was to found the Congregation of the Visitation, her son, then an impulsive lad of twelve years, so dreaded the thought of being separated from her that in the attempt to shake her resolution he threw himself across the threshold and broke into sobs, pleading with her not to go. It was a sight to move the mother herself to tears, and to tempt her to accede to her natural mother-craving. "Can the tears of a child shake your resolution?" said a holy priest who witnessed this outburst of feeling. "Oh, no," answered the mother; "but, after all, I am a mother." And then she stepped over the lad, an action indicating that she would not permit even her motherly affection for her children to stand in the way of her serving God.

When I think of St. Jane, somehow I do not recall her as the admirable mistress of novices, as the foundress of convents, as the spiritual adviser to

queens and princes and princesses; I rather picture
that incident of her stepping over the body of her son,
that son who later on was to give her so much pain.
A trivial incident it may seem out of the life of one
who did so many glorious things for the Church of
God. But is it trivial, after all? Does it not picture
the real woman, torn between love for her beloved lad
and the love of God? It was the moment of her decision. God should count even more than the son God
had given her.

In the same manner, when I think of St. Rita, there
is associated with her very name an incident in her
life that, compared with the many events in her later
life as a religious and as a saint to whom God showed
wondrous signs of His good pleasure in her, might
be regarded but as passing. It is the incident in her
life when, in her wondrous outburst of mother-love,
a love that saw beyond the preferments of this life
and regarded the few years of sojourn in this world
as insignificant beside the vast stretch of eternity, she
—a mother, mind you—prayed for the death of her
twin sons,—a prayer, too, which God in His goodness
granted to the heart-broken but joyful mother. When
I have told you the story of St. Rita's life, perhaps you
will recall her in the same manner, not as the glorious
saint, not as the ecstatic nun, but as the poor mother
torn between earthly affection for her boys and the
fear that these lads, the pride of her life, would lose
their immortal souls. What matter about her own
grief, what matter if she were left alone in the world,

so long as she might see them laid away in their graves before they had soiled their hands with the blood of a brother man. Again, like St. Jane, she would step over the bodies of the children of her own flesh and blood in order to serve God and avert any crime against His glory. St. Rita became a great saint, the saint whom the Spaniards lovingly call the "Saint of the Impossible" to show the confidence they have in her powers of intercession. She was also a great mother. It was perhaps because she was a great mother that she became a great saint. God gave her newer and greater graces because she co-operated so well with that grace that moved her to put Him above her children. All through the life of St. Rita runs the thread of the service of God. It is a thread upon which is strung the great jewel of her mother-love, surely not the least precious jewel in a life which was a veritable casket of pearls of great price.

Rita's maiden name was Mancini. There was very little about her father, Antonio Mancini, to have his name handed down to posterity. A poor farmer, he would have been the last one to take any glory to himself or to think or to fancy that his name should be kept in remembrance a day after he was dead. He was just a humble servant of God, doing his hard work and striving for the salvation of his soul. And yet his name is in lasting remembrance, for no child comes to glory without reflecting a light upon the parents to whose influence, when all is said, so much of that glory is to be attributed. Antonio Mancini was a good and just man. He was blessed, too, in having a good wife. Her name was Amata Ferri, and he had brought her from the little village of Fogliano to the other little village of Rocca Porena, situated a few miles from Cascia, then a thriving city of Umbria, at a distance of seventy-five miles from the great centre of Rome. A devoted couple they were, finding the secret of the contentment of life in the work that goes hand in hand with religion. One would not call them poor; they were just in comfortable circumstances, getting a good living out of their farm.

They had not an abundance of this world's goods, but they had enough to be able to practise charity; perhaps because they did not have an abundance they were all the more charitable, for it is from the poor, somehow, that most of the charity in the world comes. Anyway, they were noted among the people of the village for their kindness to the needy, one reason being that they did not have a large family of children like those with which their neighbors were blessed. Reading the life of St. Rita, we have no difficulty in picturing the Mancinis as the leading family in that town of small farmers. It was the custom in the village for the people themselves to be their own judge and jury. It was very likely a relic of the old freetown government. There was with the farmers of Rocca Porena no silly business of going to law. Every year a man and his wife were appointed to be referees for a period of twelve months. All the disputes that arose in the community were brought to them for settlement. It did away with a lot of legal red tape and was withal a cheaper way to get justice. Many a year were the Mancinis given this task of settling the family squabbles. And even when they were not the appointed "judges," they were always ready to pour oil on the troubled waters, so much so that they were affectionately called the "peacemakers of Jesus Christ." I fancy the wife was very much of a philosopher. "Take care," she used to say to the women of the town whenever there was any misunderstanding, "that your long tongue has not caused the trouble between you and your husband." All in all, it is a picture of pastoral simplicity—that simplicity which gets its true wisdom from the spirit of faith.

There was, however, one great sorrow to the peacemakers: they had no children. As the years went by and they passed into old age, there finally came the time when they ceased to hope for a child. But one day Amata, old as she was, realized that she was about to become a mother. It is easy to picture the amazement of the good old soul when she knew that the prayers of her young wifehood were to be answered long after she had despaired of such a blessing. The story is told, and it is not too difficult to believe in the life of one so closely united to God, that an angel appeared to her and assured her that this was a special favor from the Almighty. It is like a page from the life of the old mother of St. John the Baptist. When one is dealing with the lives of those who are great in the kingdom of God, one should not be surprised at extraordinary signs of God's approval.

The child of such especial favor was born on the twenty-second of May, in the month of Our Lady, 1381. One need not be told that the event gave rise to much gossip among the neighbors. It was good-natured gossip, more an expression of amazement than anything else, for not one but rejoiced in the fortune of Amata Mancini, who was loved by everybody. No wonder that these simple-hearted farmers and wives of farmers could see in the event nothing but a wondrous miracle. It was to them almost as much a matter of pride as to the Mancinis themselves that their little village, hidden away under the Apennines, was made the scene of such a prodigy; for all were made acquainted with the vision of the angel.

That was the first of the prodigies related of the birth of the infant. Another was to follow in that always interesting family event, the choice of a name for the new baby. What should she be called? Should it be Amata, or should it be some treasured family name, his mother's, or Amata's, perhaps? Again the angel decided, and, appearing to Amata once more, told her that the new baby should be called Rita—a strange name, a new name, a name the meaning of which they did not understand. But it was not theirs to question. Rita it should be, a name the music of which has been sounding on earth ever since it was given to the humble child of humble parents who served God five hundred years ago.

We need not, if we do not wish to do so, accept all the stories of wonderful happenings about the cradle of little Rita. There were enough of real miracles in her life subsequently, enough of graces and miracles granted through her intercession, and still granted to those who do honor to her, things that can be proved historically, to understand how she was marked by God, without troubling to prove whether this or that story is an actual happening or merely a poetic legend. There is one story, however, that is told by all her biographers to the effect that when she was five days old a swarm of white bees, the like of which had never before been seen, appeared mysteriously, and, buzzing about the face of the child, went in and out of her little mouth. The white bees have ever been connected with the life of St. Rita; St. Rita's bees they are called, and have served many an artist who has pictured some incident in her life. It is said that even to-day in Cascia, in the convent wall, midway between the place of the cell she occupied as a nun and her last resting place, the white bees still have their nest, still St. Rita's bees for these five centuries. It is a legend worthy of St. Francis of Assisi.

Like father, like son. The Mancinis were such a pious couple, it was to be expected that their child, especially a child that had been the object of such divine favor, would also give signs of extraordinary piety. One thing in Rita's favor was that there was no nonsense about her parents. They were not the kind that would be likely to have a spoiled child. They would not be slow to tell her that she was the child of humble parents, if she had any disposition to be hard to manage, as so often happens in the case of an only child. But little Rita gave no trouble to her parents. She was ever docile, ever ready to do her share of work in the household, sedate beyond her years, so serious, too, that she did not seek amusement in those things which take up the interest of the ordinary child. Even from her smallest years she sought to serve God as well as she could. At a time when other little girls are letting their fancy run away after pretty dresses, Rita used to hide herself whenever there was any attempt to deck her out in the simple finery the doting parents chose for her; at a time when others are playing with dolls, Rita was initiating herself into the wonders of serving God by prayer and fasting. Imagine a little tot wanting to fast for the good of her soul! And then, to make it more meritorious, we find her giving part of every meal to some poor child that was not as well off as this favored daughter of the Mancinis. To them she seemed as a child to be envied; but they did not see or envy the wonderful graces which she prized more than all material blessings. A precocious child, one might say; too old-fashioned. But hardly so to Him who delighted in having the little ones about Him. Sometimes, one may say, there is the disposition to underestimate the intelligence of children. They understand more than we give them credit for, and particularly in the things of faith. The sainted Pontiff, Pius X, gave the final answer to the minimizers of the child mind when, in his decree about the age at which children should be admitted to Holy Communion, he echoed these undying words, the eulogy of the child: "Suffer the little children to come unto me, and forbid them not, for of such is the kingdom of heaven." Rita was wise beyond her years, but why marvel at it when she had the God of wisdom as her teacher?

We could dwell long on the life of the child at this period. Even then she loved to meditate upon the Passion of Christ. She had a little room apart from the rest of the household, and thither, when her work of helping her mother keep house was over, she would retire and find her simple joy in the pictures of the Passion which she had placed on the walls. She never tired of being alone with God. No wonder, then, that after such a childhood of prayer she expressed the wish, when she was twelve, to leave home and become a nun in one of the convents of Cascia where so many holy men and women had sanctified their souls.

The parents must have foreseen that the day would come when she would desire to leave them for the higher life. All her training, even the training which they had given her, was to that end. Yet when the little maiden told them that she wished to enter the convent they were amazed and displeased. They loved her so much, how could they bear the thought of parting with her who was their very life?

We see the same thing so often to-day. Even pious

parents that should know better make an uproar when their daughter expresses a desire to give herself to God. They cannot bear to separate from her, forsooth; yet they will see the same girl marry and go away hundreds of miles to live where they may never see her again. They know that the girl will be happy in the convent, but they feel obliged to protest, and so in many cases, by their unreasonable opposition, spoil the girl's vocation and perhaps ruin her life forever. It is not true parental love; it is downright selfishness. Sometimes it would seem that God permits this opposition in order to test the love and loyalty of the one He calls. And it may have been that the opposition that came to Rita from her pious father and mother was in order to lead her through suffering to greater virtue. At any rate, the old folks, honestly convinced, no doubt, that Rita's duty was to remain with them in their old age, persuaded her to put aside for a time at least the thought of entering the convent. Perhaps they considered that at her tender age—she was then but twelve—she scarcely knew her own mind and was unable to judge the mighty question of a life's vocation. So, covering up her disappointment, and feeling that God would work out the matter in His own good time, the little maid assented to the will of her parents and continued to be the sunshine of their lives.

But even a greater sacrifice was demanded of the girl by her parents, who strangely thought that they were working for her best interests. Not content with having her put aside the thought of becoming a nun

during their lifetime, they determined that she should
put it aside altogether by marrying. It may have been
the wish to perpetuate their family, it may have been
the wish to put her under the protecting power of a
husband before they passed on; whatever the reason,
they informed Rita that they had chosen a desirable
young man as her husband. Her tears were unavail-
ing. What did she know about the world, what did
she know about what was best for her own good?
Parents generally think themselves so wise, and sometimes their wisdom is folly. The Mancinis were certainly foolish in their choice of a husband for Rita.
To them it seemed the finest match possible. The
young Ferdinand was well to do, a dashing fellow
whom any girl ought to be pleased to get for a husband. They were simple old folks who knew little
of the world, and imagined that everybody was as
good as themselves. They were woefully mistaken
in their chosen son-in-law.

Ferdinand was a product of the terrible time in
which he lived. It was a time when the world was
upset with political disturbance. Even the Church
was harassed by anti-Popes. Morals were free and
easy; violence was the rule of the day. Ferdinand
was hardly the man to wed a shrinking, humble maiden
like Rita. She married him, nevertheless, because it
was the will of her father and mother. But she rued
the day almost immediately. He was a proud and
haughty fellow who very likely thought that he had
made a wonderful condescension in marrying the

daughter of poor farmers. Not only was he surly to
her, but even abusive, and many a time she had to
take a blow from him. She was his slave, and not
even could she leave the house to go to church without
asking his permission. He was that worst type of
man—the man who bullies his wife. That was hard
enough to stand; but there was a more bitter drop in
the cup. The young wife soon found out that he was
dissipated. A woman can stand almost anything but
that from the man she loves. And Rita did love her
husband dearly. What a pain, then, it was to see him
dissolute, to know that he was squandering his money,
to know that he had little or no religion—in plain
words, that he was an immoral, brutal tyrant. But,
heart-broken as Rita was with the realization that her
marriage was a big mistake, she was not crushed by
it. It was then that her spirit of religion came to her
help and prevented her from being a surly and dis-
consolate wife. Rita made up her mind that she had a
work to do in the conversion of her husband. She did
not meet railing with railing. She took his abuse
silently, waited on him hand and foot, studied his
temper, and more than all prayed for him incessantly.

As one reads the story of Rita's married life one
sees why God permitted her to be married to such a
man, even while he had favored her with such wonderful graces all her life and filled her with longings to
serve him in the cloister. It was to give to ill-treated
wives a model. How many a woman has been broken
in body and soul by living with an unworthy husband!

How many have suffered and complained, yet thought it an impossibility to bring the erring one back to God! The good Catholic wife will pray for such a man in season and out, knowing that, desperate as the case may seem, all things are possible to prayer.

And Rita's prayers, her humble submission, her gentleness in suffering, were rewarded. She was making then, even when she knew it not, the novitiate to that later suffering which was to contribute so much to her sanctification. The erring husband at length had the grace to see himself in all his meanness. One day, overcome by the sudden realization of what a treasure he had in his wife, seeing her the gentle martyr to his brutality, he threw himself at her feet and begged her to forgive him for all his crimes against her, promising that never again would he offend her in any particular. He was as good as his word. He overcame his temper, was gentle with her, and returned to the practice of his religion. It was at last a marriage of love on both sides. Patience and prayer had won the day.

But Ferdinand was not as fortunate in regard to others whom he had antagonized. It was not to be expected that all should have the forgiving disposition of his wife. He had made many enemies. It was a time when enemies were readily made, and Ferdinand, with his nasty disposition, made more than his share. He paid for his temper in the end. We do not know now the details of the trouble that finally led to his death. But one day his dead body was found in a

field a short distance from the village. He had been
brutally murdered. It is easy to picture the anguish
of poor Rita when they brought home to her the life-
less form of the man she had so loved during the
eighteen years of their married life. She wept bitter
tears and was inconsolable.

Not only was there the grief at his death. That
would have been hard enough if she had seen him die
in his bed with the consolation of a last word with him,
and the greater consolation of seeing him receive the
last rites of the Church. But he had died suddenly,
had been murdered by his enemies, with scarcely time
to call to God for mercy. Had he died in the grace
of God? Had he saved his soul? That is the first
thought that comes to the Catholic on hearing of a
sudden death: did he have the priest? did he have a
chance to make his peace with God? And that was
the cause of Rita's deepest sorrow, the uncertainty as
to how it was with the soul of her husband. But again
she bowed to the will of God and took up her burden
of sorrow, determined to devote herself now more
than ever to her duty of looking after the two sons
who at the time of their father's death were just coming to their youth.

The two boys, Gian Giacomo and Paolo, are said
by some biographers to have been twins. They had
been a consolation to her, and yet a sorrow, too. Very
early the mother had discovered that they took after
their father to a great extent. They were irascible,
and besides that, they had his bad example before them

to counteract the good advice and gentle example of
their mother. Rita had many a worry over them, and
many a prayer did she say that they might not follow
in the footsteps of their father. Who could blame
her to hope, in the midst of her sorrow at the death
of her husband, that these growing youths would be
her consolation, the prop of her old age?

And one day, perhaps the saddest day in her life,
she learned that her boys were planning murder; they
were bound to have revenge for the death of their
father. They knew who had killed him, and they
would have a life for a life. Rita taxed them with
the crime they were meditating. They listened to her,
perhaps impatiently; but their hearts were not softened. What did a woman know about the manly sport
of revenge? Was it not true manhood to avenge the
blood of their father? In spite of what she said, they
would merely seem to assent to her wishes, pretend
forgiveness of their father's enemies, and then when
the opportunity presented itself they would exact justice. When it was all over she would have to put up
with it.

But mothers are wiser than sons give them credit
for. Rita knew that she had been powerless to change
their hearts. But if she could not do it, she knew One
that could. She threw herself before the feet of God
and begged Him to have pity on her mother-love. She
begged Him to change the hearts of her boys and prevent them from destroying their own souls by the
crime of murder. And then she made the supreme act

of renunciation. If God would not change their hearts, at least she begged Him to take them out of this world before they had the opportunity to commit the murder they were planning. What a heartless thing! one might be tempted to say. How could a mother ask God to have her children die? Surely she could have no love for them, to ask such a thing. But it was just there that Rita showed how much she did love her children. They were dear to her, dear as any mother's children are, but her love was not selfish. She would not keep her children to herself at any cost. Their first duty was to God. And even while they had sinned in their hearts she chose rather that they should lie dead at her feet than that they should carry into execution their wish for revenge. One is reminded of the great Blanche, who used to say to her son: "My son, you know how much I love you, but I would rather see you dead at my feet than know that you were guilty of one mortal sin." That is the real mother-love, to set itself aside and to think only of the glory of God and the salvation of the souls of those committed to its care.

It was an act of heroism on the part of Rita. To me it seems the supreme moment in her life, the thing that I always think of when I hear the name of St. Rita mentioned. And God answered that prayer. The two sons were taken ill, their hearts were freed of the desire of revenge, they atoned for their sins and died. And the strange thing is that their mother did not weep for them. Heartless? Any one that knows

Rita knows what a tender heart she had. That heart was wrenched by the parting with her two beautiful boys, but what was the grief of the world to the thought that God had reclaimed them from their sins and brought them to Himself? She had saved the souls of her boys; what mattered anything else? Supposing that they had grown to manhood, had attained wealth, yet all the while had upon their souls the sin of murder, and had as a result of that finally lost their souls? Then their lives would have been in vain. To Rita, in her wisdom, sin was the great evil, and not death. She could grieve over sin, but not over the death even of her loved ones when she knew that they were all right with God.

Rita was now alone in the world. In a short time she had been bereft of her husband and her two sons. How many a woman in her case would think that she had been unjustly visited. But she never made complaint. It was the way of the Cross along which Christ was leading her who even as a little child hid herself in her own little room in order to meditate upon His Passion and Death. Like her old mother before her, she was now more than ever the consolation of the village. In her simple manner of living she did not need much to get along with, and all that she could afford she gave to the poor. It is told of her that many a time she would take off her cloak and give it to some poor person she met on the road. Her clothes were of the simplest, and always did she wear the sackcloth as a reminder to her that she must ever be doing penance.

Rita did not remain long in the world after the death of her children. The voice that had called her to a life of religion had never been stilled. She had married out of obedience to the wish of her parents, but all the while her heart was set on serving God in the cell of some convent. Now, when her work was done, when she had fulfilled her duty to her own— for the life of this woman was ever a life of duty and self-sacrifice, whether to parents or to her husband and children—up from the depths of her heart there sounded once more the call of God.

She had often been to the neighboring city of Cascia and had envied the good holy women who had been allowed to spend their lives in the cloister. In Cascia there was a convent of nuns, at that time called the nuns of St. Mary Magdalen, who followed the rule of St. Augustine. Thither she came one day in fear and humility and asked the good nuns to let her join them. They were amazed at her request. Their convent was only for virgins; it was contrary to their custom to receive a woman that had been married. It was a terrible blow to the poor widow, but she did not complain at the refusal of the nuns to take her in. Rather did she reproach herself and seek to find in her soul the cause of her apparent rejection by God. Again she went back to them, and again was she rejected; and still again. But she was not daunted. She was the valiant woman. God had ever heard her prayers, and he would hear them now. He was trying her, leading her, as she thought, to make herself less unworthy of being admitted among his chosen ones.

It was a wondrous way in which God did finally answer those prayers. She was then thirty-two years of age, a young woman who had crowded into a few years the sufferings of centuries. One night, when she was at her prayers, she had a vision. St. John the Baptist appeared to her and gave her a sign to follow him. In fear and trembling she did so, and was led by him to a spot where St. Augustine and St. Nicholas Tolentine awaited her. These three saints had been the special objects of her devotions, and now she understood that they were to reward that devotion. They led the way and she followed, raised out of herself at the thought of the wonderful thing which was happening to her. Up hill, over the rocks they led her until they came to the convent of Cascia. Silently some unseen hand opened the gates to her and she found herself in the enclosure of the convent as the heavenly guides withdrew. It is only a saint that can imagine Rita's devotions that night, as she waited for the dawn to break upon the gray walls of the convent. Her prayers were answered at last.

Judge of the amazement of the nuns, when they rose to sing the morning office, to find within the enclosure of their convent the woman whom they had so repeatedly rejected. They were perhaps a bit indignant at what they considered her effrontery, impatient at her determination in asking for what they had told her finally was an impossibility. Many a question they put to her, and then Rita humbly told them about her vision, about the great saints that had led her from her home at Rocca Porena through the darkness of the night into the sacred precincts of the convent. Would they not now believe that it was God that was calling her and let her become one of their number? It was needless to ask. The nuns knew that they had seen the signs of God's finger. With hearts bursting with joy at the marvel God had wrought, they welcomed the widow to their home, put upon her the customary penitential habit, and admitted her to the novitiate,—her who had been through a novitiate such as few endure. It is beyond my province, dealing as I am with the life of Rita as wife and mother, to detail her life in the cloister. It is a simple life, uneventful as regards those happenings which are supposed to lend interest to a biography, but not uneventful to Rita herself. In the cloister her soul had its great chance to expand. And the striking thing about that hidden life is that it differs so little from the life she had been leading in the world. Sanctity was no sudden change for her. She had been practising all virtues as well as she could from the infant days when she wished to vow herself to God. Her ardor was but increased when she became a novice. But the good nuns, who were well accustomed to behold the operations of grace in the souls of one another, marvelled at the beauty of soul of the widow who had come among them almost miraculously. It was such great virtue that God rewarded it with many a vision. But at the same time it was not an easy virtue. Rita attained sanctity by the only road by which it is possible to attain it—by the road of the Cross. She had her temptations—temptations even against that virtue of purity which so shines out in all her life from her infancy—and she fought against them with the same old, reliable weapons of mortification, fasting, and prayer. She did not hesitate even to scourge herself, to wear the hair cloth, to keep vigil in prayer during the long hours of the night. No wonder that, as the result of this rigorous penance, the time soon came when one could almost see her bones.

So there passed thirty years. Think of it! Thirty years of fasting, of scourging, of every conceivable mortification. And then, as if this old woman—she was then sixty-two years of age—had not suffered enough, God sent her an affliction which, while it was the source of terrible suffering, was also the mark of His great love for her.

One day, she with other nuns listened to the sermon of St. James of the Marshes, who was sent forth to preach the Crusade, and as he spoke of the Passion of Christ, her heart overflowed with love for the Crucified. Returning to her cell, she cast herself at the feet of the Crucifix and begged Christ to let her taste at least of His bitter chalice. Immediately, one of the thorns detached itself from His crown and struck into the left side of her forehead, almost penetrating the bone and causing her the most exquisite pain. As the time went on the wound grew larger, festered, and became infested with worms—"her little angels," as she would call them because of the suffering and the means to do penance which they brought her. For fifteen years this continued; the sore became obnoxious to sight and smell—so much so that Rita was obliged to keep to her cell so as not to offend the other nuns. That was her dearest treasure, the proof of divine love. When she went to Rome on one occasion to gain the indulgence of the Jubilee, the sore healed miraculously, but broke out when she returned to her cloister.

So it went on till the end—suffering and still more suffering. At last she was stricken with her mortal illness, an illness that lasted full four years. During all that time she remained confined to her bed, never giving annoyance, always edifying those who marveled at such patience in the midst of terrible agony. Her only regret was that she had become so useless to the community, not realizing that the daily sight of such heroic patience was the greatest service she could render her sisters in religion.

One day, towards the end, a relative called to visit her and asked her if there were any favor she could do her. "Yes," said the old nun, "I beg you to go to the garden of my house as soon as you reach Rocca Porena and pluck a rose there and bring it to me." The visitor thought that Rita was wandering in her mind, but returning to the little village which had been the scene of so much of the happiness and the sorrow of Rita's life, what was her surprise, though it was the bitter month of January, to see one lone red rose on the bush in the garden where once Rita, the happy wife and mother, had tended her flowers and prayerfully planned the future of those children now with God these many years. It was an amazing happening to the sisters, yet they had long been aware of the special favors God was showering upon her. That miracle of the rose has often served the artists who have sought to portray the gentle St. Rita.

It was a beautiful prelude to the end. The rose was to bloom forth in undying glory. Forty-four years had Rita been a nun, and then, in the year 1457, in the seventy-sixth year of her life, this glorious rose was transplanted to the gardens of heaven.

And the rose has never lost its fragrance. Even when Rita died there was an odor of sweetness from the poor emaciated body, even from that sore which had always been so repellent to the onlooker. That odor has continued ever since. Her body has never seen corruption, and even the poor garments in which she was laid to rest have been saved from destruction.

From the very day of her death, Rita's power with God has been most manifest. Countless are the cures that have been effected through her intercession. There has been devotion to her almost since the day of her death, a devotion that has in these latter days spread with such rapidity over the face of the earth. Pope Leo XIII, in pronouncing her canonization in the year 1900, referred to her lovingly as "Umbria's

precious jewel." She is even more than that, she is
a cherished jewel, not only of Umbria, but of the
whole world.

Surely the life of St. Rita is one to marvel at, and
one cannot be surprised at the hold which her devotion
has upon the hearts of the faithful. She may be
called a cosmopolitan saint, since she is a model for
womanhood in every walk of life. The nun in her
cloister can look to her for lessons in the hidden life;
the child just beginning to understand the mysteries
of God can see in her the kind of maid that God would
have her be; the maiden can find in her an example of
humility, obedience, and sweetest purity.

But what a lesson she is to the wife and mother!
And perhaps the reason that God in these days has so
popularized the devotion to St. Rita is that wives and
mothers particularly may learn from the saint their
awful responsibility before God in this sphere. We
are living at a time when marriage outside the Church
has become a farce. The bond that was to endure till
death is severed on the slightest provocation. There
is little danger that Catholic women will ever take that
attitude towards a holy sacrament; nevertheless, seeing this disregard of the sacred bond by so many of
their neighbors, there is always the danger of being in-
fected with some of that spirit, of becoming impatient under the trials of the marriage state. What
an example is Rita the wife! For years she endured
insult and brutality; her loving affection was profaned,
yet she bore it all with patience using this suffering

to sanctify her soul, and praying incessantly for the one whom many another woman in her pride would have despised.

What an example, too, to the mothers of men! One gets a truer insight into the soul of Rita, beholding her on her knees begging God either for the conversion or the death of her beloved sons, than from all the ecstasies with which God rewarded her. Even if God had called her from earth in that moment of supreme sacrifice, we do not hesitate to say that He would have found her a saint. What a wonderful thing is mother-love even at its lowest! What a heavenly thing it is when it shines through the sanctity of a Rita! That is what we may call her, then—the Saint of Mother-love.

ROYAL LADIES

W HAT women there are among the Christians!" exclaimed a pagan in the early days of
the Church. He had known woman only in her degradation, as the plaything, the slave of man, his chattel,
his inferior. No wonder he marveled when he saw
the kind of womanhood the Church produces; for to
the man with even the smallest knowledge of history,
there is nothing more evident than the fact that it was
the Church that put woman back on the pedestal from
which she had been cast. Christ had raised marriage
to the dignity of a sacrament. In His Church His
Mother occupied a unique place. To give Mary the
honor He wished her was to glorify the womanhood
of which she was the representative. This is so true,
that history since then has shown that the dignity,
the honor given woman in any age is in proportion to
that age's veneration for the Mother of God.

The history of the Church may be traced in the
history of the women she has produced. She has
found her women-saints in every condition of life,—
in the cloister, in the world, in the palace, in the cottage. We have seen the great saints that God made
out of some of the queens. And now we would take
a rapid glance at the other great women of royal

blood who, amid the temptations that come from worldly grandeur, found the way to serve God.

Sometimes the world runs away with the idea that it is essentially an impossibility for those in high station to be "poor in spirit." How false is that notion is plain from the study of the lives of the saints. Often in life the royal robe covers the hair shirt. There is for us all an example in this. It is that if these women, flattered by the world, surrounded by all that panders to the passions, yet put aside all contentment in these things to choose humility of heart, how much is expected of us whose eyes are not blinded by the glare that beats upon thrones!

It is not only among the Roman matrons that we find these high-souled women. They flower forth in every age and in every clime. Sometimes we find them, as in the case of St. Amelia, not only attaining sanctity themselves, but also leading their family to holiness. Amelia was married to Witger. They had three children, all of whom are canonized saints—St. Gudula, the patroness of Brussels; St. Reinelda; and St. Emembertus. After the birth of their last child, Gudula, Amelia and her husband withdrew from the world, she becoming a nun and he a monk. All this happened in the seventh century,—a long time ago, you say; but life was as sweet in those days as in our own; there was the same affection between husband and wife, the same love for children. Yet this holy woman and her husband, in order to come nearer to God, made a sacrifice of their affection to each other and to their children. Little has been preserved of their history, yet what greater tribute can be paid to this mother than this, that she not only sanctified herself, but also raised up for God three saints?

In that same century we find another saintly mother, St. Rictrude. She was a grand lady of France and was married to one of the lords of the court of Clovis. Her husband was assassinated, and then she entered the cloister, where she led a life of penance. She had four children, and all four are saints.

Sometimes, too, we find both wife and husband saints. In that same century we have the striking example of St. Waltrude. She was a countess and the daughter of a princess, Bertille, who was also a saint. She had two sons and two daughters. She induced her husband to enter a monastery, and founded a religious community where she lived a life of great penance. The husband is canonized as St. Vincent of Soignies.

In later times we find another instance of this double sanctity in the case of St. Delphina and her husband, St. Elzear. He was a very charitable man and she assisted him in the work of caring for the poor. He was a count and very wealthy. It is interesting to read the rules which he drew up for the conduct of his house. "Yet I desire," says he, "not that my castle should be a cloister, nor my people hermits. Let them be merry, and sometimes divert themselves; but never at the expense of conscience or with the danger of offending God."

What a union between husband and wife when both find their greatest joy in serving God! One finds an example of it in St. Mary of Oignies in that same thirteenth century. Her parents were wealthy, but she and her husband did not think it beneath them to serve the lepers.

So with the Venerable Raingarda. A great lady was she, but her true greatness consisted in the care with which she trained her children to virtue. She and her husband agreed to leave the world and enter religion. He died before he was able to put the plan into execution, but she entered a monastery and gave herself up to a life of penance. There are so many of these cases that one can only give them the barest mention. We read in the life of Maria de Agreda that she and her mother entered the convent of the discalced Franciscans, and that at the same time her father and her two brothers became Franciscan friars.

Sometimes we find holy widows withdrawing into the convent with their children. This was so in the case of St. Bertha in the early part of the eighth century. She had been nobly born, being the daughter of a count at the palace of King Clovis II. She was married to Siegfried, a relative of the King. After twenty years of married life he died, and Bertha determined to build a nunnery and leave the world. This she did and was followed into the convent by her two elder daughters, Deotila and Gertrude. Bertha became abbess. Sometime before her death she resigned the office and shut herself up in a little cell against the wall of the church to be alone with her soul.

No doubt when these holy women made such sacrifices, there were many of their friends who laughed at them and thought them fools for giving up the enjoyments of the world. Yet, strangely enough, it is only the names of these women who hid themselves from the world that are now remembered, while those that served the world are forgotten. So it is even with the world. But what of the glory that God has shown in heaven to them that chose to serve Him rather than the world? Sometimes, as in the case of St. Ida, they lived the life of the cloister even in the midst of courtly pleasures. She was the daughter of a count, and was educated at the court of Charlemagne. She married a great lord of the court, and the Emperor gave her a fortune. It was a happy union while it lasted, but the husband died young and Ida devoted herself to penance and prayer. She lived in the world and looked after her family, yet her life was that of a nun. She suffered, too, but patiently bore her ills. She devoted the immense revenues of her estate to the care of the poor. She is a fine example of a saint, in the world but not of the world.

Sometimes the story of these saintly wives and mothers reads like a romance. That of St. Godelina is a veritable novel. She was born in 1049 in France, the youngest child of a great lord. Even in her childhood she was noted for her great piety and charity. The poor used to flock to her, for they knew she was always ready to help them. So great was her generosity that her father's steward, and her father himself, pious and charitable as he was, used to find fault with her, and seek to restrain her generosity. Soon the fame of her beauty and virtue spread over all the country, and her hand was sought by many suitors. But the girl—she was then only eighteen—did not care to marry. She wanted to enter the cloister. Finally she was prevailed upon by political influence to marry Bertolf of Ghistelles, and set out with him for her new home. It was an unfortunate marriage. Bertolf's mother at once hated her son's wife, and persuaded him, on the very day they arrived home, to put her aside, and to imprison her in a narrow cell where she almost died from starvation. But even in her want she found a way to help the poor, and shared with them what was barely enough for herself. At last she escaped, and returned to her father, brokenhearted and ashamed, for her mother-in-law had circulated the vilest calumnies against her.

Her father, indignant at the treatment accorded her, so managed things that Bertolf was threatened with all the punishments of the Church and State if he did not take back his wife and give her the honor due her. Bertolf appeared to relent, and finally took back the young wife. But persecutions again broke out against her, and Bertolf, anxious to be rid of her, arranged that, while he was away from home, two of his servants should strangle her and make believe that she had died a natural death.

And so she was murdered at the age of twenty-one. Soon Bertolf married again, and a daughter was born to him, but she was blind. It was a hopeless case. Bertolf knew it was a punishment for his sin against Godelina. He invoked her help for the afflicted child, and the child was miraculously cured. To Bertolf it was the hand of God. He became converted, went to Rome to seek absolution for his sin, and after that made a pilgrimage to the Holy Land. So sincere was he in his penitence that he entered a monastery and lived there until his death. The daughter that had been cured afterwards erected, at his request, a Benedictine monastery dedicated to St. Godelina, and into it she retired from the world. It is of such stories of suffering that the lives of the saints are made. A hard life for the young wife of twenty-one, yet by that way of the Cross she came to eternal life. There were many Godèlinas, no doubt, in those days who went through life happy, singing, without a care, and thought the life of this afflicted one a terrible calamity. Yet all are gone, not even their names remain, and she, the suffering one, has been glorified during these thousand years. God has the final judgment.

We have seen in the case of St. Bertha that she entered the convent and brought her two eldest daughters with her. Sometimes it was the other way about, and we find the daughters leading the way for the mother. So it was in the case of the Blessed Hortulana, the mother of the great St. Clare, foundress of the Poor Clares. Hortulana had belonged to a noble family, and had married Favorini Scifi, Count of Sasso-Russo. The family was very wealthy and lived in a great palace at Assisi. The mother, Hortulana, was a woman of great piety. This is as evident in the lives of her children as in her own life. She had turned their hearts to God.

It was the time of the great St. Francis of Assisi. He had come to preach the Lenten course of sermons at Assisi, and Clare, who had always longed for a life of deep spirituality, begged him to help her lead such a life of poverty as he himself was leading. The result was that she left her father's castle, and, accompanied by her aunt, Bianca, and another companion, came to the humble chapel of St. Francis, and there, laying aside her rich dress, had her hair cut off and was clothed in a rough garment, and so vowed herself to Jesus Christ. Her father was furious, and even tried to drag her home by force. His anger was all the greater when, some days afterwards, her sister Agnes—St. Agnes of Assisi—came to join her.

We have not to deal with the life of St. Clare. It was a life of extraordinary beauty and sanctity. She had the happiness of seeing not only her sister Agnes, and another sister, Beatrix, but also her mother, Hortulana, enter the Order which God had raised her up to establish. The glory of the daughter obscures that of the mother; but as we contemplate the graves of all these holy women of one family buried together in the Church of St. Clare at Assisi, we must not forget how much of the sanctity of the children was due to the pious mother who, amidst wealth and luxury, formed the hearts of her daughters to love the meanest poverty. One can never think of St. Clare without thinking of her mother, the Blessed Hortulana. Indeed, how can one think of the life of any saint without remembering her who did so much to turn the little heart to God in the days of childhood?

Queen Blanche is remembered to-day for the warning she gave the little boy who later became the great St. Louis: "I love you, my dear son, with all the tenderness a mother is capable of; but I would infinitely rather see you fall down dead at my feet, than that you should ever commit a mortal sin."

Every day, we are told, he remembered those words. St. Louis is inseparable from his mother, Queen Blanche.

One sees that same spirit of faith in the bringing up of her son in the life of the mother of St. Antonio Maria Zaccaria, the founder of the Barnabites. His father had died when Antonio was a mere infant, but the good mother set about his training, and above all else taught him compassion for the poor and made him her almoner. It was this training of childhood that turned his heart to the work that occupied his life. When his work was done, at the early age of thirty-seven, he came back to the house of his mother to die. What a reward to her to see her son die the death of a saint!

Even in the peaceful days of the Church there have

been martyrs, and as such St. Helen of Sköfde, in Sweden, is venerated. She lived in the early part of the twelfth century, belonged to a noble family, and had all that the world could give. She was married, but as soon as her husband died she devoted herself to a life of prayer and charity. She was especially fond of the poor, and her home was always open to them.

Her sorrow came through her daughter. She was married to a tyrant who was finally put to death by his servants. They declared that they had been incited to the crime by Helen, and as soon as she returned from the Holy Land, whither she had gone on a pilgrimage, she was murdered by the relatives of her daughter's husband. Many cures were said to have been wrought through her intercession; so much so that from that time on St. Helena was a favorite saint in Sweden. Near the church which she had built was a holy well, which became the scene of many miracles. It was the tribute of God to one of the world's great mothers.

A truly great wife and mother was St. Hedwig, Duchess of Silesia. She was born in 1174 at the castle of Andechs, the daughter of a count. She was one of eight children, all of whom occupied a high place in the world. Two of her brothers became bishops and one sister an abbess. All the others became rulers or were married to rulers. Her sister Gertrude married the King of Hungary and was the mother of St. Elizabeth of Hungary.

Hedwig was educated in the monastery, and at the

age of twelve married Henry, who later became Duke of Silesia. He was a splendid ruler, a man of great piety, and a fit husband for the woman that was to become a great saint. In his government he was helped greatly by the wisdom of his wife, who by her support and encouragement of the monasteries contributed much to the spread of civilization. Monastery after monastery was founded by the pious couple; hospitals, too; and we see the pious Duchess tending with her own hands the poor leper women. She had the happiness of seeing her daughter Gertrude abbess of one of the monasteries established by her. It was a life of devotion to God; yet it was a life filled with worldly duties. Hedwig was the mother of seven children, some of whom died in infancy. After the birth of the last child the husband and wife made a vow of chastity.

They were a devoted couple, but they had their trials. Once, when he was set upon by his enemies and severely wounded, we find her hastening to his side to tend him; and again, when he was taken prisoner, it was she who went to seek his release. When at last he died, she went to live in one of the monasteries she had founded, in order that she might devote the rest of her days to penance and prayer. She was to the end a lover of the poor, and used up her great fortune in acts of kindness. Of all her children, only one, Gertrude, survived her. Hedwig had many sorrows, yet she bore them all for the love of God. With all her cares, how she might have pleaded that she

[158]

had no time for prayer and charity. But she was a valiant woman. She knew that one thing only is necessary—the love of God; and so with that thought a great mother became a great saint.

It is no uncommon thing, after all, in the history of the saints to find several saints in one family. A saintly mother inspires her children. It was so with St. Kentigerna of Ireland. She was of royal blood, the daughter of Kelly, Prince of Leinster. After the death of her husband she left Ireland and consecrated herself to God in the religious life. Not only did she become a saint, but her son, Felan, the abbot, also was a saint. How much of the credit of his sanctity is due the good mother that inspired him with a love of virtue!

Frequently as this case has happened in the Church, it is always a marvel. Does it not show the importance of good example? How many a wife has sanctified her husband! How many a mother has sanctified her children! As Louis XIV said of his great queen, Madame de Maintenon, who had always been so charitable, "She helped me in everything, especially in saving my soul." One sees that power of good example manifested to a remarkable degree in the story of St. Bridget of Sweden and her daughter, St. Catherine of Sweden.

St. Bridget is the most celebrated saint of the North, due to her founding of the Brigittines and the writing of her Revelations. She was born in 1303, the daughter of the governor of the province of Uppland, a very wealthy landholder, and his wife, Ingeborg. They were a very pious couple, and it is needless to say that Bridget received a thorough grounding in piety and virtue. Even from the time she was seven years old she showed signs of one day becoming a great saint. When her mother died, she was placed in the care of an aunt, to whose wise guidance she owed much of the glory that later came to her name. When she was thirteen she was married to Ulf Gudmarsson, who was then eighteen. He was well suited to her, and she to him.

Ulf was a pious youth and became more so through the good example and prayers of his young wife. Bridget surely has every claim to be called a great mother, since she had eight children, among them St. Catherine of Sweden. But great as her home duties must have been, she had time for the service of God. Like all great saints, she had a love for the poor, and was always interesting herself in works of charity. Soon her name became a household word on account of her piety and charity. Even the learned theologians of the time looked with admiration upon her. Her influence was felt even by them; in fact, it was felt by everybody. Her husband died when she was about forty years of age, after they both had returned from a pious pilgrimage to Spain.

The widow, who had always been saintly, now devoted herself entirely to the pursuit of sanctity. There was no room in her life now for anything but prayer and penance. So holy did she become that Christ

Himself appeared to her, and made revelations to her which she wrote down, and which were widely read during the Middle Ages.

But there was practical work for her to do. She founded the new religious congregation of the Brigittines, or Order of St. Saviour, which did so much for the uplift of the society of that day. In 1349 she went to Rome and lived there the rest of her life, twenty-four years, edifying all by her piety and charity. She died in 1373, and her remains were brought back to Vadstena, one of the monasteries she had founded, where her daughter Catherine was later superior. She was canonized in 1391, only eighteen years after her death.

The example of this woman, mother of eight children, is truly remarkable. She did not allow her children to stand in the way of her sanctification.

We often see her spirit in the lives of these holy mothers. Like St. Jane Frances de Chantal, they stepped over the prostrate bodies of their beloved ones in order to come to God. They knew, after all, that the better they served their God, the better they served their children.

The youth of St. Catherine was very similar to that of her mother. Even from her childhood she showed signs of great piety. She would have liked to become a religious, but at the command of her father she married, at the age of thirteen, a German noble. He, too, was a very devout man, and was persuaded by his wife to join with her in a vow of chastity. They made the vow, and then together sought the life of perfection. Yet they both had a great love for each other. When her mother went to Rome, Catherine went with her, and while she was away her husband died in Sweden. She remained with her mother and together they lived a life of holiness. Catherine was sought by other suitors, for she was very beautiful, but she would never marry again. So she remained at Rome till the death of her mother, and then brought her remains back to Sweden. She was made the superior of the monastery at Vadstena, the mother-house of the Brigittines, of which she was an able head, and which she ruled till her death in 1381, at the age of forty-nine.

About the time that St. Catherine died, there was born in Rome a child whose life of mysticism reminds us much of the life of St. Bridget. This was St. Frances of Rome, born in 1384. She belonged to a noble family, and had all that the world could offer the rich. In spite of that, she wanted to leave the world and become a religious. But her father objected, and at his wish she married Lorenzo de Ponziani. She was then only twelve years of age. She had several children, but the care of them did not keep her from serving God in a special manner. She was a devoted mother, and perhaps on that account became a great saint. Like all saints, she loved the poor. Besides that, she had a great desire to save souls. How successful she was in that we see in her action in turning a great many of the ladies of Roman society from their frivolous amusements and associating them in a society similar to that of the Third Order, in which, without strict vows, they led lives of devotion.

Frances went further, and with her husband's consent practised a life of continence. So great was her piety that God blessed her with visions, and also gave her the power to work miracles. But the greater His gifts to her, the more humble she became. She had many trials in her life. Her husband was banished, her son was imprisoned, and finally she lost all her property. But she did not complain. Her sufferings brought her closer to God.

When her husband died she joined the Oblates, which she had been the means of establishing, and was made their superior. One day, when her son was visiting her, she fell ill and died on the day she had foretold, at the age of fifty-six, a woman who had done her full duty to her family, yet found time to help other souls and to become a saint herself. Surely wives and mothers can look to her as a grand exemplar.

In the Middle Ages the spirit of the cloister was everywhere. The flood of sanctity poured forth into the world. They were truly the ages of faith.

The life of Blessed Margaret of Savoy is representative of the times. She was born in 1382, the daughter of Louis of Savoy, Prince of Achaia, and through her mother was the granddaughter of a Count of Savoy. When she was twenty-one she married the Marquis of Montferrat, a widower. Her married life lasted fifteen years, during which time she advanced in piety; and when her husband died she decided to leave the world, gave over the management of the marquisate to her stepson, and went to join the Third Order of St. Dominic. The Duke of Milan wanted to marry her, and even asked the Pope to relieve her of her vow, but she refused. She had given herself to God, and would not take back the gift. With other women of rank, she founded a monastery, and there led a life of holiness till her death, in 1464, at the age of eighty-two. It was a calm, holy life.

But not always were the lives of these holy women calm and peaceful. Sometimes the crown of thorns was pressed down upon their heads. So was it with Blessed Seraphina Sforza, born in 1434. She was the daughter of the Count of Urbino, and her mother belonged to the famous Colonna family. Her mother's brother was Pope Martin V, and under his care Seraphina was brought up in Rome. At the age of fourteen she married Alexander Sforza, Lord of Pesaro. It was a happy marriage at first, but ten years after the marriage the husband began to lead a wicked life, so that her heart was broken. She tried to reform him, but it was a thankless task. He abused her and even attempted to kill her, and at last he forced her to enter a convent of the Poor Clares. Far from being discouraged, she prayed for him all the more fervently, and sought to sanctify her own soul. Her prayers were answered and the husband was converted. After his death she became the abbess of the monastery at Pesaro. It was a life with a heavy cross, yet it was through that suffering from the husband she loved that she became a saint.

Her story is similar to that of another saint of this same period, St. Catherine of Genoa. She was born in 1447, of the noble family of the Fieschi. Even as a child she was holy and wanted to be a nun. But at sixteen she was married to Giuliano Adorno, a gay young nobleman. He broke her heart, being a profligate, and squandering her money as well as his own. But she kept on praying for him, and he died penitent. She devoted herself to the sick in the hospital of which she became superior. It was a life of sacrifice, of penance, sickness, humiliation, yet she sanctified it, a model wife.

During the lifetime of these two good wives there lived in Brittany another holy wife whose life in its trials resembles theirs. This was the Blessed Frances d'Amboise, Duchess of Brittany. She was born in 1447, the daughter of a viscount, and at the age of fifteen was married to the Duke of Brittany. It was far from being a happy marriage as the world goes, for the Duke abused her. But she never made complaint, and her sweet disposition finally opened his eyes to his unworthiness. He did penance and then joined her in her works of charity. When he became duke she was of great service to him in the government of the duchy. In his will he testified to her devotedness. At length, when he died, she determined to enter the community she had helped to found, but was delayed in following out her plans. After years spent in charity she entered the Carmelite Order, of which she was elected prioress for life. In this office she edified all by her holiness, and died in 1485 in an ecstasy.

There is, indeed, a sameness in the lives of all these wives. Over and over again it is the story of a holy life in the world, rewarded by the opportunity to lead a life holier still in the cloister.

So with Blessed Margaret of Lorraine. Soon after her birth in the castle of her noble family, in 1463, she was left an orphan. She was then brought up by her grandfather, King René of Anjou; but after his death she was sent back to her brother, René II. When she was twenty-five she was married to the Duc d'Alençon. Four years later he died, and she governed the duchy. After her children were reared she decided to leave her high position in the world and entered a monastery, where a year later she died at the age of sixty-two, after a life of prayer and penance. At the time of the French Revolution her body was profaned and thrown into the common burying-place.

In the history of the establishment of religious communities one sees that God often chose these holy widows to do His work. It was so in the case of the founder of the great community that has done so much for the Church—the Sisters of Charity of St. Vincent de Paul. This was the Venerable Louise de Marillac Le Gras.

She was born in Paris in 1591, the daughter of

Louis de Marillac, Lord of Ferrières, a good man who educated her well. Her mother had died when she was very young, and an aunt who was a religious looked after the religious education of the girl. To her in great part the holy life of Louise may be attributed. She was a talented girl, and became very learned. When she was sixteen she wanted to be a nun, but her director advised against it, and finally she married Antoine Le Gras, a young secretary under Marie de Medici. A son was born to them, and Louise was a devoted mother to him. Busy as she was, she found time for works of charity, an inclination which finally brought her the great blessing of her life. She always felt that she should have been a nun, and she made a vow that if her husband died she would never remarry. She became a penitent of St. Vincent de Paul, and through his direction, after the death of her husband in 1625, she became especially interested in the work for the poor of Paris.

St. Vincent had founded the Association of Charity for the relief of the poor and the sick, and this led finally to the work of establishing the Sisters of Charity, which grew out of the association of young ladies whom he had brought from the provinces to look after the poor. They used to meet at the home of Louise, and thus she began what St. Vincent used to call the "little snowball." The snowball has grown mightily in all these years, thanks to the energy of the great St. Vincent de Paul and the holy widow whom God raised up to do the work. She died in 1660, a few months before St. Vincent.

Real Christian motherhood is a thrilling thing. No doubt St. Augustine was thinking of his own mother, the good St. Monica, when he declared that one woman had more humanity than a whole nation. There was many a great saint who could thank God for a holy mother. What an affecting thing is this very human prayer of thanksgiving of an old monk of the Middle Ages, the Abbot Guibert de Nogent: "God of mercy and of sanctity, I render Thee thanks for all Thy benefits. At first I thank Thee for having granted me a beautiful, chaste, and modest mother who was infinitely filled with the fear of Thy name." With such mothers the great thought was the glory of God and the sanctification of the souls of the children rather than their worldly advancement. Thus an old chronicle tells us that when the mother Willa heard that her long-lost son Theobald had been found under the cowl of a hermit, she left home and country and fled to the desert of Salonica, where side by side with him she served God till her death. Her joy was not so much that she had found her son as that she had found him trying to be a saint. It was this vigilant mother-love that made it possible in those ages to find whole families saints. It was nothing remarkable to hear of family after family, father, mother, sons, and daughters, entering the religious life. There were great mothers in those days, mothers whose first thought was of God.

But of all Christian mothers, there is none so strikingly human, and at the same time so thoroughly spiritual, as the great wife and mother, St. Jane Frances de Chantal, a woman who lived on earth and in heaven at one and the same time.

She was born in 1572, the second child of Benignus Fremiot, who was not only a great man of the world, having served as President of the Parliament of Burgundy, but also a man of great piety. His character was seen in his children, for it was to him that they could attribute all that they became, their good mother having died when they were yet almost infants. His eldest daughter, Margaret, became Countess of Effran, and his son served the Church well as Archbishop of Bourges. Whenever we think of Jane Frances—she received the name Frances at her confirmation—we think of the good father who educated her, and to whom she was the favorite.

In his worldly wisdom he sought to have her well married, and chose for her the Baron de Chantal, a young officer in the French army who was highly favored at court. The Baron was twenty-seven and Jane was twenty. It was one of the happiest of marriages, and the young Baron thought himself the luckiest man on earth when he took home his young bride to his fine home at Bourbilly. Young as she was, Jane was filled with common sense. She never was an idler, and at once she set out to be the real mistress of her home. The Baron's household during his long absence had been mismanaged, and not only did she

[169]

restore order, but she thought it her duty to look after
the souls of her charges, and saw to it that they attended Mass regularly and assisted at the daily devotions in her home. She was bound that they would
not lose their souls through any neglect on her part.
Even in those days her great aim was to please God.
When her husband was away from home, which happened frequently on account of his profession of arms,
she led the simplest life possible, cutting herself off
from company as much as she could and busying herself about her home duties and the care of her soul.
Once, when some of her friends reproached her during the absence of her husband for dressing so plainly,
she replied, "The eyes which I must please are a hundred leagues from here." Yet with all this fervor of
soul, she was a happy wife and mother,—all the happier, indeed, because she gave her greatest love to God.

But the worldly happiness was about to end. God
had chosen her to do a great work in His Church, and
to prepare her for it He required that she should
suffer in her dearest affections. He took from her
the husband she loved so dearly. One day he was
out hunting, and his companion, mistaking him for a
deer, shot him. He survived the accident nine days,
during which time he prepared his soul to meet His
God, and showed himself a good Christian, the worthy
husband of a great woman.

Jane was thus left a widow at the age of twenty-
eight, with four small children, one son and three
daughters. She had six children in all, but two had

died in infancy. She was heart-broken over the loss
of the Baron, but she wasted no time in fruitless grieving. She recognized the hand of God even in this
greatest affliction that could come to a happy wife.
She felt God drawing her closer to Him, and so she
made a vow of chastity, and led a life of true widowhood, indeed, giving her rich clothes to the poor, and
devoting herself to a life of penance and prayer. She
would have liked then to enter religion, but her duties
as mother kept her in the world as yet. For the sake
of the children she was obliged to live with her father-
in-law for seven years, during which she endured a
species of martyrdom.

In the Lent of 1604 she went to visit her father at
Dijon. There she met the great Francis de Sales,
whom she chose as her director. At once he saw in her
the special marks of sanctity. As he said of her: "In
Madame de Chantal I have found the perfect woman
whom Solomon had difficulty in finding in Jerusalem."
And a perfect woman and mother she was. Her life
was one long prayer, yet she never neglected her family duties on that account. As those of her household
used to say, "Madame prays always, yet is never
troublesome to anybody."

Every day she rose at five o'clock and made an
hour's meditation; then she called her children and
took them to Mass. She prayed with them morning
and night, and instructed them in their catechism.
Her first aim was to build up the Kingdom of God in
their souls. And all the time she was living the life

of a religious, even wearing the hair shirt. With a life of prayer went the life of charity. The poor and the sick found in her their best friend.

Leading such a life, it was no wonder that she desired to enter a more perfect state and dedicate herself to God in religion. Finally she obtained the consent of St. Francis for this, and having provided for the future of her children, she at length began the work of establishing the Congregation of the Visitation. It was not without a struggle that she was able to accomplish this. Many considered that she was a fool and wanting in motherly love to think of cutting herself from her children. On the very day that she left home her little son, thinking to keep her with him, threw himself weeping across the threshold to bar her way. She was overcome with grief; but she stepped over his body and then came back to console him. "Can the tears of a child shake your resolution?" asked a priest who had witnessed the affecting scene. "Oh, no," she replied; "but, after all, I am a mother." She was, indeed, a mother, but one who knew that God had the first demand upon her.

No need to enter into the history of the Order which she was raised up to establish. It prospered greatly because of the admirable character and the sanctity of this woman who ruled its destinies.

But her life as a religious was not without its trials. She had her temptations—violent ones that continued almost to the time of her death. Even with all the cares of her Congregation, she never forgot her duties as mother. She kept up her interest in her children, knowing that nothing could relieve her of that duty.

And at last, after a long life of service to God and her neighbor, she died in 1641, at the age of sixty-nine. Her epitaph might well be her own words: "After all, I am a mother"—a great mother because she was a great saint.

Endless is the list of these holy women of noble blood who attained a life of sanctity. Yet closely allied to them are others who, though not specially mentioned in the Church's roll of honor, deserve consideration for their great service to the Church. Such a woman was the Duchess of Acquillon, niece of the famous Cardinal Richelieu. She was born in 1604, and had married, at the age of sixteen, the Marquis of Combalet. Two years later he was killed at the siege of Montpellier, and the saddened young widow entered the Carmelite Order. When her uncle, Richelieu, was made premier of Louis XIII she had to come and live with him, and was made lady of the bedchamber to Queen Marie de Medici. She now presided over the Cardinal's house, even while her heart was in the convent. But she tried to live the life of a religious as much as possible, having no love for the vanity of the world and the high place to which she had been elevated. So great was her charity that she was known as "the great Christian" and "the heroic woman." Her charities were innumerable. She founded or helped every good work possible. The

Seminary of St. Sulpice, the foreign missions, hospitals, convents—all the religious houses of Paris regarded her as their benefactress. She had a high regard for St. Vincent de Paul, and was the very soul of his work. She helped the missions in China, but more than all she loved the missions in Canada. The Hôtel-Dieu at Quebec was erected at her expense, and it was at her request that Richelieu sent the Jesuits and Ursulines to Canada. In a word, charity dominated her life. Princes of the royal blood sought to marry her, but she preferred to remain a widow and to lead her life of charity.

When Richelieu died he made her his heiress and she devoted all her great fortune to the interests of charity. Well was she called "the Almoner of God." When she died in 1675, at the age of seventy-one, the Church of France sustained a great loss.

Such were some of the noble women who served the Church,—noble not only by blood, but more than all by their deeds. They could have pleaded their position, their dignity, their care for things of state, as reasons for leading a worldly life. Yet their greatest glory was to be humble wives, humble widows, humble servants of the poor, humble servants of God. Their lives are well described in the picture which Spenser paints of the Matron in his *Faerie Queene:*

"Whose only joy was to relieve the needes
  Of wretched soules, and helpe the helplesse pore.
  All night she spent in bidding of her bedes,
  And all the day in doing good and godly deedes."

Surely one of the greatest glories of Catholic womanhood, something in which every Catholic wife and mother can take pride, are these noble wives and mothers who, amid all their dignities, showed a great example of poverty in spirit. What a reproach are their lives to those who set aside their devotions, their very salvation, in the vain pursuit of the unreal glory of life!

ISABELLA THE CATHOLIC

(1451-1504)

THE reign of Isabella of Castile is of the utmost importance in the history of Spain, and indeed of the whole world. It saw Spain, which from the time of the invasion of the Saracens in the eighth century had been divided into numberless small states, now made one great nation. It saw that nation extended by the discoveries in the New World by the immortal Columbus, who owes so much of his glory to the patriotism and faith of Isabella; and with the union of states it saw the domestic institutions of Spain and its literature moulded into what is practically their present form. For these reasons alone Isabella would be a figure of world-history. Yet it is not as a great ruler that we would view her, but as a great woman, a great wife and mother, a great soul, who well deserved the title which has become a very part of her name—Isabella the Catholic.

She was born in 1451, the daughter of John II of Castile and his second wife, Isabella of Portugal. He was an intellectual man who wrote and spoke Latin, and even composed verses; it was a time of literary activity in Castile, and it had its lasting influence on the young Isabella. Castile always had pre-eminence among the states of Spain; and even when the various states were consolidated into one, the capital of Castile became the capital of the new kingdom, and its language that of the court and the people. Spain was always *par excellence* the land of chivalry; and patriotism, religion, and a proud sense of independence were traits of the Castilians even in those days.

But when Isabella was born there was little prospect that she would ever rule as queen. She had two brothers who were older than she—Henry, her stepbrother, and Alfonso, her full brother. It was Henry that succeeded to the throne on the death of his father. Isabella was three years of age at the time, and had been taken by her mother, a woman of noble character, from whom Isabella inherited her many striking virtues, to live in the little town of Arevalo, where she was brought up in seclusion, far from the court, which during the reign of her brother Henry was a licentious one. Her mother was filled with piety, and it was her first care to train Isabella in practical piety, to fill her with that spirit of religion which was the most evident characteristic of her reign as queen.

When Henry's daughter Joanna was born, Isabella and her brother Alfonso were brought back to court from their retirement, this being a move of Henry's to prevent the attempt of any faction to aspire to the throne on their behalf, on account of the belief then prevalent that Joanna was not really his own daughter and consequently not the legitimate heir to the crown.

It was a licentious, frivolous court, as we have said, but the little Isabella had been well grounded in piety, and her life was kept pure amid the bad examples ever before her eyes.

It was no wonder that she had many suitors. She was very beautiful, with a clear, fresh complexion, light blue eyes, auburn hair inclining to red, a style rare in Spain, and of great dignity of bearing. But, more than that, she was closely allied to the crown, and therefore considered a great catch. At first her hand was sought for the very Ferdinand to whom she was later married, but for reasons of state that match was set aside, and then she was betrothed to Ferdinand's brother Carlos, the heir-apparent to the throne of Aragon, who was persecuted by his father and his stepmother, and died in his prime, supposedly of poison administered to him.

After the death of Carlos, Isabella was betrothed to Alfonso of Portugal, a man many years older than herself, for which reason she bitterly protested against the proposed marriage. Henry was now in danger of losing his throne, and in order to strengthen himself politically, caring little about her personal choice in the matter of choosing a husband, he arranged a marriage between her and the grand master of the Order of Calatrava. Isabella protested against this arrangement also, but Henry was bound that she should be sacrificed for his own interests. She detested the man chosen for her, for he was inferior to her in birth and was notorious for his evil manner of life. When she heard that the King was insistent she kept to her room, refused to eat or sleep, and prayed unceasingly to God to preserve her from such a marriage. She was saved from the disgrace of this merely political and unworthy union by the sudden death of the grand master, who was supposed to have met his untimely end by poison at the hands of some of his enemies.

His death put an end to all hopes of conciliation of the two factions. War broke out between Henry and the confederates, who had declared him dethroned and Alfonso king in his stead. But Alfonso died at the age of fifteen, being also poisoned, it was supposed; and now the eyes of the confederates were turned to the young Isabella, then living at the short-lived court of her brother Alfonso, to which she had come out of disgust at the corruption prevalent in Henry's court. When Alfonso died she retired to the monastery of Avila, and there she was visited by the confederates, who begged her to let them proclaim her Queen of Castile. But she refused, replying that while her brother Henry lived no one else had a right to the crown; and, moreover, she declared that the country had been divided long enough by factions, and that the death of Alfonso should be interpreted as the expression of the will of Heaven to show its disapproval of the cause of the confederates.

She expressed herself as willing to effect a reconciliation between the two parties and to work with her brother the King for the removal of abuses in the government. But nothing could move her to take a

throne to which she felt she had no right; and even
when the confederates, disregarding her wishes, proclaimed her Queen of Castile, she refused to accept
the dignity, which might well have turned any girl's
head. As the result of her persistence, which amazed
everybody to think that any woman would refuse a
kingdom, matters were finally arranged peaceably,
one of the conditions being that Isabella should be
recognized as heir to the crowns of Castile and Leon,
and that she should not be forced to marry against
her own choice. Such magnanimity is rare in the history of the world, but, knowing the character of Isabella as we do, any other course would have been impossible to her.

Now that she was heiress to a great throne, she was
again sought by many suitors. But she refused them
all. Her heart was turned towards Ferdinand, who
was related to her, both being descended from the
same great-grandfather. There were many reasons,
political, geographical, racial, and others, to make
such a union desirable; but what decided her more
than anything else, perhaps, was the fact that the
young Ferdinand was handsome and in every way an
excellent prince, a fit husband for any princess.

Like Isabella, when he was born there had been little
prospect that he would ever be King of Aragon. His
stepbrother, Carlos, was the heir-apparent, but, as we
have said, met an untimely death, and so cleared the
way for Ferdinand. King Henry, however, was not
in favor of the match with Ferdinand, and even

threatened to have Isabella imprisoned in the royal fortress at Madrid if she did not change her mind. And this would have been done, only the common people were very much in favor of the marriage with Ferdinand, regarding it as the most desirable union for every reason. Isabella now showed her strength of character, took matters into her own hands, and gave her consent to the marriage with the man she loved. She fled to Valladolid from fear of her enemies, who were determined to stop the wedding at any cost; and there she was joined by her future husband, who had come thither in disguise. He was at the time eighteen years of age, a year younger than his bride, a handsome prince, bronzed by his life in the camp. No prince ever received a greater treasure. She was, says one of her household, "the handsomest lady whom I ever beheld, and the most gracious in her manners." She was dignified and modest, even reserved. And so these two lovers were married, a marriage that meant so much to Spain and to the whole world. Yet at the time they were so poor that they had to borrow money to defray the expenses of the ceremony!

This poverty of the young couple continued for some time, and there were occasions when they were hardly able to meet the expenses of the table. The reason was that Henry and his confederates objected to the succession of Isabella. They desired that his daughter, Joanna, should succeed him. Marriages were arranged between Joanna and princes of different nations, but nothing came of any of them, since the prospective husbands were afraid of a union that promised a civil war. So Isabella grew in power. It was her own character more than anything else that contributed to strengthen her cause. Her little court was a great contrast to the frivolous, luxurious one of her brother. And the thinking people knew that her rule would be more desirable than that of her rival.

And then, in 1474, Henry died. It was the end of a reign of weakness. Castile in his time had been dismembered by factions, her revenues squandered till the treasury was bankrupt, and public and private morals had come to degradation. Never since the time of the Saracen invasion had the condition of the kingdom been so bad. And in the time of this darkness the sun of the young Queen Isabella began to shine. In her rule one has little difficulty in discovering the providence of God.

Isabella succeeded to the throne by the right that she had been recognized by the Legislature. And so she was proclaimed queen in the city of Segovia, where she then resided, with simple but magnificent ceremonies in the public square, after which she went with a great procession to the cathedral, where a Te Deum was chanted. She prostrated herself before the high altar to thank God for the past and to invoke His protection for the future.

Her succession was not without its troubles. The King of Portugal thought it a good chance to gain new power by espousing the cause of Henry's daughter, Joanna, his niece, and so led an army against Castile. It was a surprise to Isabella, but historians tell us that she acquitted herself well during this her first care of state, sometimes sitting up all night to dictate despatches, and even making long journeys on horseback. We do not need to enter into details of the War of the Succession. After the first great battle, which was won by her soldiers, she ordered a procession to the Church of St. Paul, in the suburbs of the city of Tordesillas, where she was then staying, and she herself joined in it, walking barefoot as a pilgrim, and thanking God for the victory He had given her arms. The effect was that in a little more than six months the whole kingdom practically acknowledged the supremacy of Ferdinand and Isabella. But the war broke out again, and lasted in all four years, ending in complete victory for Isabella. Her niece Joanna, her rival for the throne, finally withdrew into a monastery and consecrated herself to the service of religion. Shortly after this the old King of Aragon died in 1479, and the crown came to Ferdinand. And so Castile and Aragon, which had been separated for more than four centuries, were now reunited forever, and the foundations laid of the kingdom which for a time was to overshadow every other European monarchy.

As soon as Isabella was on her throne, she set to work to be a real queen. She was filled with the spirit of justice, and justice she gave to all her subjects, rich and poor alike. She went from city to city, reforming abuses, and sat on the judgment-seat to hear all the cases brought before her. She was a fearless woman, and when occasion required rode with her retainers to put down the petty rebellions that still arose from time to time. The country, which had been infested with robbers in the previous reign, was soon rid of them by her efforts. It was the same in other things. She was always looking after the interests of her subjects. It could hardly be believed, historians tell us, that in a few short years so many changes could be effected. Yet all these changes were due to the character of the woman who was more than all else a great, practical Catholic.

One of the greatest accomplishments under her reign was the destruction of the Moslem power in Granada. In that war we see her real character. She was solicitous for all that concerned the welfare of her people, even visiting the camp in person to encourage the soldiers and to relieve their necessities. She had a large number of tents reserved for the sick and the wounded, which were called the "Queen's hospitals" and which she herself supported. This is the first record in history of a regular camp hospital. Her whole soul was in this war, not from a desire for conquest, but to replace the crescent by the Cross and to retrieve for Christianity the beautiful domain it had lost long before. And so great was her own enthusiasm that it won her that of the people. It was a war that appealed to the best instincts of a people always noted for chivalry. The noblest of the youths of Spain rushed to the standard to serve their country and their religion. It was a veritable Crusade, and the inspiration of all was Isabella.

The history of the siege of Baza in the campaign against Granada shows clearly her influence. It was she who renewed the courage of the leaders. She procured all the supplies, constructed the roads, took charge of the sick, and furnished the sums necessary for the conduct of the war. When the hearts of the soldiers were growing weak, she visited the camp to cheer them and fill them with some of her own energy. It was easily done, for the attachment to her was universal. They looked to her as to a superior being, and she held their hearts in her hands. And so, on the second of January, 1492, the submission of Granada was made, after having been a Moslem kingdom for nearly eight hundred years.

But that year was famous for another event that has given more glory to Isabella than all the other events of her great reign—the discovery of America. We would be unable to magnify too much the place which Isabella holds in the discovery of America. Columbus had come to the court of Spain in 1484. It was hardly a propitious time. Ferdinand and Isabella were then engaged in the war against the Moors, and all their resources were used in that undertaking. And though they were interested in nautical enterprises, as was Portugal, it was more important for them to press the war than to take chances with a possible discovery. And while Columbus had the best of recommendations, while he had a good friend in Isabella's former confessor, Father Juan Perez, the sovereigns could not arrive at any decision until the war was over.

Meanwhile Columbus stayed in Spain, serving in the army, and all the while considered highly by the King and Queen and helped by them.

Worn out by waiting, he at last determined to leave Spain and offer his services to France. But on the way he was stopped by Juan Perez and brought by him to Santa Fé, where the court then was previous to the fall of Granada. Columbus and his friends so pleaded his cause that even while Ferdinand refused to give any sanction to the plan, Isabella, to whom Columbus appealed not only on the score that it would bring wealth to Spain, but would also extend the Gospel, decided to aid him.

"I will assume the undertaking," she said, "for my own crown of Castile, and am ready to pawn my jewels to defray the expenses of it, if the funds in the treasury shall be found inadequate." It was not necessary to pledge the jewels, however, as funds were advanced from the Aragonese revenues, though all the charges of the expedition were made to Castile. "This," says Washington Irving, "was the proudest moment in the life of Isabella; it stamped her renown forever as the patroness of the discovery of the New World."

The great glory, of course, belongs to Columbus of entertaining and carrying out an enterprise which no one else had the hardihood even to conceive. Yet

we must not ignore the part of Isabella. She was
the only sovereign of the time that gave countenance
to the project. And when she gave her word to Columbus she remained ever after his steadfast friend,
shielding him against his enemies, believing in him,
and helping him financially. She was enthusiastic
about the work, for she believed that she had been
raised up at this time to spread the light of the faith
into unknown lands. Indeed, one can see the providence of God in raising up Columbus and Isabella at
the same time.

When Columbus returned and announced his discoveries the sovereigns sank to their knees, raised their
clasped hands to heaven, and with eyes filled with
tears gave thanks to God. When he set forth on his
second voyage the most explicit directions were given
him by Isabella as to the conversion of the heathen.
She ordered him to treat them well and lovingly, to
give them presents which she and Ferdinand sent them,
and to punish any Spaniard that dared molest them.
The paramount thing to Isabella was the civilization
and conversion of her new subjects, for she beheld
them as having been committed to her by Heaven. So
during all her life she fought against the enslaving of
even one of them. All this was due to the kind heart
of Isabella as well as to her zeal for the faith.

And with that thought there was also the zeal for
the welfare of her country. Even from a worldly
point of view, she was a wise ruler. Nothing was
foreign to her so long as it concerned the advancement

of her people. So it is that we see her taking a lively interest in the cultivation of letters. Her father's reign had given great promise in literature. But during that of his son there had been no thought for such tame amusement. When Isabella came to the throne she aimed to increase the love of literature. She herself, in those years when she had led a life of retirement with her mother after the death of her father, had the chance to cultivate her mind. She had learned several modern languages and could write in her own with great elegance.

We are told that when she came to the throne she did not know Latin, which was then the language of diplomacy. But she set herself to learn it immediately, and soon became as proficient in that as in other languages. She collected books and soon had a library which may justly be called fine for the times. She took great pains, too, in the instruction of her children, and had for them the best masters obtainable, so much so that the acquirements of her daughters created surprise even among the learned. The same care she exercised with the young nobility. She delighted in gathering them about her and urging them to study. It was a complete reform for the nobles, who previously had considered learning as beneath their notice. But she soon made them understand that with her intellect was to count more than blood, and that if they hoped for any advance at her hands they must cultivate their minds. Soon there was a real enthusiasm for learning, and it was no strange thing to find women lecturing in the great universities.

It is beyond our scope to give a lengthy narration of the literary achievements of Isabella's reign. Suffice it to say that in every branch there was a progress that was astounding. And all was due to the enthusiasm of this one woman.

The King and Queen of Spain were successful not only in arms, but also in the matrimonial alliances they made for their children, although in several cases it was but a prelude to sorrow. They had one son and four daughters, whom they educated thoroughly, and who repaid them by their fine characters. They inherited the virtues of Isabella. The eldest daughter, the Princess Isabella, was married to Alfonso, the heir to the throne of Portugal, but he died soon after, and the broken-hearted widow returned to Spain and devoted herself to religion and works of charity, refusing many brilliant offers of marriage. She was afterwards married to Emmanuel of Portugal.

Isabella's son, Prince John, was married to the Princess Margaret, daughter of the Emperor Maximilian, and her daughter Joanna was married to Maximilian's son Philip. Katharine, immortal in history as Katharine of Aragon, was married to Prince Arthur of England, and, after his death, to Henry, later Henry VIII. Happily, Isabella was spared the knowledge of her daughter Katharine's repudiation. But, somehow, Katharine in her woes reminds us, by her fine spirit of faith, of the mother from whom she inherited her genuine womanliness.

In the midst of the rejoicings at having settled her children so well, there came sadness. Prince John died at the age of twenty, a terrible blow to the mother who so loved him. Ferdinand had gone to see him in his illness, and tried to break the news gently to Isabella, for he feared the effect the shock would have upon her. But, like a good Christian, she received the tidings religiously, with resignation to the will of God even while the heart within her was crushed. Great as this affliction was, a greater soon came in the death of the Queen of Portugal, her beloved daughter Isabella, who had always been her bosom friend as well as daughter. The grieving mother still devoted herself to her duties. Externally she was calm, but her health gradually sank beneath the weight of woe. Not only did death come to her loved ones, but a greater affliction came when she realized that her daughter Joanna was insane. Yet no grief blunted the energy of her mind. She was not only a mother: she was a queen, and she had duties as queen to her people with which her personal sorrow should not interfere. And so she sacrificed her feelings to her duty as ruler. Her character was so great that she rose triumphant over every ill, while her truly religious spirit made her realize that the sorrows of this world, like its joys, are but passing.

It was this great character that made her age the

golden age of Spain. It is this same character that has led even hostile critics to regard her as one of the greatest rulers of all time. As Irving sums it up: "Contemporary writers have been enthusiastic in their descriptions of Isabella, but time has sanctioned their eulogies. She is one of the purest and most beautiful characters in the pages of history."

The year 1504 witnessed the death of Isabella. For some time her health had been failing; indeed, she was never careful about her health when duty demanded her presence. We have seen her, even when she was about to become a mother, riding out to the field of battle in order to stir her soldiers to fight for her cause. To this activity of body there was added a ceaseless activity of mind. She had the cares of state, and she attended to them as only a great statesman could. And with all that there came the sorrows which are the portion of a mother. Some of her children died; the others married and went to live far from her. It is the lot of queens to be separated from their children. But Isabella, the great queen, was also the great mother. No mother ever took more interest in her children; no mother ever loved her children more, or was loved more in return by them. For that reason she felt in a special manner the blow of the death of her daughter Isabella, from which she never wholly recovered. Yet the combined sorrows did not break her spirit. She knew to whom she would go in her sorrow. To God she went, and, as ever, put her trust in Him. Pious as she always was, she now became more pious, though all the time her heart was sick and weary of the world.

The affliction which came to her daughter Joanna had brought only abuse from her husband Philip. When the news of this came to Ferdinand and Isabella both were sorely afflicted. It so affected Ferdinand that he became ill. So also with Isabella, and to this was added her worry over Ferdinand's condition. But he recovered and she failed. It was not only worry over the condition of her beloved daughter, but also over her beloved Castile, for which she had labored so hard and which now, when she should be gone, was to suffer for lack of a fit ruler.

Most of each day in those declining months she had to lie down, but even in that position she attended to the business of state despite her mortal malady. It is interesting to note a letter written at this time by her faithful follower, Peter Martyr.

"You ask me," he writes, "respecting the state of the Queen's health. We sit sorrowful in the palace all day long, tremblingly waiting the hour when religion and virtue shall quit the earth with her. Let us pray that we may be permitted to follow hereafter where she is soon to go. She so far transcends all human excellence, that there is scarcely anything of mortality about her. She can hardly be said to die, but to pass into a nobler existence, which should rather excite our envy than our sorrow. She leaves the world filled with her renown, and she goes to enjoy life eternal with her God in heaven."

It was at this time that Isabella made her famous will. First of all she provided for her burial, ordering that her remains be transported to Granada to the Franciscan monastery of Santa Isabella in the Alhambra, and there placed in a low and humble sepulchre with only a plain inscription. "But," she added, "should the King, my lord, prefer a sepulchre in some other place, then my will is that my body be there transported and laid by his side; that the union we have enjoyed in this world, and, through the mercy of God, may hope again for our souls in heaven, may be represented by our bodies in the earth." She then ordered that her funeral be as simple as possible, and that what was saved by this economy be given to the poor. This she did not only out of her own simplicity and humility, but also to set an example to her subjects, who were accustomed to extravagance in funerals.

She then made bequests to charities, among others settling marriage portions on poor girls, and also money for the redemption of Christian captives in Barbary. Then she settled the crown of Castile on her daughter Joanna, and urged her and her husband to live with the same conjugal harmony that had always existed between her and Ferdinand, and urged them also to look after the welfare of their subjects. Finally she said: "I beseech the King, my lord, that he will accept all my jewels, or such as he shall select, so that, seeing them, he may be reminded of the singular love I always bore him while living, and that

I am now waiting for him in a better world; by which remembrance he may be encouraged to live the more justly and holily in this." In a codicil to the will she urged her successors to hasten the work of converting and civilizing the poor Indians, to treat them kindly, and to repair any wrongs they might have suffered.

When this work of disposition was done, she gave herself over to the care of her soul. "Do not weep for me," she said to those at her bedside, who were afflicted at the thought of losing her, "nor waste your time in fruitless prayers for my recovery, but pray rather for the salvation of my soul."

And so, having received the last sacraments, she died November 26, 1504, aged fifty-four, and in the thirtieth year of her reign. "My hand," says Peter Martyr, "falls powerless by my side for very sorrow. The world has lost its noblest ornament—a loss to be deplored not only by Spain, which she has so long carried forward in the career of glory, but by every nation in Christendom; for she was the mirror of every virtue, the shield of the innocent, and an avenging sword to the wicked. I know none of her sex, in ancient or modern times, who in my judgment is at all worthy to be named with this incomparable woman."

On the news of her death, Columbus wrote to his son Diego: "A memorial for thee, my dear son Diego, of what is at present to be done. The principal thing is to commend affectionately, and with great devotion, the soul of the Queen our sovereign to God. Her life was always Catholic and holy, and prompt to all things in His holy service; for this reason we may rest assured that she is received into His glory, and beyond the care of this rough and weary world. The next thing is to watch and labor in all matters for the service of our sovereign the King, and to endeavor to alleviate his grief."

So passed away Isabella the Catholic, one of the greatest rulers that ever lived, a great ruler because she was a great Catholic. She was every inch a queen, but withal she had great simplicity of character. She lived frugally; she spun and sewed all the clothes her children wore, and it was said that she even mended the King's doublet seven times. She herself dressed simply, except on state occasions, and even gave away her jewels and her fine clothes to her friends. She was a big-hearted woman. There was nothing petty in her make-up. Once a friend, always a friend, as she proved in her dealings with Columbus.

But her chief characteristic was her piety. As Prescott says: "It shone forth from the very depths of her soul with a heavenly radiance which illuminated her whole character." It was the piety which had been implanted in her heart by her good mother. With all the cares of state—and one gets some idea of them when one considers all that she accomplished for Spain—she saw to it that she had plenty of time to give to prayer. She said her office every day like a nun. She built hospitals and churches, and endowed monasteries; in a word, she did all she could for the

Church and for the sanctification of her own soul. She had all the strength of a man and all the gentle piety of a woman. No wonder that when she died it was amid the cries of woe of her people.

A great queen, indeed, a great wife, a great mother, and all this because she was first of all a great Catholic—Isabella the Catholic.

MARGARET ROPER

(1505-1544)

WHEN the Spirit of God would describe the ideal, the valiant woman, it uses these beautiful words: "The heart of her husband trusteth in her. . . . She will render him good, and not evil, all the days of her life. . . . She hath opened her hand to the needy, and stretched out her hands to the poor. . . . She hath opened her mouth to wisdom, and the law of clemency is on her tongue. . . . She hath looked well to the paths of her house, and hath not eaten her bread idle. Her children rose up and called her blessed; her husband, and he praised her. Many daughters have gathered together riches: thou hast surpassed them all." (Proverbs xxxi.)

To read these words is to read the epitaph of Mistress Margaret Roper, the gentle lady, the learned scholar, the charitable Christian, the noble daughter of a noble father, the ideal wife and mother. If Sir Thomas More stands for glorious Catholic manhood, his daughter Margaret, who was so like him in many ways, stands for glorious Catholic womanhood. It is a story filled with sadness; yet, too, with that joy that comes only from the service of God. To tell the story of Margaret, it is necessary to tell the story of her father. Their lives were intimately bound together; she was his favorite daughter, and indeed resembled him closely both physically and mentally.

Sir Thomas More, now Blessed Thomas More, was born on February 7, 1478, the eldest son of John More, a gentleman who afterwards, in the time of Henry VIII, was a judge on the King's Bench. It was a family, as More used to say, "not illustrious, but honourable." More loved his father dearly, whom he called, "a man, courteous, affable, innocent, gentle, merciful, just, and uncorrupted." As he loved his father, so Margaret in turn loved him. It was a family of affectionate nature.

The Mores in the beginning were not rich. John More at first was but a poor lawyer, so that for his early education the young Thomas was sent to a free school. From there he was transferred to the house of Cardinal Morton, Archbishop of Canterbury, as in those days the houses of ecclesiastics were schools of learning and good breeding for the sons of the gentry and even the higher nobility. The Cardinal, a learned and good man, took a great interest in the young Thomas, and prophesied remarkable things for him. It was through him that the lad was sent to the University of Oxford in 1492, the year of the discovery of America.

More was there two years, studying hard, full of ambition, learning everything he could, even to play on the viol and the flute, enjoying a joke as few enjoyed one. From Oxford he passed to New Inn, and there studied law, becoming proficient in that branch, and all the while devoting his spare time to other studies, even to the study of theology. It was not surprising that a youth so piously inclined thought of becoming a priest. He even went to the Carthusians to try his vocation, but at last, by the advice of his confessor, he decided to stay in the world.

So at the age of twenty-six he decided to take a wife. He was a handsome, intelligent, refined youth; but there was little romance in his courtship. More, while visiting the home of a man named Colt who had three daughters, fell in love with the second eldest, and determined to marry her; but then, as he thought that the eldest would take it ill if her younger sister were married before her, he turned about and asked the eldest to marry him. Not very romantic, but it proved one of the happiest of marriages. Of this union four children were born—Margaret, Cecily, Elizabeth, and John. Margaret was born in 1505.

The happiness of the More family was short-lived. The young wife died six years after marriage, leaving her husband with four small children to care for. It was, no doubt, the thought of the welfare of these children that induced More to marry again. His second wife was a widow with one daughter, Mrs. Alice Middleton, seven years older than himself. He had no children by the second wife. But they were extremely happy together, and though she had the reputation of being close in money matters and feared that

her husband would beggar himself and his family by
his great charity, she proved to be an admirable
mother for his children. It was one of the happiest
families that ever lived.

More himself was ever affable and courteous, witty,
full of jokes and banter, especially with the women-
folk; and he was kind to animals, of which he had a
great many as pets. He arose at two o'clock in the
morning, studied and prayed till seven. Every morning of his life he heard Mass. There is a story that
one day he was at Mass when the King sent for him;
but More would not come. A second and a third time
the King summoned him, but he would not go till the
Mass was ended, saying that he was paying court to
a greater and better Lord, and must first perform
that duty. He made many pilgrimages on foot, sometimes walking seven miles to a shrine. He loved
prayer, and whenever he entered on a new office or
undertook a difficult business, he received Holy Communion. Yet, while exhibiting such great and unaffected piety, he was always of a joyous character,
happy and prosperous, enjoying life to the full even
while he was detached from the world, a truly model
married man. No wonder his kind disposition dominated the family. All the relatives lived together in
the great house which he had built—More and his
wife and children, his father and his father's third
wife, his daughter Margaret and her husband, and
later on, when the other children were married, their
families, too. More actually poured out his affection

upon his children. He personally looked after their education, and imparted to them so much learning that their reputation was known all over Europe.

But though he loved all his children, he made a special favorite of his daughter Margaret—his Meg. She was always his confidante, always the one to whom he told his troubles. Perhaps it was because she was so like him in character, and because she responded so readily to his teaching. More was a firm believer in the education of woman, at a time when little attention was paid to it. He set his daughters heavy tasks in learning, supervised their education himself, and while he was away from home on affairs of state when he became Lord Chancellor, wrote to them and had them write to him so that he might watch their improvement. His first duty was to his children; nothing could take the place of that. And it was always good advice he gave to them, and to the man he had engaged as their tutor. In one of his letters to the tutor he writes as follows: "I have often begged not you only, who out of your affection for my children would do it of your own accord, nor my wife, who is sufficiently urged by her maternal love for them, which has been proved to me in so many ways, but all my friends, to warn my children to avoid the precipices of pride and haughtiness, and to walk in the pleasant meadows of modesty; not to be dazzled at the sight of gold; not to lament that they do not possess what they erroneously admire in others; not to think more of themselves for gaudy trappings,

nor less for the want of them; neither to deform the
beauty that nature has given them by neglect, nor to
try to heighten it by artifice; to put virtue in the first
place, learning in the second, and in their studies to
esteem most whatever may teach them piety towards
God, charity to all, and modesty and Christian humility in themselves. By such means they will receive
from God the reward of an innocent life, and in the
assured expectation of it will view death without
horror, and meanwhile, possessing solid joy, will
neither be puffed up by the empty praise of men nor
dejected by evil tongues."

No wonder that such watchfulness over his family
produced good results. All of More's children grew
up learned and of fine character. The great scholar,
Erasmus, who was the dear friend of More, expressed
his amazement that the girls could write such fine
Latin. But while More was pleased at this, it delighted him more to know that they were pious. As an
instance of what good reason he had to rejoice in their
learning, it is related that in 1529 the fame of these
girls had so spread through Europe by the talk of
Erasmus that they were invited—they were all married then—by the King himself to appear before him
and hold a philosophical tournament in his presence.

So that the home in which Margaret Roper was
brought up was such a one as to develop in her all
those fine characteristics which she had inherited from
her learned and saintly father. She was sixteen years
old when she fell in love with and married William

Roper. Roper belonged to distinguished legal families both on the side of his father and on that of his mother. He was educated at one of the English universities, and received his father's office of clerk of the pleas in the Court of King's Bench, an office he held till shortly before his death. When he was about twenty-three he was taken into More's home, no doubt on account of associations at court. He is described by Erasmus as a young man who "is wealthy, of excellent and modest character, and not unacquainted with literature." Later in life he served four times in the Parliament of Queen Mary. We are not surprised that the brilliant and wealthy young man soon fell in love with Margaret More. She was of the character, refined, pious, and learned, that would appeal to him. And so at the age of twenty-six he married her. She was then but sixteen.

It was a happy marriage, yet in the beginning it threatened to be disrupted by differences in religion. It was the time when the new doctrines of Martin Luther were becoming popular in certain quarters. Young Roper took kindly to the novelty, and soon became a zealous Protestant, anxious to talk the new religion to everybody he met, so much so that he was arrested on the charge of heresy and brought before Cardinal Wolsey, then chancellor. Wolsey, out of regard for his friend More, gave the youth a friendly warning and discharged him. But Roper kept up the talk at home. He affected to despise the religious life of More, and assumed a superiority to him. More argued with him, but finally saw that he was wasting his time in so doing. "Meg," said he to his daughter one day, "I have borne a long time with thy husband: I have reasoned and argued with him in these points of religion, and still given to him my poor fatherly counsel, but I perceive none of this able to call him home; and therefore, Meg, I will no longer dispute with him, but will clean give him over and get me to God and pray for him."

What More could not do with his son-in-law by argument he did by prayer. Roper soon returned to the faith, attributing his conversion to the prayers of More. And he ever remained faithful after that to the old religion, so much so that in later times, when Elizabeth ruled, he was summoned before her council for being a Catholic.

Roper made a good husband for Margaret. He had the same tastes. We find both of them, even after their marriage, studying the same branches together. He could give her all that the world held dear, for he was wealthy; yet we never find her losing her head over her prosperity. She was always content to be the humble, studious, diligent wife. She was never idle, being either engaged in her studies, or in looking after the affairs of the house, or in attending to the charities which were so dear to her father's heart.

More was noted for his charity; he was the greatest lawyer of his time, making an income of what would to-day amount to twenty-five thousand dollars a year, but, sought as he was on all sides, he was always at

the call of the poor; from them he would never take
a cent as fee, even while he devoted himself to their
cases with as much care as if he expected to be paid
well by them. But not only did he exercise charity
in this manner: he even went so far as to hire a house
in the parish where he lived, to care for the sick, the
poor, and the old, and tended them himself. When
he was away on business it was the special privilege
of Margaret to tend them in his place. It was the
greatest proof of love he could give her. There is
one of his letters to her which specially shows his admiration for her. "You ask, my dear Margaret," he
writes, "for money with too much bashfulness and
timidity, since you are asking from a father who is
eager to give, and since you have written to me a
letter such that I would not only repay each line of
it with a golden philippine, as Alexander did the verses
of Cherilos, but, if my means were as great as my
desire, I would reward each syllable with two golden
ounces. As it is, I send only what you have asked,
but would have added more, only that as I am eager to
give, so am I desirous to be asked and coaxed by my
daughter, especially by you, whom virtue and learning
have made so dear to my soul. So the sooner you
spend this money well, as you are wont to do, and
the sooner you ask for more, the more you will be sure
of pleasing your father."

Once, when she was at the point of death with the
sweating sickness, and the doctors had given up all
hope of her recovery, the grieving father went to the

chapel, and on his knees begged God to spare her if it were His blessed will. The prayer was answered, and Margaret recovered, even though it had been seen that all the marks of death were on her. More at the time said that if she had died, he "would never have meddled in worldly matters more."

It was a family of joy and prosperity, a home with all those things that make life worth living. But even then the shadow of death was nearing.

In 1509 Henry VIII had come to the throne of England. More was then famous as a lawyer, so much so that he attracted the notice of the King, who told Wolsey, then chancellor, to do his best to have More enter the service of the court. But More was not a bit anxious to come to court; he was happy as he was, independent, without taking upon himself the burden of affairs of state. But it was hard for him to avoid the demands of the court. He was sent on a mission to Flanders, on which he was absent six months; and so well did he acquit himself of the task, that more than ever the King desired to secure his services. More put it off as long as he could, but fearing that refusal would finally mean his destruction, he obeyed the summons of the King and came to court.

More was now a statesman, beginning the career that was to last twenty years, and that was to end with his death at the hands of the King who was now so anxious to advance him. But while answering the command of the King and coming to court to serve him, More never lost his independence of soul. He always spoke out his mind on public affairs, even when he knew that his views were not pleasing to the King. In 1518, when he was forty years of age, he was appointed privy councilor, and in 1521 was elevated to the rank of knight. But the new honors did not change his character a bit. He was the same simple man in the days of glory as he had been in the days of struggle.

In those first years of public service More was pleasing to Henry VIII. Henry was then an amiable prince, affable and courteous. This was before he became a slave to his passions and fell in love with Anne Boleyn, who later on was to work such havoc in the kingdom and in the Church. More traveled with the King, especially during the terrible days of tne sweating sickness, a plague which destroyed multitudes of lives. The King sent him on legations, even honoring him by making him the royal secretary. Wolsey, too, admired More, and their relations were always most cordial. The King was so proud to have such a man at court that he often made him come and dine with himself and the Queen; and, more than that, came himself to visit at More's house, where they could be seen walking in the garden, the arm of the King about the neck of More.

It was too good to last. Henry, who had once been the defender of the faith, was now to become its persecutor, and all through his impure passions. It was a strange friendship, that of More and the King. While all the time More was advancing in

virtue, the King was advancing in sin. The reason
of the decline was this. After the end of the war
with France, the King and his courtiers had little to
do. There was nothing for them now but to seek
amusement. The courtiers had no education to serve
as diplomats. And so with Henry, who was now
thirty-six. He began to pay less and less attention
to the business of state, and spent his days in hunting and gambling. More did not care for the society of men to whom impurity did not seem much of
a crime; and so he kept away from the King as
much as possible, even though the King, secretly ad-
miring his virtue and his ability, liked to keep him
near him. And then came the time when Henry
thought he could use More to further his own selfish ends. He was going to make him return all the
kindness which he had shown him. The occasion was
the divorce which Henry sought from his lawful wife,
Katharine.

The story of the divorce is this. Henry was the
second son of Henry VII. The eldest son was Prince
Arthur. Arthur had married Katharine of Aragon.
It was an international marriage, but it had never
been consummated, and Arthur died in 1502. When
Henry VII died, Henry VIII, then a young man of
eighteen, succeeded to the throne. Katharine, his
brother's widow, was five years his senior; but Henry
determined to marry her, and in order to do so a dispensation from Rome was obtained. Henry was now
content and happy. He always, even after the divorce,

had the highest regard for Katharine. At any rate, he had no scruples then about the legality of his marriage with her. It was only years after that he began to express his worry that he was living in sin by having as his wife the widow of his brother, even though a dispensation had been granted by the Church. One reason for his desire to get rid of Katharine was the fact that he had by her no male children. All her children but Mary, afterwards queen, died in infancy. But the chief reason for his wish to be divorced was Anne Boleyn. It is doubtful if Henry's married life was ever pure. He had had impure relations with Mary Boleyn, a sister of Anne, a fact which made his marriage with Anne later on invalid, apart from the question of Katharine being alive, on account of the impediment of affinity.

Anne had been in the employ of Henry's sister Mary in France at the time she married the French King. After his death she came to England and was made a lady-in-waiting to Queen Katharine. The strange thing which shows the hypocrisy of Henry is that he had no conscientious worries about his affinity with her. But Anne was very wise. She had the example of her sister Mary to guide her. Henry had thrown Mary aside. Anne was determined that he should marry her or she would have nothing to do with him. He must get a divorce from Katharine.

No need to go into the details of the fight for and against the divorce. The great universities of the world were approached, but after serious investiga-

tion the majority were for the validity of Henry's
marriage with Katharine. Rome could do nothing
but decide for the Queen against the King out of pure
justice. Wolsey had tried hard to have the marriage
annulled, even while he had no notion that the
King was inclined towards Anne Boleyn. He was
looking towards a union with France. He hated Anne
Boleyn, and she hated him. But Wolsey failed in
his effort, and was obliged to resign the chancellorship in 1529.

A week after his retirement as chancellor, the seal
was given to Thomas More. He was now Lord Chancellor of England. Everybody, even Wolsey, was
pleased. But More himself was not pleased. He saw
the way the wind was blowing. He knew that he
had received the great honor as a bribe to induce him
to come out in favor of the divorce. He knew that
Henry then was trying to find flaws in the dispensation that had permitted him to marry Katharine. But
he refused to discuss the matter, saying that he was
incompetent to judge. Even after the marriage with
Anne he refused to give his opinion. He was virtually obliged to accept the chancellorship. If he had
refused he would have gone to the block sooner than
he did go. More had attained the highest point in his
career. He was now the chief adviser of the King and
the council. He had a great income, but he still continued to live a simple life, knowing that every moment he was in danger of death. He was then fifty-
two.

In 1531 Henry took the title of "Supreme Head of the Anglican Church." It was at the time rather an ambiguous title and was not in opposition to the supremacy of the Holy See. But More did not like the whole business, and he even thought of resigning, seeing that the King was beginning to usurp the authority that belonged to the Church alone. Finally, in 1532, he resigned. He saw that he could not retain the office in conscience, and that he would have to displease the King by refusing to side against the clergy. It was a great sacrifice, leaving More with an income of only five hundred dollars. It necessitated the breaking up of his family circle, since he was unable now to keep up the great establishment he had maintained for years.

Even after the resignation the King continued to have the deepest respect for More. But More had many enemies at court in the party of Anne Boleyn, who was still waiting for the divorce to be pronounced. Charges were brought against him, but he was exonerated from them all. Added to his poverty, his health began to fail. But he did not complain. He was glad to be free from the world in order to attend to his soul.

The divorce was not granted, but Henry and Anne were married in 1533, and at the Pentecost of that year she made a magnificent entry into London to be crowned queen. More refused to be present—another reason why Anne determined to be revenged for his slights against her. Plots were now set on foot for his ruin. The occasion of the plots was the case of "the Holy Maid of Kent." The woman was one Elizabeth Barton, a servant-maid, who was said to have been cured of the falling sickness in a chapel of Our Lady. She became a nun at Canterbury, and soon got the reputation of having received revelations, from which she was known as "the Holy Maid of Kent." Soon her supposed revelations took a political turn. She declared that she had had revelations about the divorce, and warned the King and Wolsey, who was then chancellor. She was the tool of the anti-divorce party, and as the result of it she and several others were convicted of treason and were executed at Tyburn in 1534. More was charged with misprision of treason in not having had her apprehended, but he proved that while he had regarded her as pious, and all that, he had never heard any treasonable statements from her. His name was put in the bill of attainder with others, but finally was stricken from it for lack of evidence.

But he was not yet safe by any means. Henry, who had thought so highly of him, now grew to hate him for his very goodness and the impossibility of corrupting him. In order to win him over to the cause of Anne and to approve of his marriage with her, he had More accused of treason. But the council feared public sentiment if this were done, and it prevailed upon the King to spare More. A turn in affairs now took place, for the marriage had been celebrated and the work was begun of confirming Anne's offspring in the succession to the crown. This was done by requiring oaths. A bill was passed in Parliament, and received the royal assent in 1534, making it high treason to oppose the succession, and misprision of treason to speak against it. A preamble was drawn up by the commissioners, and was therefore invalid, as the Parliament alone had the right to do this, declaring the first marriage illegal, and that with Anne Boleyn legal. It implied a rejection of the Pope's authority, since he had given the final decision that Katharine's marriage had been valid; moreover, the preamble included the repudiation of any oath taken "to any foreign authority, prince, or potentate." This was, of course, directed against the Pope. An oath was administered to the clergy rejecting the authority of the Pope, whereas the form chosen for the laity dwelt rather on the succession of Anne's children to the crown. The oath was taken by the members of both Houses of Parliament.

One day, when More came to London to hear a sermon at St. Paul's, he was cited to appear before the royal commission to take the oath. Feeling that trouble was approaching, he went to confession, heard Mass, and received Holy Communion. He read the oath and the Act of Succession and refused to sign. He found no fault with others who signed it, but he declared that it was against his own conscience to sign. He refused to give his reasons, saying that he would give them to the King if he wanted them. He was willing to sign for the succession, but would not sign the preamble rejecting the authority of the Pope. And so for his refusal he was sent to the Tower. Cranmer suggested to the King a modification of the oath in order to get More to sign it; but the King refused. He wanted to humble More.

In the winter session of Parliament, More, together with Bishop Fisher, was charged with misprision of treason. More had been in the Tower all this time. He was a prey to physical sufferings; but that was not enough penance. He wore the hair shirt as usual, and gave much time to prayer, rather pleased with his imprisonment, as it gave him more time to devote to his soul. His wife came to him, and begged him to sign the oath, but he turned her off in a bantering way. Even his beloved daughter Margaret came to him and pleaded with him to have pity on himself and his family and do as the King required. She herself had signed the oath, "as far as it would stand with the law of God," and she could not see why he also could not do the same. It was not surprising. So many high in the Church had signed it that it was not strange that women felt it all right to do so. More told her that she did not know what she was doing in tempting him; as for himself, he said that he had counted the cost long ago. His conscience would not permit him to sign it, and that was all there was to it.

The family pleaded with the King; but he was obdurate. More's property at Chelsea was confiscated, that home which had been the scene of so much happiness, into which Henry himself had so often been welcomed. Parliament now passed a new statute asserting that Henry was the only Supreme Head on earth of the Church of England.

There is no need to go into all the details of those last days of More. His trial was a farce. On the day that the Carthusians and others were put to death on the same charge of misprision of treason, Margaret came to visit him in jail. Her husband, Roper, tells us of that interview. "As Sir Thomas More was looking out of his window, he chanced to behold one Master Reynolds, a religious, learned, and virtuous Father in Sion, and three monks of the Charterhouse, for the matter of the supremacy and the matrimony going out of the Tower of execution; he, as one longing in that journey to have accompanied them, said unto my wife standing there beside him: 'Lo, dost thou not see, Meg, that these blessed fathers be now as cheerfully going to their deaths as bridegrooms to their marriage? Wherefore, thereby thou mayest see, mine own good daughter, what a difference there is between such as have in effect spent all their days in a strait and penitential life religiously and such as have in the world, like worldly wretches (as thy poor father hath done), consumed all their time in pleasure and ease licentiously. For God, considering their long-continued life in most sore and grievous penance, will no longer suffer them to remain here in this vale of misery, but speedily hence taketh them to the fruition of His everlasting Deity. Whereas thy silly father, Meg, that like a wicked caitiff hath passed the whole course of his miserable life most sinfully,—God, thinking him not worthy so soon to come to that eternal felicity, leaveth him here still in the world further to be plagued and turmoiled with misery.' "

More answered the charges against him by saying to the court that he knew the reason of his condemnation was his refusal to agree to the King's second marriage. The beloved Margaret, it can well be imagined, was near to distraction during these days of the trial. Eagerly she waited for every word from the jail. She could not content herself at home, but must come forth, eager to give help to the man who loved her so dearly. As More was being brought back to the Tower from the place of trial, Margaret rushed through the crowd of guards, and threw herself upon his neck and kissed him with all the affection of her heart. Again she ran back to him, and again embraced him. So affecting was the scene that as the father blessed his daughter the bystanders were moved to tears.

More was sentenced to be hanged, drawn, and quartered at Tyburn. The sentence did not alarm him; it drove him to give more time to the care of his soul. In the midst of his cares he wrote to his family. His letter to Margaret, written with a coal, is so touching that we give it entire. It was the last he ever wrote:

"Our Lord bless you, good daughter, and your good husband, and your little boy, and all yours, and all my children, and all my godchildren, and all my friends. Recommend me, when ye may, to my good

daughter Cicily, whom I beseech Our Lord to comfort. And I send her my blessing, and to all her
children, and pray her to pray for me. I send her
an handkerchief; and God comfort my good son her
husband. My good daughter Dance hath the picture
in parchment that you delivered me from my Lady
Coniers; her name is on the back. Show her that I
heartily pray her that you may send it in my name to
her again, for a token from me to pray for me. I like
well Dorothy Coly; I pray you be good unto her. I
would wit whether this be she that you wrote me of.
If not, yet I pray you be good to the other, as you
may in her affliction, and to my good daughter Joan
Aleyn, too. Give her, I pray you, some kind answer,
for she sued hither to me this day to pray you be good
to her. I cumber you, good Margaret, much, but I
would be sorry if it should be any longer than to-
morrow. For it is St. Thomas's eve, and the Utas of
St. Peter: and therefore to-morrow I long to go to
God: it were a day very meet and convenient for me.
I never liked your manner towards me better than
when you kissed me last: for I love when daughterly
love and dear charity hath no leisure to make look to
worldly courtesy. Farewell, my dear child, and pray
for me, and I shall for you and all your friends, that
we may merrily meet in Heaven. I thank you for
your great cost. I send now to my good daughter
Clement her algorism stone, and I send her, and my
godson, and all hers God's blessing and mine. I pray
you at time convenient recommend me to my good son

John More; I liked well his natural fashion. Our
Lord bless him and his good wife my loving daughter,
to whom I pray you to be good, as he hath great cause:
and that if the land of mine come to his hand, he
break not my will concerning his sister Dance. And
Our Lord bless Thomas and Austen and all that they
shall have."

More, as stated above, had been sentenced to die as
a traitor—that is, to be hanged, drawn, and quartered
—but the King commuted the sentence to beheading on
Tower Hill.

When the news came to him one morning that he
was to die that day, he thanked the messenger for the
good news, and begged that his daughter Meg might
be allowed to be present at his burial; and he was told
that all his family might assist at that last service.
He had sent his hair shirt to Margaret; she used to
wash it for him, and was the only one he permitted
to see this instrument of penance.

And so he was led forth to die. We get a picture of
the noble man that morning, going to his doom, his
face pale, his body emaciated from the long imprisonment, in his dress of frieze, carrying in his hand a
small red cross, his eyes turned to heaven. When he
had ascended the scaffold, he asked the people to pray
for him, and called them to witness that he died for
the Catholic faith. He then knelt and recited his favorite prayer, the Miserere. Then he bound his eyes
with a handkerchief, placed his neck on the block,
and in this manner gave up his soul to God.

After the execution, the head of More, according to the custom of those days, was parboiled and then fixed on a stake on London Bridge as a warning to traitors. There it remained a month, till Margaret bribed the man whose business it was to throw it into the river after a certain time to give it to her. It was the dearest treasure she possessed. She had it preserved in spices, and kept it while she lived. Later on she was summoned before the council to answer the charge of keeping the head as a relic. She answered that she had procured it so that it might not be the food of fishes. She desired that the head should be buried with her when she died. There is an old tradition that when she was buried the head of her father was laid on her bosom. Tennyson beautifully describes that incident in his "Dream of Fair Women":

> "Morn broaden'd on the borders of the dark
> Ere I saw her, who clasp'd in her last trance
> Her murder'd father's head. . . ."

When the news reached Margaret that her father had been beheaded, her first thought was to prepare his body for burial. So, accompanied by her maid, she came to St. Peter's chapel in the Tower, where the headless body was lying. It is related that when she arrived there she realized that she had come without a sheet in which to wrap the body. She was without a cent, as all the money she had had she had given to the poor in aid of her father's soul. The maid went out to a draper's shop to get the linen, and when she looked into her purse she found the exact sum that the cloth cost.

After the burial Margaret watched for the time when the head would be disposed of. We can fancy her coming to London Bridge to gaze with love on the adored head, and the eagerness with which she bought the dear treasure from the keeper. As we have said, she was later on summoned before the council on the charge of keeping the head as a relic, and also that she had the intention of publishing her father's writings.

"It would be well to remember," said the Chancellor, "that he suffered death as a traitor, and to be cautious, fair mistress, lest thou thyself be condemned."

"I procured my father's head," she answered, "lest it should become food for fishes, hearing that an order had gone forth that it was to be cast into the Thames; and for the rest, I have buried it where I thought fit. Methinks, my lords, I speak to such amongst ye as have daughters; they could scarce do less than I have done, if the hard hap of life should render them fatherless in such a way. Alack, they would not stop to reckon up the cost to themselves, nor care whether in the eyes of the law you had been deemed guilty. I did procure that venerated head, my lords, it listeth me not to tell you how. Nevertheless I glory in the deed, and if for such I be deemed worthy of punishment, I am in your hands; do with me as it pleaseth you. Moreover, I will publish his works when opportunity shall serve."

She was dismissed while the council held a conference as to what should be done to punish her. It was decided to cast her into prison. There she remained, however, but a short time, as it was feared that the people, who were indignant at the imprisonment, would show their resentment. Margaret would have been pleased, no doubt, to go the way of her father. But it was not the will of God. She had her work to do in the world, the work of caring for and educating the children God had sent her.

She lived nine years after her father. They were sad days for her, yet by degrees peace returned to her soul. She watched over the education of her children, as her father had watched over hers. Her husband prospered in his profession, and she always had an abundance of this world's goods. But their riches were used by them in open generosity. She rejoiced in distributing his alms, as she had distributed those of her father. And more than all else, she had time to give to prayer, remembering the wonderful example of her sainted father.

Her last years were spent at her husband's estate in Canterbury, where she gave the example of a model wife and mother, ever generous to the poor. When she died, a great throng came to her funeral, prominent among them the poor whom she had befriended. We are told even of those who constituted her funeral procession. First walked the poor, two and two. To these succeeded servants with black staves. The brothers-in-law of the deceased lady. Her brother. Her sons. Then was borne, covered with black velvet, the leaden box containing the head of Sir Thomas More. Then the corpse borne on a bier, men on either side bearing staves. William Roper walked at the head of the coffin. Then came distant relatives and friends, men with staves keeping back the throng. And so, all chanting the De Profundis, they carried the remains of Margaret Roper to the little church of St. Dunstan, which she loved so much, and where she had spent so many hours in prayer. And there, after the Requiem Mass, she was buried in a large vault beneath the Roper chancel, the burial-place of all the family. In a small niche in the wall of the vault was placed the box containing the head of the father she had so loved in life and in death. The following is the epitaph in the church:

"Here lieth interred Thomas Roper, a venerable and worthy man, the son and successor of the late W. Roper and Margaret his wife, daughter of Sir Thomas More, knight, a woman excellently well skilled in the Greek and Latin tongues. The above mentioned William Roper succeeded his father in the office of Prothonotary of ye Bench; after having discharged the duties of it faithfully for 44 years he left it to his son Thomas. The said William Roper was both liberal in his domestic and public conduct, kind and compassionate in his temper, the support and preserver of the poor and the oppressed. He had issue by Margaret, his only wife, two sons and three daughters, whose children and grandchildren he lived to see. He lost his wife in the bloom of his years, and lived a chaste widower 33 years. At length, his days finished in peace, he died, lamented by all, in a good old age, on the 4th of January, 1577, and of his age 82."

One of their daughters, Mary, was maid of honor to Queen Mary Tudor. She also, like her mother, was learned, and translated into English part of one of her grandfather's Latin works. Even to-day in England there are many families that can claim descent from Sir Thomas More through his beloved daughter Margaret.

So died Margaret Roper in the prime of life. We would wish to know more about her personally, so appealing is her story to every lover of the good and the beautiful. Her life, as we have seen, was bound up in that of her martyred father. We know her through her intimate and beautiful association with him. But little as we know of her personally, that little is enough to paint a picture of a true Catholic daughter, mother, and wife, not only the "ornament of Britain," as Erasmus called her, but an ornament of all true womanhood, the beautiful, charitable, learned, pious, and, above all, loving Margaret Roper.

MARGARET CLITHEROW,

(1556–1586)

THE English Reformation, if it has perpetuated for all time the picture of degraded womanhood in Queen Elizabeth, so also has it immortalized the memory of many a noble woman. How time shows the real value of things! Back in the year 1586 there were living in England two women: one was queen of a great kingdom, seated upon her throne, listening to the voice of flatterers, trembling for her very crown, which had come to her through the lust and dishonesty of the miserable Henry VIII. Her dainty fingers held the sceptre; she was a fortunate, a successful ruler. But in the eyes of God those dainty fingers were the fingers of a Lady Macbeth, red with blood which all the seas of the world could never again make white. Yet to the world of her day she was the most happy of women.

The other woman was deemed the most unhappy of women; a traitor to this great queen, a woman, too, whose gentle body was covered with blood, but blood that is the sign of glory unending. She was Margaret Clitherow, the first woman martyr in the reign of Elizabeth, a gentle wife and mother crushed to her death because she followed her conscience and served her God. An unfortunate woman to her age, a fool to lay down her life for such a simple thing as religion, when but a word would have saved her to years of happiness. But the centuries have gone by; and as we look across them to behold the queenly woman on her throne and the disgraced martyr on her bed of death, do we need to say which of them was the happier, which the more to be envied, the Queen who risked her eternal salvation for the bauble of a crown, or the young Catholic wife who chose to serve God rather than an earthly ruler, and so went the way of suffering and death to reign with Christ in Heaven?

Margaret Clitherow, whose maiden name was Middleton, was born and lived all her life in the city of York. Her father was Thomas Middleton, a waxchandler, evidently a man of means and of some importance in the community, for we find him holding various offices, acting as sheriff for one year, and at different times a member of the Common Council. After his death his widow did not long remain inconsolable, for four months later she married a man named Henry May, who by a strange circumstance was lord mayor of the city at the time his stepdaughter Margaret Clitherow was put to death for her faith.

With her mother and her stepfather Margaret made her home for four years, until the time of her marriage in 1571 to John Clitherow, a wealthy butcher, who established her in a magnificent home which later

on was to be the hiding-place of many a poor priest
with a price on his head. It is said that she was very
beautiful, the fairest of brides. It was a happy marriage, a home with all that the world could give, money,
position, and love, with never a trial until the day when
God tested her in his fiery furnace.

For some years now the Protestant religion was
dominant in England. The revolt that had been begun by Henry in his lust and covetousness of the
Church's goods had been consummated by his illegitimate daughter Elizabeth. She had succeeded to the
throne in 1558, two years after the birth of Margaret
Middleton. Thomas Middleton, judging from the
offices he had held, had evidently conformed to the
new religion with his wife. At any rate, Margaret
was brought up in the queer new Protestant religion.
She knew no better. The old Catholic religion was a
despised thing by those who sought preferment in
holding to the new faith which Elizabeth set up in
order to make her position secure. In a worldly sense
she was driven to it, though she had little religion of
any kind in her own make-up. Rome had in justice
branded her as illegitimate from the fact that her
mother's marriage with Henry was null. Catholics in
general regarded her as a usurper of the throne, which
they declared belonged by right to Mary Queen of
Scots. Hence her aim was to banish the old religion
for her own safety.

And little Margaret Middleton, as she grew up, was
made to conform to the new order of things. At the

time she was married to John Clitherow there were in York many signs of the passing of the old order. The altars in the churches were being torn down, the altarstones turned into pavements; the rood-lofts with their great crucifixes were burned, the glorious windows of stained glass broken, the gold and silver altar vessels melted down to enrich the destroyers, and the Scripture scenes that had been painted on the walls obliterated by coats of whitewash. There was an effort to make the people forget all the beauties that had been, and this with such diabolical hatred that in York itself no less than nineteen churches were destroyed.

But, try as she might, Margaret found no consolation in the new religion. For three years after her marriage—she was but fifteen when she married—she followed the new faith. But all the while it palled on her. Her soul was not satisfied. All the more was she discontented as she heard the touching stories about the priests and laymen who went to their death in defence of the old religion. She little thought that the day would come when she, too, would be called upon to lay down her life in defence of it. Even in those days the martyrs of the faith made an appeal to her. Surely, she thought, the faith must be true that could inspire such heroism. And so, after earnest prayer and study, the light of faith came to her, and she was received into the Catholic Church.

Even if Margaret Clitherow had never died the martyr's death, her name would deserve to be held in everlasting remembrance as that of an exemplary wife and mother. Perhaps it was because she was such, corresponding so perfectly to all the graces of God, that she was at length enriched with the glorious privilege of martyrdom. From the time she became a Catholic her life was one great act of love for God.

We get a beautiful picture of her in the midst of her family. John Clitherow, her husband, belonged to the established church, though he had a brother a priest. He did not interfere, however, with her in the practice of her religion; and, moreover, he permitted her to bring up her children in the Catholic faith, a sign of the firm character of his wife at a time when a father knew that the Catholic faith was a handicap for his children. They had three children, two boys, Henry and William, who became priests later on, and one daughter, Anne, who became a nun at St. Ursula's, Louvain. They were blessed for their mother's loyalty to the faith.

The Clitherows had an abundance of the goods of the world, but that did not make the young wife feel that she could be an idler. She was an example of the busy housewife who, with all her cares, could find time for the special service of God. She arose early every day, and spent an hour and a half, sometimes two hours, on her knees, praying and meditating. She had a room in her house set aside as a chapel, and there very often Mass was said by her spiritual director or by one of the missionary priests who, with a price on their heads, sought a refuge in her house, which was a centre of Catholicity, a refuge for all the priests who went up and down the country, looking after the spiritual wants of those who remained true to the old Church. What a happiness it was to her to harbor the ministers of God, finding her great reward in the blessing of having the Holy Sacrifice offered up in her own home! It was like a page from the story of the Catacombs, where the first Christians worshipped in secret. She was again the Roman matron presiding over the destinies of a proscribed people.

Mass over, she busied herself with the management of her household, striving to do the humblest tasks for the glory of God.

"Now for God's sake pray for me," she used to say to Father Mush, her director, who later wrote the story of her life and sufferings. "Methinks I do nothing well, because I overslipped this right intention, which God's servants should always have actually, to refer all my doing to His glory."

Her greatest joy was to serve the meals to the priests who sought her protection. She had many servants, but she did not disdain helping them in their work. Many a time did she spare them, and perform herself the humblest duties of the household, saying, "God forbid that I should will any to do that in my house which I would not willingly do myself first." Nor did she hesitate to correct them when they needed it. Her confessor, noting this, asked her one day: "How is it that you dare speak so sharply to these servants, when they are careless in the performance of their duty? Have you forgotten that they have it in their power to revenge themselves on you by making it known that priests are concealed in your house?"

And she would reply: "God defend that, for my Christian liberty in serving Him in my House, I should neglect my duty to my servants, or not correct them as they deserve. God shall dispose of all as it pleaseth Him; but I will not be blamed for their faults, nor fear any danger for this good cause."

The servant problem would be settled very easily if there were more mistresses like Margaret Clitherow.

This valiant woman knew all the while that her life was in danger, but the thought did not make her morose or sad. She was always cheerful, always with a smile on her lips, and ready to take part in any fun. She reminds us of the dear St. Elizabeth of Hungary, who, even while she wore the hair shirt of penance, could take part in the dance and bring pleasure to others. The only sorrow she had to drive the smile away was the fear for the life of the priests who left her house to go forth on their missionary journeys. Many a time, too, she was found weeping when her house was without a priest to say Mass, thinking that some fault of hers had made God take from her that grace.

At four o'clock in the evening, when most of the day's work was done, she would spend an hour in prayer with her little ones gathered about her. We can fancy the things she talked about to them, telling them of the blessings of the faith, relating the hero-

ism of the martyrs of their own times, and implant-
ing in their souls the seeds that in later years were to
give such abundant harvest. Then at eight or nine
she would seek her spiritual director and get his blessing, after which she would spend an hour in prayer
before retiring. And along with this life of prayer
she practised severe mortification. Perpetually she
curbed her appetite. Four days of the week she kept
strict abstinence, and on Monday, Wednesday, and
Saturday took but one meal. On Friday she fasted
on bread and water, and scourged herself with the discipline whenever her confessor permitted her to do so.
Busy as she was, she found time for the reading of
pious books, her favorites being the New Testament,
the *Imitation of Christ,* and Perin's *Exercise.* She
even learned by heart the Little Office of the Blessed
Virgin in Latin, saying, "If it please God so to dispose,
and that He sets me at liberty from the world, I will
with all my heart take upon me some religious habit,
whereby I may ever serve God under obedience." She
little guessed in what way God was to set her at liberty from the world.

Twice a week she confessed, weeping over the smallest faults; and when she went to Holy Communion
she took her place far from the altar, bowed down
with her own unworthiness, and the tears would
stream from her eyes as she received the Bread of
Angels.

Such was the daily life of this wife and mother,
more like the life of the nun in her cloister away from

[231]

the cares of the world. So that I say, even if Margaret Clitherow had not died the martyr's death, she would still deserve everlasting remembrance as an exemplary woman in the world.

But even while she busied herself in her home and served God lovingly and whole-heartedly, martyrdom was coming near. Even if she had known that, it would not have frightened her; rather would it have given her joy, for if there was one thing that this beautiful, wealthy, happy young wife prayed for, it was that she would be permitted to suffer death for the sake of Christ. One day she related to her little daughter, Anne, the story of the martyrdom of Father Lacy, an old priest who had spent many days under her roof. He had been sentenced to death for high treason because in his trial he refused to acknowledge the Queen as the Supreme Head of the Church. "God be forever blessed," he said; "I am now old, and by the course of nature cannot expect to live long. This will be no more to me than to pay the common debt a little before the time."

"Mother," said little Anne, "if you had stood at the bar and been sentenced to death like Father Lacy, would not you have been frightened and sad?"

But the mother answered: "Why should I be frightened and sad if I were condemned to die for the Catholic faith? Methinks I would die any death for so good a cause."

With Father Lacy there was martyred another priest, Father Kirkeman, who, too, had enjoyed the hospitality of the Clitherow home. And when she had finished the story of these men of God, dragged on a hurdle through the streets and finally hanged at Tyburn, where criminals were put to death and their poor bodies drawn and quartered, she cried out, "Oh, children, how glorious a privilege it is to die for Christ! How sweet would it be to pour out every drop of blood for the Church He came on earth to found! Happy martyrs! who have merited the favor I, alas, am unworthy to obtain. From my heart I rejoice and am exceeding glad that these two blessed priests have suffered and died with courage, patience, and heroic constancy. Ah! it shall still, as heretofore, be my daily prayer that I may be worthy to endure whatever may betide for God's sake and the Catholic faith!"

After the execution of these two priests in 1582, in the month of August, there followed in a few months' time the martyrdom on the same spot of three other priests, Father James Thompson, Father William Hart, and Father Richard Thirkill, all of whom had been at one time or another her spiritual directors. It was only natural then that she, who had such a desire of martyrdom, should feel great devotion to the place where these her friends had laid down their lives before her. Tyburn, where stood the gallows, was situated about half a mile outside the city of York. Very often at night, either alone or with some of her Catholic neighbors, she would make a pilgrimage to this now hallowed spot, in order to spend some time in prayer where her priests had shed their blood. Always she went barefoot, considering the way they had gone to their death holy ground. Imagine her, if you can, this tender young wife, putting her little ones to bed, and then, close to midnight, tramping in her bare feet along the sorrowful way to kneel in the darkness beneath the gallows-tree where in ages gone by the worst criminals had forfeited their lives in payment for their crimes! It was an experience to bring terror to a gentle woman, but she thought not of the awful dreariness, the horror of the place; she thought only that on this spot men had died for God. So at the foot of the gallows she and her companions knelt in prayer, not mourning the martyrs, but thanking God for them, and begging their help for themselves and their families, praying for their poor country, now gone astray in heresy and crime, and even begging God to grant them, too, the grace of martyrdom.

In such devotion these short years went by. All the while the laws for the elimination of the very name Catholic became more brutal. And, indeed, for a long time these laws had been severe enough. Elizabeth, as we have said, in order to make her crown more secure, felt obliged to espouse the Protestant cause, even while, personally, religion bothered her very little. It was in 1559 that the law took effect—three years after the birth of Margaret Clitherow—abolishing the old worship and setting up the new. From that time Catholic worship could be held only in secret and at the risk of heavy punishment. For the first two years, however, there was a tendency not to push the law to extremes. Catholics were treated with comparative leniency; they were fined occasionally, had their goods confiscated, or were themselves imprisoned. But there was no shedding of blood. Elizabeth had the idea then that when the old priests died there would be none to take their place, and consequently the people now remaining Catholics would gradually come over to the new religion.

But she reckoned not with the zeal of the Catholic faithful. A seminary was established at Douai, and here were trained the missionary priests who for so many years, through suffering and death, were to come in secrecy to England to break the Bread of Life to the Catholics. Such an action roused the wrath of Elizabeth, and immediately she increased the severity of the penal laws. Catholics who would not acknowledge her as the Supreme Head of the Church in England were put to death as traitors. But in 1581 a man was considered a traitor who absolved or reconciled others to the See of Rome, or was willingly absolved or reconciled. And even a person who had harbored a priest was deemed guilty of treason. In the four months between July 22 and November 27, 1588, twenty-one of these seminary priests, eleven laymen, and one woman—our own Margaret Clitherow—were put to death for their religion. The total number of Catholics who suffered under Elizabeth was one hundred and eighty-nine, of which number one hundred

[235]

and twenty-eight were priests, fifty-eight laymen, and three women, the other women being Margaret Ward and Anne Line, besides thirty-two Franciscans who were starved to death.

Every one of these martyrs might well be the subject of a book as well as Margaret Clitherow, but in telling her story of faith we tell the story of them all. There was none of them that prayed more earnestly for the gift of martyrdom, and at last her prayers were answered.

It was not the first time that a woman's blood had flowed in these terrible days of the persecution of the Church. Elizabeth was but carrying out the policy of her bloodthirsty father. The first woman martyr of that period was the Blessed Margaret Pole, who was put to death in 1541, in the reign of Henry VIII. She was the daughter of the Duke of Clarence, and in 1491 had been given by King Henry VII in marriage to Sir Richard Pole, the son of the half-sister of the King's mother, the sainted Margaret Beaufort. Her husband had died in 1505, leaving her a widow with five children, one of them being Reginald, afterwards Cardinal Pole. Henry VIII had great admiration for her, and considered her the saintliest woman in England. He made her Countess of Salisbury, restored her property to her, chose her as the sponsor for his daughter Mary, and made her governess of that princess and her household. There was even talk of marrying Mary to Reginald Pole. At the time of the divorce Reginald did not scruple about coming out against it, in spite of the bribes that were offered him to side with Henry. He fled to Rome and was there made cardinal. By his representation of the case, the excommunication of Henry was hastened. When Henry's daughter Mary was pronounced illegitimate so as to favor the issue of Anne Boleyn, Henry removed the Countess of Salisbury from her position as governess, and she lived in retirement until the death of Anne, whereupon she returned to court.

But Henry was turning against the Poles. Soon after the passage of the Act of Supremacy steps were taken to despoil the smaller monasteries on any pretext. These monasteries were the only support of the poor, and the only places for education, but they were suppressed and the monks and nuns thrown out on the street to become beggars. The people in the North, seeing this, rebelled and, united in an army, thirty thousand strong, demanded redress for the Church they loved. The government was frightened at this display of strength, and promised everything. But as soon as the army disbanded the hypocritical government turned against those who had rebelled, and farmers and yeomen were hanged by the hundreds. This was so encouraging to Henry that he determined to strike at the Courtenays and the Poles, families that were staunch defenders of the Catholic Church. Henry Courtenay was next in succession to the crown after Henry's children.

When, in 1530, Cardinal Pole sent to Henry his defence of the Church, Henry went into a rage. He

determined to be revenged on the Poles and especially
on the Countess, whom he had once so admired. Her
eldest son was executed on the evidence given against
him by a younger brother, Sir Geoffrey Pole, and
she and others of her relatives were executed. When
the old woman—she was then nearly ninety—was
arrested she said nothing, being so old that she
scarcely knew why she was arrested. She was treated
with indignity and was kept a prisoner in the Tower
for two years. And then this noble, saintly old woman,
herself a royal princess, was sent to the block. She
walked to her death calmly, her last words being,
"Blessed are they who suffer persecution for righteous-
ness' sake."

So that Margaret Clitherow had, besides the example of her good priestly friends, that of a weak
woman like herself who thought little of the hardships
that bring one to God.

It was in 1585, when Elizabeth had been reigning
twenty-seven years, that there was enforced the statute
which made it a crime to give shelter to a seminary
priest or a Jesuit, these men upon whose heads a price
had been set. Now not only was the priest to be put
to death, but even the one who harbored him. Some
of the neighbors, knowing that Mrs. Clitherow was
accustomed to have priests in her house, came to her
to warn her of the new law that made her charity a
crime. Her only answer was: "If God's priests dare
venture themselves in my house, I will never refuse
them shelter." She had no fear; in fact, being ar-

rested for her faith was no new experience to her. Many a time had she been imprisoned, sometimes for two years at a time, and there were other Catholic wives and mothers who were persecuted in like manner.

One day she asked the advice of her confessor as to whether it was right for her to harbor the priests without asking her husband's consent; and he assured her that it was not only her right but her duty. She was overjoyed at the decision.

"But," said the priest, merrily, "you must prepare your neck for the hangman's rope."

"God's will be done," said she; "but I am most unworthy of that honor."

But even then there was about to dawn the day when God would show this woman that she was worthy of the honor. For a long time the Clitherow house had been marked as a rendezvous for missionary priests where the Catholic inhabitants of the city might hear Mass and receive the Sacraments. Even those who had fallen away from the faith knew that almost at any time a priest might be found in some secret chamber. But, in spite of all that, she did not become cautious. No doubt her apparent boldness was merely her confidence in God, her faith that He would save her house from harm as long as it was His good will. More than that, she had such a winning way that even her heretical neighbors could not bring themselves to accuse her before the law. There were a few, however, so filled with hatred of the old religion that they watched every opportunity to betray her.

She had two rooms fitted up where Mass was said, one adjoining her own dwelling and the other at a short distance from her house. The latter was used only in the very dangerous times, when her own home was unsafe. Both chapels were beautifully fitted with religious articles, vestments, etc., so much so that the authorities were amazed when the discovery was made. It was a proof of her wonderful love for the altar of God. All that she could spare went to its adornment.

About a year before her arrest she had induced her husband to send their eldest son, Henry, over to France, so that he might receive a Catholic education in one of the English seminaries abroad, an education such as it was impossible to get in England at the time. This was deemed a crime, and as soon as it became known to the Council which managed such affairs in the northern part of the kingdom, they cited John Clitherow to appear before them to be questioned as to his part in the crime against her Majesty's statutes.

As soon as he left the house, two sheriffs of the city, accompanied by other men, came to search his home. His wife was busy about her duties when they arrived. She was not surprised at the visit; all these months she had expected it. Her fears were not for herself, but for the good priest, Father Mush, then in his room talking with some Catholics who had come to consult him, perhaps to go to confession. Before admitting the searchers she managed to go to the room to warn her dear friends, and to hide them in another secret chamber, where they escaped the spies and so saved their lives. She was calm as she admitted her enemies. They immediately arrested her, and asked her where she had secreted the traitor-priests, Mush and Ingleby.

"I shelter no traitors here," she answered; "the members of my household are loyal subjects." But the searchers proceeded to search the house for the concealed "traitors." There were at that time many Catholic children in the house, her own and those of the neighbors, for she always dearly loved children, being instructed by a schoolmaster, a loyal Catholic who had been seven years in prison for the faith. Among them was a little Flemish boy whom she had charitably taken under her care. The authorities seized him, and threatened him with death unless he told them all that he knew about the visiting priests and their hiding-places. The boy, trembling for his life, told everything, and led his captors to the secret chamber in the house and then to the other chapel at a distance, telling them, too, the names of the Catholics who from time to time assisted at Mass there. They gathered together all the vestments and church articles, and carried them away, leading off as prisoners Mrs. Clitherow, her two children, and all the servants. The children and servants were sent to different prisons, but Mrs. Clitherow was brought to the Common Hall to be questioned by the Council. But, finding the questioning of her useless, they sent her a prisoner to the Castle.

It was a loathsome place, that dungeon, filled with dirt and swarming with vermin, its only furniture a hard pallet, the only food bread and water, which in her love of fasting she did not touch. Yet in the midst of such squalor she did not grumble, but even smiled and was joyous, singing hymns, so much so that the jailers were astounded that any woman in such circumstances could be so brave. Her only worry was for her husband and children, all in prison, and for the safety of the priests she had sheltered. Her prayer was that her little ones might not be led to deny their religion through persecution. And earnest was this prayer as she knelt through the night upon the cold stone floor, happy to begin her sufferings for God. Two days later her sister, Mrs. Ann Tesh, was thrown into the same prison for the crime of hearing Mass, and kept there till her fine of five hundred marks was paid. Strange to say, it was a joyful time, and the two sisters, one of them in the shadow of death, laughed and made merry as they tried to keep up their strength by eating the humble supper of bread and water. Those who love God can find joy even in affliction, and there were not on earth happier beings than those two sisters as they laid them down on the hard bed to sleep the sleep of the just.

It was a beautiful spring day when Margaret was led from prison to the Common Hall to be placed on trial. The streets were thronged as she walked along, most of the multitude filled with sympathy for this mother who had been torn from her children. She did not flinch as she faced the Council, though she knew she could expect little justice from these paid persecutors. She was accused of harboring priests, of hearing Mass, and of sending her son to be educated in a foreign Catholic college, and then she was asked to plead guilty or not guilty. Margaret Clitherow threw back her head and stood erect, a woman of striking beauty.

"I know of no offence," she said, "of which I should confess myself guilty."

Again and again they tried to persuade her to have a trial by jury, but she refused. She knew that the only witnesses against her would be her servants and her own children, and she wished to save them from having any part in her condemnation.

Long did the officials harass her, insulting her religion, and then, seeing that their urging was of no avail, they ordered her to a private jail, there to await sentence. It was night as she was conducted to the jail, but the streets were still crowded as she passed along, her face beaming with joy while she scattered money to the poor, now as always the angel of charity.

The next day she was brought again before the Council. Again they pleaded with her to stand trial. Again she refused, and the judge, seeing that it was a waste of time to seek to break her will, pronounced the terrible sentence.

"If you will not stand your trial," he said, "this must be your sentence. You must return from whence you came, and there, in the lowest part of the prison, be stripped naked, laid down, your back upon the ground, as much weight laid on you as you are able to bear, and so continue three days without water, and the third day to be pressed to death, your hands and feet tied to posts, and a sharp stone under your back."

As this terrible sentence was pronounced, she stood with head uplifted, a smile upon her lips, as she said, "I thank God heartily for this."

"Have you no consideration for your husband and children?" they asked.

"I would to God," she said, "my husband and children might suffer with me for so good a cause."

They bound her hands with ropes, and sent her back to jail, where the Protestant ministers and the minions of the law vainly tried to shake her faith. For several days this situation continued. There was dissension in the Council as to putting her to death. One of the judges in particular sought to defer action. All humanity was not dead in him, for Margaret Clitherow was with child, and he dreaded the wrath of Heaven in putting to death not only the mother, but also her unborn child. But he was not strong in character, and feared the wrath of the crown if he let pity persuade him against this awful crime; and so he tried to assuage his conscience by letting the other judges settle the question. And settle it they did. Margaret Clitherow was to die.

Meanwhile the condemned woman was preparing for death. Tranquil and cheerful she was, as if in her own home instead of the jail. All her time was spent in prayer, fearing that God might deny her the crown of martyrdom which was so near. She managed to get word to Father Mush, begging him to pray for her martyrdom, and telling him that the heaviest cross she had to bear was the fear that she would be set free. In those last days she longed to see her husband before she died, but they refused her this consolation unless she would consent to hear a sermon from one of the Protestant ministers, a condition to which she would not listen. Her husband meanwhile had been let out of prison, but he was warned to keep out of the city for some days. When he heard that his wife was condemned to death, he raved as one mad.

"Alas! alas!" he cried, "they will kill my poor wife! She has been the best wife and the best Catholic in the whole country. The Council may have all my goods if they will but spare her."

When one of her neighbors told her this, she said: "May God enlighten him to see the true faith, that so at least his soul be saved." She sent to him her hat as a sign of her duty and obedience to him. At the same time she sent her shoes and stockings to her daughter Anne, saying, "Tell her they are to remind her to serve God and to practise all virtues. I trust to God that she will leave this wicked world, so full of snares for one so young and fair, and consecrate herself to her Divine Spouse in some fervent community abroad." Ten years later Anne joined the

English Augustinians at Louvain. Her mother's prayers were heard.

At last the day of her martyrdom dawned. It was Good Friday, and also Lady Day, March 25, 1586. Through the crowds, congregated to see the strange sight of a woman led to slaughter, surrounded by the officers of the law and by her executioners, she was led from the private jail where she had been guarded to the tolbooth, or prison, where she was to lay down her life. Four women attendants unrobed her, and then put on her a linen garment which she herself had made. She lay down upon the ground, and a sharp stone was placed under her back. She was calm and peaceful, her soul rapt in prayer, so that the very light of Heaven shone from her face. So beautiful was her countenance that the sheriff ordered a handkerchief to be spread over it, fearing the effect her glorified look would have upon the spectators, many of whom were Catholics. A heavy door was then placed upon her, her hands were bound to two posts on either side, and then every one of the four executioners, at the command of the sheriff, raised a heavy weight and let it fall forcibly on the door. It was the work of barbarians, of devils. Her bones were broken, but she made no outcry of pain.

"Jesu! Jesu!" she pleaded. "Help me, blessed Jesu! I suffer this for Thy sake."

She still lived. The sheriff ordered more weights to be thrown upon her. The bones burst through the skin. She still lived. "Jesu, Jesu, Jesu, have mercy on me!"

Those were her last words, the words of one of the sweetest and gentlest of women, done to death with unbelievable brutality because she would not be false to her conscience.

We are told that her body remained in the press till three o'clock in the afternoon. Then the poor blood-covered mass was taken out and rolled up roughly in a sheet. At midnight the executioners buried the body secretly, lest the Catholics might claim her bones as relics. And they buried it beneath a dung-heap. Some weeks later the Catholics discovered where the body had been buried, and in the dead of night rescued it from its ignominious grave and brought it, still incorrupt, to some point far distant. There, in a grave now unknown, they reverently buried this noble woman, Margaret Clitherow, the Pearl of York.

There are other stories of the heroism of womanhood that could be told of these days. Margaret Clitherow was not the last to suffer. How inspiring is the story of Margaret Ward! She was companion to a Catholic lady of London, and having heard that a certain missionary priest, Father William Watson, was in jail and in danger of perversion, she determined to come to his help. Taking a basket of provisions, she bribed the jailer's wife, and so was able to succor the poor priest.

She finally arranged to help him escape, and got the aid of a young Irishman, John Roche, to further her plans. The priest escaped, but Roche and Margaret Ward were arrested. Roche was executed at Tyburn. Margaret was thrown into prison, where she was flogged and hung up by her wrists, the tips of her toes only touching the ground, for so long a time that she was crippled and paralyzed. Liberty was offered her if she would ask the Queen's pardon and promise to go to the Protestant church. She declared that she had committed no offence against the Queen. "With regard to my going to church," she said, "I have been convinced for many years that it is not lawful to do so, and I would lay down many lives, if I had them, rather than act against my conscience or do anything against God and His holy religion." And so she was put to death.

Another woman who was very like Margaret Clitherow was Mrs. Anne Line. She was the widow of a staunch Catholic who had given up a big estate rather than sacrifice his faith and had lived abroad until his death. Then she had returned to England, and had been chosen to manage a house in which priests might find a refuge during the days of persecution. She was physically weak. "Though I desire above all things to die for Christ," she said to Father Gerard, "I dare not hope to die by the hand of the executioner; but perhaps the Lord will let me be taken in the same house as a priest, and then be thrown into a chill and filthy dungeon, where I shall not be able to last out long."

She was at last arrested for harboring priests and asked to plead guilty or not to the charge.

"My lords," she exclaimed, "nothing grieves me but that I could not receive a thousand more!"

She was so weak that she had to be carried to court in a chair. She was condemned. On the day of her execution, kissing the block with joy, she knelt to pray, and kept on praying till her head was struck off. This was in February, 1601, fifteen years after the death of Margaret Clitherow.

What noble women were they all! But none is quite so appealing as Margaret Clitherow. What a glorious example is she to the wife and mother! Her heart was filled with love for her husband and her children. Yet willingly she parted even from these dear ones, willingly let her home be broken up, willingly let her little flock be scattered, for the glory of God. When God showed her the way of the Cross and commanded her to take it, she did not plead that she was a wife and mother, that her duty was to stay with them, her loved ones that so needed her. No. It was enough that God called. He had a greater claim even than her little ones. She would seek first the Kingdom of God and His justice, knowing that a greater love than hers would come to care for her children when she was gone, even the love of Him who so loved the little ones.

Blessed the children that have a mother who loves God even more than she loves them!

THE VENERABLE ANNA MARIA TAIGI

(1769–1837)

G OD calls us all to sanctity. It is our blessed
privilege that we all are the children of God,
sharers in His abundant graces, and that no matter
what our state in life, we can aspire to be great in His
kingdom. Sometimes one is apt to think that the
present circumstances of life are not conducive to
sanctity. The mother of a family, for instance, is apt
to think that the care of her children is an excuse for
her coldness in the service of God. "How can I be
devout, let alone aspire to sanctity," she asks, "when
all my life is filled with the cares of the home? Now
if I were in a convent, I would have more time to give
to God, and I am sure that in such an atmosphere of
sanctity my soul would grow in holiness." Always
the same old excuse—if I were somebody else, I would
be better than I am now.

But that is only a way to deaden the conscience.
A woman—even while we know that the virgin life in
itself is a higher life—may be married, may be the
mother of many children, may be obliged to lead a
life that is full of the trivialities incident to the bringing up of those children, may find her days but "the

trivial round, the common task" of baking and clean-
ing and mending, may have to struggle against poverty,
and yet may so use that life that it becomes doubly
dear in the sight of God. There have been great saints
who have been great mothers, toiling mothers, ordinary
mothers in the eyes of the world. From every walk
of life they come, these saints of God, so that we all,
no matter what our station in life, may take courage
in doing His work. After all, the Queen of all saints
was a mother,—Mary, the Mother of God. Hers was
a humble life, a humdrum life if you will, a life of
simple duty,—the handmaid of the Lord. And while
there is a vast difference between the life of the Mother
of God and the life of the mothers of men, still may
the mothers of men look to her to learn from her
motherhood the way to sanctify their own.

And so that we may not be discouraged by the
sight of her great glory, God has raised up lesser
glories of motherhood in order that mothers may emu-
late them, knowing that what has been possible to the
saintly mothers raised to the altars of God is still possible to the most lowly mother of to-day.

The story of Anna Maria Taigi is a glorious one for
this reason—it is a glorification of the simple life, the
life of a poor woman, the mother of seven children,
with all the cares which that implies, yet of one who,
while neglecting none of her duties to her family,
realized that even more than to them her first duty
was to God and her own soul.

The whole of this woman's life is well summed up

in the Decree of the Sacred Congregation of Rites regarding her beatification and canonization. It may be taken as a sketch which we shall try to fill in later. It reads: "He who, when He would show forth His power and wisdom, hath been wont for the most part to use the weak and foolish things of the world to confound the haughtiness of man, to frustrate the designs of the impious, and bring to naught the efforts of hell, hath in this our age, when human pride and infernal power have seemed to combine to subvert, if it were possible, the foundations, not only of the Church, but even of civil society itself, opposed a poor, weak woman to the floods of impiety bursting in on every side. He hath employed for this work Anna Maria Antonia Gesualda Taigi, born, indeed, of honest parentage, but poor, married to a common man, hampered with the cares of a family, and fain to seek wherewith to support herself and them by the constant labor of her hands. This woman, whom He hath chosen for Himself to be an attracter of souls, a victim of expiation, a bulwark against plots, a warder-off of evils by her prayers, He hath first cleansed from the dust of this world and then hath united to Himself by the strictest bond of charity, hath adorned with wonderful gifts, and hath replenished with such virtues as to draw to her on all sides, not pious persons only, from every rank of society up to the very highest, but even the impious themselves, and to inspire all with the highest opinion of her sanctity."

It is remarkable that the cause of this poor woman,

who died in 1837, was introduced in 1862, only twenty-five years afterwards, at a time when her husband and some of her children were still living, a proof at least of the reputation for sanctity she enjoyed among her neighbors.

Her maiden name was Giannetti. She was the only child of Luigi Giannetti, who was by profession an apothecary in the city of Siena. He and his wife, Santa Maria Masi, were people in good circumstances, highly respected by their friends, Giannetti being especially noted for his absolute honesty and trustworthiness in his business.

The child was born May 29, 1769, and was baptized the next day, receiving the name of Anna Maria Antonia Gesualda. The little girl was barely six years of age when misfortune came upon her parents. They lost all they had of this world's goods, and rather than face poverty among those who knew them in their days of prosperity, they left Siena and came to Rome, where, too, the apothecary knew there would be a better chance for him to get employment. So poor were they that they had to make the journey on foot, and yet we can well believe that the hand of God was directing them in what they considered a severe trial.

Giannetti and his wife soon found employment as domestic servants, and took a small lodging in humble quarters. Their hearts were centered in their little daughter, who was a pretty child of attractive manners. They gave her an excellent education, as far as they could, sending her to the nuns to school, with whom she soon proved to be a great favorite. But better than all else, the good nuns as well as the parents laid in the child's heart the deep foundations of solid piety. The parents, before going to work, took her with them to Mass every morning, while at home they faithfully trained her childish lips to pray and to repeat often the names of Jesus and Mary.

Those years of childhood were uneventful. She was simply a poor child of poor parents. She would have to make her living in the world; and so, when she was thirteen, she was taken from the good nuns who had taught her so many things to be of service to her in later life, and put to live with two old women, along with other girls, where her work was to wind silk in preparation for manufacture. She made a few cents a week at this work, which she gave to her parents. For six years she was thus employed, and then she got tired of it and wanted to come back home to help her mother. She was now a young woman, grown tired —and no wonder!—of the humdrum life of silk-weaving. She wanted, too, to see something of the world. She loved dress, and later reproached herself that during these days she was vain of her personal appearance. Still, withal, she remained a good, virtuous girl, an ordinary, good Catholic girl, faithful to her religious duties, but with no remarkable piety. Her parents succeeded in placing her as lady's-maid in the house where they were still employed as domestics. She was under their protecting eyes, and yet an attractive, refined girl like Anna was not free from danger.

She realized this, knew the temptations, and as a result was more earnest in her prayers, more ready to seek the advice of her confessor, who counseled her to marry.

She was about twenty-one when she was married to Domenico Taigi. He was descended from a good, even an illustrious Milanese family, but was a poor man, a domestic servant. He was, however, a good man, religious and of excellent character. But he was uneducated, even a rustic boor, far inferior to his young wife in point of breeding, and so in many cases a trial to her.

He asked for her hand. They both prayed to ascertain the will of God, and finally, after a month, they were united in a marriage which, with all its trials, proved particularly happy. She was loving, faithful, industrious, and studied all his wishes. He was proud of his beautiful young wife, and liked to show her to his friends. She was gay and happy, attractive and vain of her beauty and her dress. But all the while she was displeased at her own worldliness, for she felt in her heart that God was seeking to draw her to a more devout life.

One day, when she was praying in St. Peter's, the grace of God touched her. She realized her vanity and frivolity, her passion for amusement, and determined to put it all aside. She had not committed any serious sin, but she felt that such a frivolous life was wrong. From the day she made her confession to the Servite priest, Father Angelo, to whom God had led her almost miraculously, this young wife of twenty-two entered upon the road to perfection, from the pursuit of which she was never to swerve during the long years of her married life. She put aside the life of pride and pleasure for the life of mortification. When she returned home from confession, she threw herself before the crucifix and scourged herself, and struck her head against the floor many times, exclaiming, "Satisfy to God, impure head, for so many frivolous ornaments with which you have dared to adorn yourself." God rewarded this self-abasement with many graces, and in particular with the gift of a luminous disc in which, as in a mirror, she saw the past, present, and future, a gift which she enjoyed for the remaining forty-seven years of her life. Shortly afterwards she was given the power of healing with the touch of her hand, could read the secret thoughts of others, was granted the privilege of ecstasies, and all this at the very beginning of her conversion to a more earnest life. God thus rewarded early her love for Him.

At once she put aside all her ornaments of vanity, her rings, her ear-rings, necklaces, and fine clothes, and dressed herself in the commonest and coarsest of garments. She joined the Third Order of the Trinitarians, and wore the habit under her other clothes. She put aside all her worldly amusements and even denied herself the simple pleasure of visits to her friends. There was no half way about her giving herself to God. She punished herself, used the discipline, wore a hair shirt, and even an iron chain. She fasted rigorously, sometimes for a period of forty days, and went for days without a drink of water, a terrible penance in a hot climate, and especially for one who worked as hard as she. As she used to say, "The more greedy the ass is, the more needful is it to draw the rein tight." She mortified her sight, too, and was as modest as a young girl. Not only did she not criticize anybody, but she would allow no one to make in her presence depreciating remarks about others.

"My mother," said one of her daughters, "scarcely slept at all. She spent most of the night in prayer, and was up early in the morning to go to Mass, after having slept but two hours." In a word, she lived in God and for God. "To acquire the love of God," she used to say, "we must always be rowing against the current, and never cease counteracting our own will."

If this woman had not been married, no doubt she would have entered the religious life. It is useless, however, to speculate on that, for it was the will of God that she should be a wife and mother, no doubt, in order that she might show that it is possible to lead a holy life even in the lowliest surroundings. And this poor woman became, says one of her biographers, "the rampart of the Holy See, the oblation of sinners, the consolation of the afflicted, the succorer of the poor, the guider of the learned, and the counselor of priests; she was a theologian, a doctor, a mother in Israel, a seer of the ancient days, an inspired prophet, a true wonder-worker." What a panegyric for a poor, hard-working mother of seven children! Yet it was because she was a devoted wife and mother, faithful to the duties of her home, that God raised her to such heights.

Her religious ardor was never an excuse for neglect of duty. Not even her husband or her children knew to what heights of sanctity she had reached. It was only after her death that her instruments of self-mortification were discovered. Her penances, like her trials, she hid in her own heart.

And she had her trials. She was refined and sensitive; her husband was rough, coarse, and uncouth. He was self-willed, easily angered, and would fly into a rage if contradicted. She never argued with him or contradicted him. She was always patient, silent when he was angry, and in such a way that he soon became ashamed of himself, fearing that he had distressed her.

Domenico Taigi, with all his faults, had a good heart. His wife always sought to please him, would even set aside her devotions in order to accompany him or to do some service for him. As he said, long after she had died, at the time of the opening of the process of her beatification—he was then ninety-two— "I always found her as docile and submissive as a lamb." It was a touching tribute to a loving wife, words that could be taken to heart by many wives of to-day, when we are hearing so much about women's rights and so little about their duties.

And this docility and simplicity on her part are all

the more remarkable when one knows that the humble home was always crowded with persons of distinction, ecclesiastical and lay, come to seek her advice; for by her great sanctity, her charity to the sick and poor, her ecstasies in the churches, and her ability to give the soundest advice, she was renowned all over Rome.

And yet, in spite of that popularity, her first thought was for her husband. "It happened to me frequently," he said, "when coming home to change my clothes, that I found the house full. Immediately she would leave everybody, whatever lord or prelate might be there, and hasten to me with the greatest cheerfulness and pleasure, that she might brush my things and wait upon me, even to the tying of my shoe-strings. In short, she was my consolation, and that of all the world."

In her he had the greatest confidence. "I let her manage everything," he said, "because I saw that she acquitted herself perfectly of the task." Yet she would never do anything unusual without first of all consulting him. What a simple tribute are the words of the old man of ninety-two, looking back over the past happy years. "She was always cheerful and pleasant," he said; "yet she had a host of maladies. This, however, did not hinder her from putting her hand to work; she looked to everything and had hands of gold. As for me, I did not give a thought to anything. She made pantaloons for me, and overcoats. I do not well know how to express myself. To cut the matter short, I am old; but if I were young, and were minded to travel over the whole earth to find such a woman, it would be impossible to meet with her. I have lost a great treasure."

She was the mother of seven children, four boys and three girls. Camillo, the eldest, died at the age of forty-two; Alessandro at thirty-five; Luigi at a year and a half; and Pietro at two years. Two of the daughters were living at the time of the process of her beatification, one unmarried, the other a widow.

It can be easily believed that this mother, holy as she was, took a deep interest in her children. She nursed all of them, taught them their catechism, and instructed them how to read and write. Morning and night, the whole family had prayers together, and always she taught the children to thank God that they had been born in the Catholic Church. She prepared them for Confession and Communion, and saw that the girls frequented the sacraments once a week, and the boys two or three times a month.

She arranged that all the boys should learn a trade according to their station in life. She had no foolish ideas about their becoming wealthy. The girls she sent to school. Over them all she exercised a watchful care. She guarded their modesty even in their own home, and kept them from bad companionship. In a word, she was a hard-working, prudent, common-sense mother, devoted to her children. "I will save your children," Our Lord said to her one day, "because they are of your blood, because they are poor, and the poor are my friends. Yes, I will save them, although they have many faults."

She did not hesitate to punish the children when they needed correction. She always insisted that they give their father strict obedience. She would allow no one to criticize others in the presence of the children. In fact, she would not listen to remarks about others, anyway, and especially about priests. "They are God's ministers," she would say, "and therefore always worthy of our respect; at the hour of death whom shall we need save the priest?" And this reverence for priests she instilled into the hearts of her children.

It was a happy household, a home simple in its furnishings,—poor, even,—but rich in its simple, unaffected piety. As soon as she awoke the children in the morning, they all would kneel about the little altar and say their morning prayers, together with her old mother, who lived with them. And after supper all would gather and listen to the reading of some pious book, and then before retiring there would be family prayers, the recitation of the Rosary, and other devotions. In her family God was the first consideration. And yet it was not a gloomy household. There was nothing unhappy about her. She was always pleasant, always could enjoy a good joke, and always sought to provide simple amusement for the children, taking them on picnics and otherwise seeking to make them light-hearted.

We get a good picture of her as manager of the

home. Her husband received small wages, scarcely
two dollars a month, so one can imagine how she had
to plan in order to bring up her large family. She
always stood and served the others while they sat at
meals. Difficulties came upon the family when the
husband lost his position through the removal to Paris
of the family he worked for, at the time the French
army in 1798 occupied Rome. It was discouraging
to Domenico, but the wife urged him to put his trust
in God; and then, to help out in the care of the family's
support, she learned to make women's shoes and stays
and worked at the new trade night and day. So successful was she that soon she was able not only to
support her own family, but also to feed a great number of poor people.

It was at this time that she met the Princess Maria
Luisa, afterwards Queen of Etruria, who came to her
assistance in helping the poor. It was the time of
the terrible famine in Rome, and Mrs. Taigi, delicate
of health, through the long cold days would stand in
the bread-line before the baker's so that her children
should not go hungry. Yet she was always calm and
patient. She was never idle, and even when confined
to the bed with torturing illness would do the family
mending.

Besides the care of the children, she also had the
care of her father and mother, who in their old days
had been obliged to give up their work. The mother
was hard to get along with, a woman with a bad
temper, but her daughter was ever kind to her and

tended her devotedly to the end. So, too, with her father. In the last years of his life he was afflicted with a horrible leprosy, but she would wash and comb him and attend to all his wants. Added to that, her son Camillo brought his wife to live with them, a woman who was a trial, since she wanted to be the mistress of the house, always looking for trouble. And then, when her daughter Sofia lost her husband, she came with her six children to live with her parents. It was a patriarchal way of living, but it brought its trials. Yet the good mother who was the head of the house never complained, but tried to make everybody feel at home.

To bear such trials and petty hardships she needed a lively faith. And surely she had that. She ever thanked God for the gift of faith, and had the utmost reverence for everybody and everything connected with religion. She had a special devotion to the Blessed Trinity, and soon after her conversion, as we have seen, became a member of the Third Order of Discalced Trinitarians, founded in 1198 for the redemption of captives, which may be called a religious order for those who live in the world.

And with it all there was that same confidence in God which knows that He will help those who help themselves and pray. "She did not," says her husband, "wait for the basket to come down from heaven without doing anything herself. She joined labor to prayer in order not to tempt God by seeming to expect that He would work a miracle for her. When she found herself in a position of real necessity, she addressed herself to God with all the greater confidence, and the Lord helped her so well that the maintenance of her numerous family without their ever suffering want was a continual miracle." And then he asks very simply, "What could I do with my salary, if I had not the servant of God?"

It was all her simple trust in the providence of God. They were always on the verge of poverty, but always managed to get along. The wealthy who came to the house to consult with her wished to make presents to her, but she would have none of that. God was the only help she wanted. Even when her daughter Sofia brought home her six children to increase the family burden, and began to weep and to wonder how they would all be fed, she was reproached by her mother. "What are you thinking about?" she asked. "You must know that God never abandons any one. You will have what you need. Place your trust in God, and give no thought to anything else; as for me, I will never forsake you."

One day, when she called to see the Princess Luisa, the latter opened a drawer full of gold, and said to her: "Take, take, Nanna *mia,* what you will." But the poor woman merely smiled and answered: "How simple you are, madam! I serve a Master richer than you. I trust and hope in Him; and He provides for my daily necessities." It was not pride that made her refuse help from others; it was just her simple trust in God and her desire to remain always poor.

Later on, when she was unable to work, the family was in great poverty, and, painful as the humiliation was, the poor woman had to accept alms. She was poor in everything but the grace of God. And how rich she was in that! She lived in the presence of God, and endeavored to please Him in all things. This love of God made her endure physical and mental suffering, calumnies, contempt, harshness, not merely with resignation, but with joy. Her life was one long martyrdom gladly borne. Hers was a soul that God loved exceedingly, and He showered His choicest blessings upon it. Sometimes, when she was busy sweeping the floor or cooking, she would go into an ecstasy. At times even the note of a bird would transport her, so tenderly did she love God. Yet some of her neighbors, seeing these things, used to say that she was possessed, or that she was a hypocrite. Even her husband used to think, when these ecstasies came upon her, that she had a fit of convulsions, and would try to shake her out of them. So little even he suspected the wonders God was working in the soul of this humble wife of his.

And through it all was her intense hatred of sin. She told her confessor that rather than commit a venial fault, she would mount a scaffold and endure all its shame, together with the infliction of every conceivable torture. As her love for God, so her love for her neighbor. Even out of her poverty she helped the poor, spending some of her time at night working for them, taking into her house the chance wanderer to feed and clothe, always seeing in the poor Jesus Christ Himself. "Never send the poor away," she would say to her family; "when you have nothing else, give them a bit of bread." When sent for by the sick, she always went, no matter what the weather. And she was always being sent for. She had a special gift for consoling the afflicted, and if she found poverty she would herself go begging alms for the destitute ones, and even take the bread out of her own mouth to succor them.

Hers was a charity that extended even to the dumb animals. "These poor beasts have no paradise save in this world," she would say, and would even use the power she had to cure them. It is said that she would leave her own dinner to feed a hungry cat. She saw all animals as creatures of God. In her was renewed that love for animals so characteristic of St. Francis.

If there was one virtue for which she was especially noted, it was her patience. Sometimes her neighbors insulted her, so much so that the angered Domenico had to defend her. But the more she was insulted, the more she rejoiced. For years she endured bodily ills, constant sick-headaches, neuralgia, rheumatism, asthma, gout—in fact, all the ills to which the flesh is heir. But never a murmur from her. Despite her sufferings, she kept at her devotions. She had a special devotion to the Infancy and Passion of Our Lord and to the Blessed Sacrament. And she had a tender devotion to the Blessed Virgin and the poor souls in Purgatory.

Many a sinner she converted, offering up herself in expiation, and God accepted the sacrifice, sending her all manner of trials, and permitting her to be sorely beset with temptations of every kind.

It was a time of trial for the Church, a time of persecution, and she was a victim of penance for the sins of the world and for the evils affecting the Church.

But with her sufferings God gave her great privileges. There is no doubt, in reading her life, that she had the gift of prophecy, and also worked miracles of healing. "Anna Maria the Saint," was what the people called her, and high and low came to her, begging her advice and her prayers.

For eight months before her death she was confined to her bed of pain—of torture, rather—for every member suffered as if on a rack. And with what patience!

She did not fear death. She even announced her approaching end to her family with great cheerfulness. Then she called Domenico, her husband, and thanked him with tenderness for all the care he had taken of her, and all his kindness to her. Then she called her children and gave each of them advice. "My children," she said, "have Jesus Christ always before you; let His Precious Blood be ever the object of your veneration. You will have to suffer much, but sooner or later the Lord will console you. Keep His com-

mandments, cherish devotion to the most Holy Virgin,
who will be your mother in my place."

She left them nothing; rather, she left them poverty.
But she did not bemoan that. She knew that God
would take care of them.

And so, in poverty and alone, the good wife and
mother died in 1837, at the age of sixty-eight. On
that occasion the following letter was written by her
confessor, Father Filippo, to the Pope's vicar, Cardinal Odescalchi: "It is very just and proper season-
ably to reveal the works of God, for His greater glory
and for the edification of the faithful. Yesterday,
Friday, the ninth of the current month (June), passed
to eternal rest the soul of Anna Maria Taigi, who lived
in the parish of Santa Maria in Via Lata. I know
that the secretary of his Eminence Cardinal Barberini,
D. Raffaele Natali, who has lived with her nearly
twenty years, has addressed, in conjunction with other
persons, a petition to your Eminence, to the intent that
regard should be had to the body of this holy woman,
which merits all respect. As for me, who have been
her confessor for more than thirty years, until the day
before yesterday, when she received the last sacraments, I believe myself to be bound in conscience to
make known to your Eminence that not only did she
exercise the Christian virtues in an heroic degree, but
that God favored her also with special graces and
extraordinary gifts, which will excite admiration,
should it please God to publish them authentically before the whole Church, as I hope. I should have

much to say on this head. I content myself with testifying to the charity of this holy soul, which constituted itself as a victim before God, and which obtained signal graces for Rome. I hope that God will cause this to be recognized later. The mortal remains, therefore, of so virtuous a soul, and one so highly esteemed by Pius VII and Leo XII, by Monsignore Strambi, Monsignore Menacchio, and a crowd of persons of every rank and every country who obtained extraordinary graces through her intervention, seem to merit special regard, in accordance with the constant practice of the Church."

The same priest said: "Well, a woman replenished with so many merits, virtues, and supernatural gifts lives unknown and dies abandoned by every one; having round her bed of suffering only a poor family whom she leaves in destitution, and recommends to a priest, equally poor, who is to continue collecting daily alms for them. She blesses her children, and leaves them, as her sole bequest, piety, religion, devotion to the Virgin, to the saints, and particularly to St. Philomena, her patroness, whom she constituted the guardian and protectress of her poor and numerous family. After which, recollected in God and animated by the fortitude which resignation imparts, she drinks to the very last drop the bitter chalice of a painful death."

When this poor woman died there was universal sorrow throughout the city as soon as the sad news was learned. "The saint is dead," was heard on all sides. High and low visited the house where she had died, and many, in spite of the fear of cholera then prevalent, went to pray at her tomb. Her work went on even after her death. The sick were healed through her intercession, sinners converted, and many other graces granted. So general was the opinion of her sanctity, that the Cardinal Vicar commissioned Raffaele Natali to collect all the documents relative to her life. When her biography was written shortly afterwards, seventeen thousand copies of it were sold in Rome alone. It was translated into many languages and spread over all the world.

For eighteen years the body lay in the common cemetery, and then there arose a desire to remove it into Rome. It was found incorrupt, and the clothes in perfect preservation. It was then placed in the Church of Santa Maria della Pace. Ten years later, on the occasion of the removal of the body to its last resting-place in the Church of the Trinitarians, it was still incorrupt. Her tomb was ever after a shrine at which the faithful prayed. The process of her beatification was begun in 1863, and it has not yet been finished.

So passed a poor, simple woman; so passed a great servant of God. What an example, we say, to all, but especially to the mothers of whom she may well be patroness! What mother ever had a harder life, one of continual toil, continual pain? Yet she was always rapt in God. Faithful to her husband, faithful to her children, and, above all, faithful to God, surely the venerable Anna Maria Taigi understands the difficulties of mothers, and will help those that pray to her.

ELIZABETH SETON

(1774–1821)

THE Catholic Church is comparatively young in this country. Her history here is but as the story of a day in her long life. But it is a story to thrill the heart of her children. We have had our martyrs for the truth, many of them; we have had our confessors of the faith, confessors without number. The same spirit of religion which has made saints of God in the Old World has made them in the New. From every quarter of the globe our people have come, and in every quarter of the globe has flourished that faith that makes saints. The old countries have their national litany of saints. It is the growth of the ages. But are we to be less blessed than they? Are we to have no special litany of our own? We cannot think that. The ages of faith are not to be confined to one people or one period. The Litany of the Saints is not a sealed book of the dead past. It is a never-ending scroll to be written on until the day of judgment. "A great multitude, which no man could number, of all nations, and tribes, and peoples, and tongues, standing before the throne, and in sight of the Lamb, clothed with white robes, and palms in their hands." (Apocalypse vii, 9.)

We have scarcely begun to make our own national litany. The Church, which knows herself to be of and for all time, is never in a hurry. She thinks in centuries, rather in eternity, not in days. Sometimes she has canonized her saints almost before the body was cold in death; sometimes she has waited for centuries to pass before raising them to her altars. In God's own good time it is all done. It is not for us to anticipate the judgment of the Church. The making of a saint is a wonderful thing. No human power, no admiration even for service done to the Church, can place man or woman on that Church's calendar. Even the great Constantine, who was so blessed with heavenly vision and heavenly aid, to whom the Church owed so much, is still but Constantine the Great, not St. Constantine.

But we may hope—we have, indeed, every reason to hope, judging from the past—that America, too, will have its saints. And surely we may hope and pray that one day we may, after Holy Church, give the glorious name of saint to that noble woman of our own land, wife and mother and religious, Elizabeth Bayley Seton.

Her maiden name was Elizabeth Bayley, and she was born in New York City on August 28, 1774, at a time when New York was still an English colony, a short time, as the date shows, before the outbreak of the Revolutionary War.

Her grandfather had come as a young man of good English family to make a tour of the American colonies some years before, at a time when the colonies were deeply attached to the mother country. He met his fate on that tour in the person of a young lady of New Rochelle named Lecomte, descended from one of the Huguenot families which had settled that place.

One of his sons was Richard Bayley, who became a doctor, and was later the first professor of anatomy at Columbia (then King's) College. After the war, during which he had been a staunch royalist, he was appointed health officer of the port of New York, and filled that office in an admirable manner. It was a tribute to his character that in spite of his former political affiliations he was deemed worthy of the appointment. In 1781, when Sir Guy Carleton succeeded Clinton as commander-in-chief of the British forces in America, he had joined his army as surgeon. And so close was his friendship with Carleton that he called one of his sons Guy Carleton Bayley, who became the father of James Roosevelt Bayley, who at Rome in 1842 became a convert from the Episcopal Church, and was later noted as Archbishop of Baltimore.

Young Dr. Bayley married Catharine Charlton, daughter of an Episcopalian clergyman of Staten Island. Three daughters were born to them, Mary, Elizabeth Ann, and Catharine, and then in 1777 the young wife died. Dr. Bayley was devoted to his little ones, and for that reason, perhaps, more than any other, he married again, taking for his second wife a Miss Barclay of a well-known New York family. She was a good mother to the two stepchildren—little

Catharine had died at the age of two—and Elizabeth especially loved her.

We get a charming picture of the little Elizabeth when she was nine years old, after the dread days of the war had passed. She tells us herself of the visits she used to make to her mother's people in the country. "I delighted to sit alone by the waterside," she writes, "or to wander for hours on the shore, singing and gathering shells. Every little leaf and flower, or insect, animal, shades of clouds, or waving trees, were objects of vacant, unconnected thoughts of God and heaven."

Even in those young days the grace of God was working in the soul of her who later on was to do such great work in His kingdom. She was her father's favorite, and much of her strong character was due to his loving interest in her, and withal his firmness in the manner of educating her. Even in her childhood it is said that she edified her elders by her recollection and fervor in the services of the Episcopal Church, of which her stepmother was a devout member. It was this good woman who gave Elizabeth a taste for the Bible, a book she loved and read daily, together with the *Imitation of Christ*. And even as a child, she tells us, the crucifix was especially dear to her. One is surprised at the Catholic spirit of the child, seeing her writing out every night her examination of conscience, a practice she kept up even when she was grown and had taken her place in the brilliant New York society of those days.

It was a time when little attention was paid to the education of girls, but Elizabeth managed to get more than her share by browsing in her father's excellent library, a course which had its dangers, too, considering that the Doctor's library contained many infidel books. But God kept innocent and religious the soul of this little girl who was trying so hard to do His will.

Elizabeth at an early age took her place in society. New York even then had its very exclusive circle, wealthy, brilliant, and refined. The beauty and smartness of Elizabeth Bayley made her a favorite at once. One of her biographers describes her as she looked at that time. She was small in stature, with finely cut features, slenderly and gracefully formed. Her face, lit by brilliant black eyes, inherited no doubt from her Huguenot grandmother, was framed in masses of dark, curling hair, arranged in the simple, graceful fashion of the close of the eighteenth century. Combined with this youthful loveliness was the charm imparted by intelligence of mind, perfect womanliness, and vivacity, which was no doubt also a heritage from her French ancestry.

It is not strange that this beautiful young woman of fine family, vivacious, educated, ready to take her part in everything, an accomplished horsewoman even, soon attracted the attention of men. But of all the suitors young William Seton, son of a wealthy merchant of New York, won the prize. He had spent several years abroad, had served in the business house of the Filicchis in Leghorn, Catholic gentlemen of wonderfully great faith, who were to be the cause, under God, of Elizabeth's conversion, and besides that, he had traveled extensively, and was therefore well equipped to win his way into the heart of such a girl as Elizabeth Bayley.

They were married in January, 1794, when Elizabeth was a few months over nineteen years of age. It was a happy marriage. William Seton was an excellent man. He adored his wife, and she responded with a like adoration. The young husband took his wife to live with his own family in the big New York mansion which was like a patriarchal establishment. Elizabeth was at once a favorite with all, from her father-in-law, who made her his confidante, to her husband's many brothers and sisters. The oldest of the unmarried ones became "the friend of her soul." She was deeply spiritual like Elizabeth, and devoted to charity. Often the two were to be seen making visits to the poor, until at last they came to be lovingly called "the Protestant Sisters of Charity."

In the fall after the marriage the young couple went to live in a house of their own, and here in the following May, 1795, their first child, little Anna Maria, was born. Their cup of joy was now full.

But the happy marriage did not remain long unclouded; for in the summer of 1796 the husband's health began to fail. To this affliction was added the fear of business troubles, threatening the ruin of the house of Seton, so long prosperous. And meanwhile a second child, William, was born. The elder Seton died under the strain of financial difficulties, and William Seton and his wife took charge of the family mansion and assumed the burden of caring for the many little ones whom the elder Seton—he had been married twice—had left. It was a heavy task for them, but they did not complain. It was their duty, nothing more. Who knows what great graces were given to Elizabeth Seton for this work of mothering the orphans? It was here that, in 1798, their third child, Richard, was born.

The young mother had no easy life in those days. Not only did she have her own little ones to mother, but she had also to care for those that were not her own. So devoted was she even to those who were not her own flesh and blood that she inspired a devoted love in them. Her husband's little sisters, Harriet, then eleven, and Cecelia, seven, were particularly fond of her, the beginning of that attachment to her which ended in both of them later on becoming Catholics, following her example, and moved to it, under the grace of God, by their complete confidence that what she did was always right.

In June, 1800, the fourth child, Catharine, was born, and at the same time William Seton was financially overwhelmed by new disasters at sea. It was a time of worry for the young mother, a time of sorrow increased by the death of her own father, whom she so deeply loved. He had been a man of little religion, and the devout daughter feared for his eternal future, a fear so great that she often raised the new-born infant from the cradle and offered its life to God for the salvation of her father's soul. Before his death, she tells us, he spoke several times the Holy Name of Jesus, which he had never before done, and so passed away, a man of upright life and of wonderful charity to the afflicted, having projected and conducted for five years a Lazaretto on Staten Island. Somehow his death brought Elizabeth nearer to God, and she sought more and more to know and do God's will. In 1802 the fifth and last child was born, whom she named Rebecca, after her beloved sister-in-law and companion in charity.

Meanwhile William Seton, worn out by business troubles, decided to take a trip to Italy for his health, and Elizabeth, knowing that he was not fit to go alone, prepared to go with him. And so, in October, 1800, after dismantling their home, they took passage for Leghorn, facing a long, hazardous voyage in a sailing-vessel of the period, and bringing with them their eldest child, little Anna, then eight years of age.

Yellow fever had been prevalent in New York, and when the vessel arrived at Leghorn the Setons, who were the only passengers, were obliged to go into quarantine in the Lazaretto for forty days. It was a time of severe trial for the young wife, in a foreign country, virtually in prison, and seeing her husband very ill as a result of the voyage and the confinement in the cold, cheerless Lazaretto.

When the quarantine was over they were removed to an apartment which their friend, Antonio Filicchi, had obtained for them; but the poor invalid did not rally, and two days after Christmas, praying to God to look after his dear wife and little ones, and calling, "My Christ Jesus, have mercy on me and receive me," he died, a stranger in a strange land. Elizabeth herself had to perform the last offices of love to the dear dead body, so afraid were the people of the tuberculosis of which he had died. Then they proceeded to Leghorn, where, in the Protestant cemetery, William Seton was laid to rest far from his native land.

The young widow then went to live with the Filicchis. It was the beginning of her grace. The Filicchis, of an excellent Catholic family, were wealthy merchants who were forever performing works of charity. One of the brothers, Filippo, had married a Miss Cooper of Boston, and as representative of the chief banking-house of Leghorn had been to America to discuss commercial questions for the new government after the Revolution, and was well known to Washington and to all the other noted men of the time. Washington had appointed him consul-general for the United States at Leghorn.

It was then, while living with this fine Catholic family, that Elizabeth Seton got her first insight into the faith and practice of the Catholic Church. She accompanied the Filicchis to Florence, and was thrilled by the beautiful churches, the magnificent ceremonies of worship, and the simple devotion of the people. Yet during that month in the Filicchi household, piously Catholic as it was, she had no doubts about her own faith. Zealous for the truth, her hosts sought to convert her, giving her good books to read, and even having her meet the pious Father Plunkett, a Jesuit, then in Leghorn. But it all seemed in vain. "Keep on praying," was the advice of the good Antonio Filicchi to her.

But Elizabeth, with her little daughter Anna, set sail for home, and apparently nothing had been done towards bringing her any nearer to the Catholic Church. But the grace of God intervened in a simple manner. Scarcely had the vessel set sail than it collided with another and was obliged to put back for repairs. Little Anna was suddenly stricken with scarlet fever, and when she recovered Elizabeth herself fell ill with the same sickness. It was but another grace to her soul, as she felt the wonderful charity of the good Catholic family in which God had placed her in order that she might witness their unstinted devotion to their faith. Even at that time, writing to her sister-in-law about the Catholic privilege of assisting at daily Mass, she said, "Why, they must be as happy as angels, almost."

At length the travelers sailed for home, Antonio Filicchi accompanying them to protect them and also to continue the work of conversion he had begun. It was a long voyage, lasting fifty-six days, and many an hour of it was employed by Antonio in explaining Catholic doctrine and practice to the young widow, the salvation of whose soul he so desired.

Scarcely was Elizabeth back home when a new sor-

row came to her in the death of her sister-in-law, the
devout Rebecca. In the midst of that grief, Elizabeth
made up her mind to enter the Catholic Church at once.
But Antonio advised her first of all to tell her family
of her intention. It was hardly good advice. It raised
a storm of indignation. It was a time when everything
Catholic was despised, and the Setons and the Bayleys,
high in New York society, deemed the contemplated
action of Elizabeth an insult to their position in society. This opposition, however, had no effect upon
her. The greatest obstacle, the thing that delayed
her embracing the faith immediately, was her consideration for the Rev. Mr. Hobart, the minister of
Trinity Church, who had ever been kind to her, and
for whom she had a great reverence. If a good man
like him was satisfied that he had the true faith, why
should she worry about her position? she asked herself. So she wrote to him of the sufferings of her
soul, drawn as it was to the despised Catholic Church,
yet held also to the faith of her childhood.

He pleaded with her to put the design out of her
mind, and finally she agreed to read the books he
would give her, hoping to satisfy her that her duty
was to remain in the Episcopal faith. It was for her
a time of groping in darkness, a time of wavering,
moved as she was by the dread of breaking the family
ties always so dear to her. She did not know what to
do. Mixed with this spiritual unrest was the worry
about the support of her little ones. There was
nothing left of her husband's business. She and her

children would have to depend on the charity of her own and her husband's family. These were willing to care for them, but only on condition that Elizabeth would not disgrace them by joining the Catholic Church. If she took that step, she and her children must take the consequences of her folly.

She was now living in a little cottage a mile outside the city. Mr. Hobart still corresponded with her and satisfied her conscience that she should remain an Episcopalian. Meanwhile her good friend, Antonio Filicchi, who had been visiting other cities, returned to New York. She showed him Mr. Hobart's manuscript, and Antonio persuaded her to let him show it to Father William O'Brien, then pastor of St. Peter's Church on Barclay Street. She owed her conversion, under God, to the same Antonio. He kept writing to her, and got Bishop Carroll to write to her, convinced that she should become a Catholic.

Finally she stopped going to the Protestant church, but her soul was unhappy, in spiritual darkness and misery. So it continued for several months, but at last the grace of God triumphed. Despite all opposition, notwithstanding the bitterness of her relatives, and the fact that she was facing destitution not only for herself but for her five children as well, she made up her mind to enter the Catholic Church. She was baptized into the Church at St. Peter's, in Barclay Street, New York, by Father O'Brien, on March 14, 1805, Antonio Filicchi being present; and on the Feast of the Annunciation she made her first Holy Communion. Her soul had found its peace at last.

But with the new peace came worldly troubles. How was she to support her little ones? Most of her friends had deserted her. Filicchi, ever kind, had placed a sum of money at her disposal, but she did not wish to be a subject of charity without first trying to help herself.

Everything looked promising in the establishment at this time of a school for boys by a Catholic gentleman, an Englishman named White. She was to have charge of the younger boys and in return receive education for her own children. But the bigots killed the school. It was rumored about that the object of the school was to proselytize, and this, together with the presence of the "renegade" Mrs. Seton, sealed its fate after a few months. Then she took in boy boarders from another school, and was happy at being able to earn her own living, until her persecutors destroyed this work, too. God was making her suffer for her loyalty to her conscience, and yet He was using these sufferings to bring her to the work for which He had chosen her.

What renewed this persecution was the announcement made by young Cecelia Seton, her husband's sister, that she wished also to become a Catholic. She went for instruction to Father O'Brien, and again the storm of bigotry broke forth. Elizabeth, who a short time before had nursed Cecelia through sickness, was now denounced as a corrupter, and the Seton family threatened to obtain her expulsion from the State by the Legislature as a dangerous character. Cecelia was kept in close confinement, and was even threatened with deportation to the West Indies if she did not give up the outrageous idea of becoming a Catholic. It seems almost incredible that good people could descend to such persecution. What made the persecution harder for Cecelia was that Elizabeth was not permitted to write to her.

About that time Bishop Carroll made a visit to New York. Elizabeth met him, and derived much consolation from the wise advice of the old man, besides receiving Confirmation from him. He also met Cecelia, and perhaps as a result of his priestly counsel she soon entered the Church, though in doing so she had to leave her home, where she had been persecuted, and seek an asylum with Elizabeth.

Elizabeth at this time thought of taking her loved ones to Italy, where her staunch friend Filicchi offered her a home. He again showed his practical kindness by putting another sum of money in the bank for her to draw on. But Father Cheverus, afterwards Cardinal, and Father Matignon persuaded her to remain in America. The hand of God was directing things.

The decision to remain at home in America brought hard days for the converts. The bitterness of the Seton family was simply the prejudice general at the time against the Catholic Church. On Christmas eve of that year a mob attempted to tear down St. Peter's

Church, Barclay Street, or to set it on fire. One constable was killed and others were wounded while dispersing the rioters. However, the animosity of the Setons wore away somewhat, and when one of the family was taken ill they gladly accepted the offer of Elizabeth and Cecelia to do the nursing.

After that Cecelia went to keep house for her brother, whose wife had died, but soon it was said that she was trying to pervert his children. It was the talk of New York society, and Elizabeth received all the blame. Her opponents were determined to break her; all the pupils she was boarding were taken away from her, and again she was dependent upon the charity of Filicchi. She thought of going to Canada to teach in some religious community, yet cultured and educated though she was, she dreaded her inefficiency. Bishop Carroll, too, advised her against the plan. God had other designs, and soon it was arranged that she should come to Baltimore, where a two-story brick house was rented for her with the purpose of opening a school for young ladies. There she found an asylum for herself and her girls, the two boys being taken into Georgetown College through the kindness of Father Dubourg, who had been instrumental in getting her away from New York. It was a relief of soul for her to escape from the persecution she had suffered in her native city and at the hands of her own people.

It was soon made possible for Mrs. Seton to start her plans for the establishment of the religious community upon which she had set her heart. A Mr. Cooper, a convert to the Catholic Church, and at that time a student at Mount St. Mary's, where he was preparing for the priesthood, desired to give his wealth to some worthy cause, especially for the instruction of poor children. By his generosity it was made possible to purchase a farm at Emmittsburg, fifty miles from Baltimore, and soon work was begun on the house for the new community. Several young women had joined Mrs. Seton, thus making the beginning of what was soon to be a most flourishing institution. To start the work, Mrs. Seton, in the presence of Bishop Carroll, took the vows of poverty, chastity, and obedience, and while waiting for the drawing up of a permanent rule the new sisters called themselves the Sisters of St. Joseph.

The cup of spiritual joy was now filled for Mother Seton, and especially so when she had the happiness of welcoming to the Baltimore house the beloved Cecelia, who had been nigh to death's door. With her came her sister Harriet, still a Protestant, however, but allowed to take the trip in order to care for Cecelia. It was a happy reunion.

Soon the house at Emmittsburg was ready, and Mrs. Seton, accompanied by Cecelia, Harriet, her daughter Anna, and another sister of the community, went there to prepare the place for the coming of the other sisters. In those days it was a long, hard, uphill journey, but their hearts were light as they thought of the Holy Land to which they were going. The ac-

commodations in the new house were primitive, but
the determined women did not mind the inconven-
iences. They were missionaries in a new work. Mrs.
Seton was of course the happiest one of the lot.
Founder of a religious community, she knew now what
her life's work was to be, and she had the blessed
privilege of keeping her children with her.

One of the most touching incidents in the life of
Mother Seton is the story of Harriet Seton, her sister-
in-law. When Harriet came down to Emmittsburg to
accompany the delicate Cecelia, she had left the centre
of New York's most fashionable circle. She was
indeed the belle of that city. Many had sought her in
marriage, but for several years now she had been
engaged to Barclay Bayley, Mrs. Seton's half-brother,
a man who hardly seemed worthy of such a woman
as Harriet.

The zeal and patience of Mrs. Seton and Cecelia in
the Catholic faith had impressed her, and she, too,
had the longing to embrace the faith. But family ties
held her back. And even when she was allowed to
go south with Cecelia she had been warned not to go
into the Catholic church for fear of the machinations
of Elizabeth. So for a long time at Emmittsburg she
would accompany the others to the door of the little
church, and then spend her time in the fields and woods
until the services were ended and the others rejoined
her. One evening, when Mother Seton came from
the church, she found Harriet on her knees at the foot
of a tree, sobbing her heart out because she could not

enter the church. It was the coming of grace. Soon the young woman made her decision, a decision that caused her much pain. She was willing even to give up the man she loved to follow the will of God.

But she was not long for this world. In the December of that year, after nursing the sick, she was taken ill herself and died a most edifying death, a true child of the Church, the first one of the little community to be laid at rest in the new cemetery. She had given up a luxurious home, the love of the man to whom she was engaged, all that this world prizes, for suffering and sacrifice; but she had received in return the pearl of great price. There is no sweeter character in all history than Harriet Seton, once the belle of New York.

It is not my purpose to detail the religious life of the new community. It was for the ten sisters a life of hardship, but with never a murmur. They suffered from the cold, their habits were coarse and patched, they had not enough to eat. On the Sunday before Christmas they feasted on a herring; their coffee was made from carrots and molasses, but they laughed at all the discomforts, for their souls were at peace. They went about their work, teaching the poor, spinning, knitting, praying, grateful to God, who had been so good to them.

And thus in poverty and lowliness was established that great work of the Sisters of Charity which was to be a tower of strength to the Catholic Church in America.

Death again came soon, this time for the saintly Cecelia, and she was laid away in the grave next to Harriet's. As Mother Seton said of her: "She was innocence and peace itself."

These deaths were sore trials to Mother Seton, but God required a greater sacrifice still. Elizabeth was to be wounded in her great mother-love. Anna Seton, or Annina, as the mother called her, was her pride and consolation. She had been with her in the days of sorrow in Italy, and had never been separated from her. She had grown into a girl of great beauty, and as good as she was beautiful. She sought admission into the community, but even before that, while a pupil, she arose every morning at five and passed an hour in meditation on her knees before Mass. But her health failed. She showed her father's weak constitution, but in spite of that went out in all weathers to nurse the sick. Drenched with rain one day, she caught cold, and soon the dread consumption claimed her as a victim. She made her vows on her death-bed, and while the little Catharine and Rebecca, her sisters, knelt at the foot of her bed and sang her favorite hymn at her request, she went to her reward. The following day she was buried beside Harriet and Cecelia.

Mother Seton's heart was broken at the death of the beloved daughter, but she bore the grief with sweet resignation to the will of God. Her mother-love had been purified. She knew that she could procure for her darling Annina nothing more glorious than the death of a saint. "O mother, mother," she wrote in her journal, "give a thousand thanks all your life, every day of your life, until you meet with her again."

A few years more, years of hard labor for the new community, years of prayer and sacrifice, and again God afflicted the mother's heart by taking from her the little Rebecca. She had fallen one day and had become a hopeless cripple. But she never complained. All medical skill had been tried in vain. For six months before her death she knew no ease from pain. One day she said, "If the doctors were to say to me, 'Rebecca, you are cured,' I would not rejoice. My dearest Saviour, I know too well the happiness of dying young and sinning no more." Sometimes she would worry over the sorrow her death would bring her mother. "You will return alone, dear mamma, and there will be no little Bec behind the bed-curtains. But that is only one side; when I look at the other side I forget all else. You will have consolation, for you hope that my salvation is assured."

It was a long death-agony for the young girl. "Think only of your Blessed Saviour now, my darling," said Mother Seton as she held her in her arms. "To be sure," she answered, and dropped her head for the last time on her mother's breast.

As her daughters had gone, so was Mother Seton soon to go. She did not complain; indeed, she was glad to go. Her two boys had been provided for, and she felt that little Catharine would enter a religious community. The same little Catharine died, at the age of ninety, as Mother Catharine of the Sisters of Mercy in New York. Mother Seton knew that her work was done, and she longed to go to Rebecca and Annina and to God. During those days of her last illness and decline she would visit every day the graveyard and gaze at the resting-place of Annina. Many graves were there now, the graves of her children, of Harriet and Cecelia, and of many of her sisters in religion. And she knew that she herself would soon be lying beside them. It was not long. She died on January 4, 1821, and was laid to rest beside the dear Annina.

So passed the great Mother Seton, one of the most beautiful characters that ever lived. Her cause has already been taken up, and one day we may have the privilege of calling her St. Elizabeth Seton, one of the greatest glories of the Church in America.

Mother Seton is she called on account of her office in the community which she established. But it is a title that belongs to her in another sense. She was the mother of children, and as such shines forth, a glorious example to all mothers.

Elizabeth Seton loved her children. But she loved them with a holy love. She considered little their worldly advancement. She knew the real value of things, and sought first of all the welfare of their souls. What was death, even, so long as it meant the going of her little ones to God? When she embraced the Catholic faith she knew that it would mean suffering, not only for herself, but for her children. But she chose for herself and them the way of the Cross.

Better to serve God and save one's soul than to gain the whole world and lose heaven.

Surely our Catholic mothers have a glorious patroness, a shining example, in Elizabeth Bayley Seton.

JERUSHA BARBER

(1789–1860)

THE history of the Catholic Church is a history of noble men and women. Page after page is filled with the story of sacrifice demanded by a jealous God, Who requires that hearts shall be His alone. And what sacrifices He has asked of His avowed lovers! He has asked the wife to leave her husband, the mother to leave her little ones. Again, He has asked mother and children to give their life as a proof of love.

There is no end to these sacrifices. Not only does one find them in the martyrs, in the days of the Cecelias, the Felicitas, the Symphorosas: they have been asked in our own land, in our own time, as in the case of Mother Seton. Sanctity belongs to no age, to no country. As long as the Holy Ghost abides with the Church, so long shall we see the flowering of sanctity.

In all the history of the Catholic Church in the United States there is nothing more romantic and at the same time more inspiring than the story of the Barber family, among the very first of the converts from Protestantism, and the example which those men and women have handed down to posterity of a de-

votion to the truth, of an answer to the call of God,
even though the way led through sacrifice and pain.
To read the story of this family, and especially of
Jerusha Barber, is to fancy one's self back in the ages
of faith. Her story is like a page from the life of
St. Jane Frances de Chantal, or St. Elizabeth of Hungary, in its renunciation—or, rather, sanctification—
of a mother's love.

When Bishop Carroll made his first visit to Boston in 1791, he found there, all told, one hundred and
twenty Catholics. Father Thayer, Boston-born and
a convert, was then the only priest in New England.
One can judge from these facts what the condition of
the Church then was in a place where it is now so
strong. Bishop Carroll had been received kindly by
the Protestants, and was even the guest of honor at
the annual dinner of the Ancient and Honorable Ar-
tillery Company. "It is wonderful to tell," says he,
"what great civilities have been done to me in this
town, where, a few years ago, a Popish priest was
thought to be the greatest monster in creation. Many
here, even of the principal people, have acknowledged
to me that they would have crossed to the opposite
side of the street rather than meet a Roman Catholic
sometime ago. This horror which was associated with
the idea of Papist is incredible; and the scandalous
misrepresentations by their ministers increased the
horror every Sunday."

But up in New Hampshire, which witnessed the first
step of the Barber family towards the Catholic Church,

[295]

there was none of that incipient Boston broad-mindedness which Bishop Carroll had discovered. Catholics in New Hampshire were ostracized socially and, of course, politically. There was that old unreasoning, ignorant hatred of everything Catholic. For that reason it is evident that the Barbers, who faced that spirit unflinchingly, were of heroic courage.

Daniel Barber was then an Episcopalian minister in Claremont, New Hampshire. He was born in Connecticut in 1756, one of nine children, of parents who were both very religious. He had served two short terms in the War of the Revolution. He had been a strong Congregationalist, but, as his father before him, he had reached the conviction that there was in that body no ecclesiastical authority or priesthood. It was a sacrifice for him to part from friends, from old customs, but he manfully made the sacrifice, and joined the Church of England, which in those days was quite as much despised as the Catholic Church by the Puritans. He was made an Episcopal minister at Schenectady, New York, in 1783. From there he came to Vermont in 1787, where he spent a few years, and finally took a church in Claremont, which he served for twenty-four years. He had married Chloe Chase, daughter of Judge Chase, and at the time he settled in Claremont had three sons, the youngest of whom died at the age of three, and one daughter.

It was during this ministry that in 1808 he baptized Fanny Allen, a daughter of the famous General Ethan Allen. Her story is worthy of more than passing mention. She was the youngest daughter of the General, and had been born in 1784. She was a remarkably beautiful girl and had inherited much of the firmness of character of her father. The General had died when she was about five years old, and her mother had married again. When she was twenty-three she determined to go to Montreal to study French; and her mother and stepfather, before letting her go, decided that she ought to be baptized. For that purpose they invited the Rev. Daniel Barber to the house. He was shocked on that occasion, for Fanny during the ceremony did nothing but laugh, and he reproved her for her levity.

On arriving at Montreal, she went to board with the Sisters. One day one of the Sisters asked her to bring a vase of flowers and place it on the altar, telling her to adore Our Lord at the same time. Fanny had no notion of adoring the Blessed Sacrament, but she brought the flowers nevertheless. As she tried to enter the sanctuary she felt repelled. Three times she renewed the attempt, but all in vain. And then she fell on her knees and adored Jesus in the Eucharist. She determined then, as she wept, to give herself to the Lord. So she was instructed and admitted to the Church.

There was of course great consternation at home. The parents brought her back immediately, and by every means sought to dissuade her from becoming a nun. They took her traveling to different cities. Admirers sought her hand, gay social parties were arranged in her honor. But all to no purpose. After the year which she had promised to give her parents was over, she returned to Montreal. And her mother not only gave her consent for her to become a religious, but even accompanied her to Montreal, inspected the convent, and was pleased at the good home her daughter was to have. She was finally received into the Hôtel-Dieu, and was visited there by her parents, who were delighted with the place. When, in 1810, she made her profession, the chapel was filled with American friends, among them Daniel Barber, all of whom wondered at the strange life chosen by the beautiful Fanny Allen. There she lived nine years, a life of suffering, always patient and happy, and died at the age of thirty-five, the "First New England Nun." The sight of her happiness, her determination, her sacrifice, had its influence, no doubt, in the conversion of Daniel Barber.

It was about the time of Fanny Allen's baptism that Daniel began to have doubts about the validity of his Orders, doubts that had been occasioned by his reading a Catholic book against the validity of Anglican Orders. He had made inquiries among those of his own faith, but could receive no satisfactory solution of his difficulties.

Finally, in desperation, he decided to consult Father Cheverus, afterwards Bishop of Boston, one of the priests who, as a result of the French Revolution, had come to America to labor for the faith. Father Matignon had come in 1792, and Father Cheverus in 1796.

When Boston was made a separate diocese from Baltimore, Father Cheverus was chosen bishop and was consecrated in 1810. In 1812 he had come to visit New Hampshire, which he had visited before when he was only a missionary priest. Father Cheverus was the first priest Daniel Barber had ever seen, and it took great courage for him to consult him. But the saintly Cheverus received him kindly, gave him to read certain books explaining Catholic doctrine, and answered all his questions as best he could. Daniel brought the books home, and not only read them himself, but gave them to his family and to members of his congregation, who were evidently as broad-minded as their pastor.

The good work towards conversion was furthered by no less a person than Daniel's own son, the Rev. Virgil Barber, who had come home with his wife to pay a visit to the old folks. Daniel was so enthusiastic over the books which Father Cheverus had given him that he delighted in reading them to the family, to the great pleasure of Virgil; so much so that when he and his wife left home they asked to be allowed to take with them one of the books, which was Milner's *End of Controversy.*

Virgil at that time was principal of an academy at Fairfield, New York, about fifteen miles from Utica, and was also pastor of the Episcopal church of that town. His maid at that time was a good, pious Irish Catholic girl. He had seen her reading her prayer-book, and curiosity induced him to take it up and read it. It was a Novena to St. Francis Xavier. So struck was he by the life of the Saint that he got the complete life, and after reading of the miracles of the extraordinary man of God and his wonderful sanctity, he began seriously to consider it.

He himself tells the story: "How could a religion which forms such men be a mere human institution? Peace then departed from my soul. I had doubts concerning the truth of my Protestant faith. I began to study very seriously, and the more I studied the more my doubts increased. These doubts I submitted to my bishop (Dr. Hobart), hoping thereby to find peace; but he gave me no light on the subject, and rather strengthened my doubts, as he paid no serious attention to my objections. We were at this time standing at the window of a room whence we could hear the singing going on in a Catholic church near by. I took occasion to ask the Bishop, 'Do you think that those can be saved?' At this question of mine he could not help smiling, and answered, 'They have the old religion, don't you know? But they do too much, and one can be saved without so much trouble. Do not distress yourself about such matters. Go back home in peace, and if you choose to do so, consult your brother ministers and your religious scruples will soon vanish.' I returned home from that interview more distressed than I was before. I put down on paper my objections against the Protestant religion in the shape of fourteen questions, and I invited many ministers of the Episcopal Church to come and visit me. To each of them, as they came, I presented the terrible sheet of paper. They all glanced at the questions, and none failed to say, 'Well, well, we'll see after tea'; but after tea music was had at the piano; and as no one attempted to answer the questions, I then resolved to see and consult the Bishop of Boston."

This was Bishop Fenwick, then Father Fenwick, an assistant to Father Kohlmann in New York City. To him came Virgil Barber with his difficulties. Father Fenwick received him kindly and answered his questions. A few months afterwards he came to him again. He was now convinced that the Catholic Church alone was the true Church. But he hesitated to take the step. He had a wife and five small children, and he worried as to how he could support them if he gave up his fine living as pastor and president of the academy. Father Fenwick, however, pointed out to him his duty, regardless of the consequences. "Trust your affairs to the management of a beneficent Providence," he told him. "Embrace the truth, now that you have found it, and leave the rest to God. He has led you on to make this inquiry. He has followed you step by step, and now that you yield to this grace, will He abandon you? No; believe me, you were never more secure of subsistence."

It was enough. He saw his duty, and he did it. A few days after this interview with Father Fenwick he renounced Protestantism and was received into the Catholic Church. Meanwhile a change was also tak-

ing place in the soul of his wife, Jerusha. She had
been born in New Town, Connecticut, in 1789. Her
parents were models of domestic virtue, and her
mother had been regarded as a saint by her Protestant
neighbors. Jerusha was the youngest of four children, and at the time of her father's death, when she
was sixteen, she gave herself more and more to piety,
and was the great consolation of her mother. When
she was nineteen she married Virgil Barber, then
twenty-five. It was a union of deep love. There was
perfect devotion on both sides, and not only did she
love him, but she was also his chief adviser even in
spiritual matters. At the time he read the life of St.
Francis Xavier he remarked to her that "his parallel
could not be found in the whole Protestant Church."
So great was his admiration for the Saint that when
their son was born shortly after this he wanted to
name him Francis Xavier Barber. But she was indignant, and refused to have the "Popish name," calling him Samuel instead. But still, in spite of her in-
nate repugnance to the Catholic Church, she took part
in his investigations. He used to tell her the results
of his studies, and she soon saw whither he was tending. She saw the ground giving beneath her, and
it brought consternation. He never suspected the pain
she was suffering as she saw him drawing near to the
Catholic Church and away from the living upon which
she and her little ones were dependent. When the
Episcopalian bishop and the ministers, seeking to
deter him from taking the step, came to him and

told him that of course he would have to resign the academy if he persisted in becoming a Catholic, he came to his wife for advice. "If," said she, "I were to become a Catholic, I would go where I could practise my religion." And she also continued to study the Catholic doctrine, principally, perhaps, to please him, for she loved him greatly. It was a great blow to her prospects for her family when he announced to her his decision, but she made no objection. She hid her grief in her heart.

Once he had become a Catholic, he knew that it was useless to seek to hold his school, and so, with her consent, he resigned; for so great was the bigotry that after he had given up his pulpit all his parishioners turned against him, and would have compelled him to resign from the academy had he not done so voluntarily.

It was a hopeless future they faced, with the five little ones to feed. Again he turned to Father Fenwick, who had promised him that God would not fail him in this sacrifice. Father Fenwick welcomed them to New York, opened his house to them and started a school which he gave into the charge of Virgil, and thus provided him with the means to support his family.

It was an answer to the man's faith. During the time of trial, Virgil Barber found strength in his good wife. She entered heart and soul into all his plans, and great as was her inherited prejudice against the religion he had adopted,—and that, too, with such a sacrifice imposed on her,—she listened to his talk about the claims of the Church, and was soon received herself into the faith. They both made their first Communion together in St. Peter's Church, Barclay Street.

Jerusha was not one to refuse to do the will of God. It meant a great deal to her. She had given up good society and a position of ease. She had put aside all the worldly prospects of her children. But she knew that God would provide. She said at the time that she considered the children as God's rather than her own, she being only the temporary agent. If the children were God's, surely He would provide for them. It was a simple but a great faith.

The Barbers continued their school for five months. And then they were called on by God to make a sacrifice of their very hearts. On the day that Virgil Barber received his first Communion side by side with his wife, he was filled with the desire to consecrate himself wholly to the service of God, impossible as that seemed at the time. Father Fenwick was at this time rector of Georgetown College, having returned there after his work as administrator of the New York diocese was ended, in 1816, on the appointment of a new bishop. He was still mindful of the Barbers, and perhaps a bit worried over their future. The school had been prosperous, and numbered among its many pupils children from some of the most influential New York families. But he knew not how long that would continue, and wrote to Virgil, asking him what were his

plans for the future. All the time the new converts
had been studying and reading the *Lives of the Saints*.
Virgil wrote to his good friend, Father Fenwick, and
told him that he felt a call to the religious life, and
that were it not for his wife and children, he would
think of becoming a priest. Before he sent this letter, he read it to his wife, as he was accustomed to
read to her all his letters. To her it was a new
thought, and it stunned her. She could not get it
out of her mind. It seemed to her as a death-blow.
She could not bear even the thought of separation from
the man she so tenderly loved, the father of her children. Her daughter, later Sister Josephine, tells the
story of that trial.

"The letter was the death-blow to her happiness.
'From that hour,' she said to me, 'I enjoyed not a
moment's peace. The thought that God wanted my
brother (for so she called Mr. Barber after their en-
trance into religion), and that I was the obstacle, pur-
sued me day and night.' But she did not at first reveal her trouble to him, hoping time would dissipate it.
But it proved the reverse. Everything she read, everything she heard, seemed to bear upon the one point,
and to fasten upon her heart with a tenacity from
which she was unable to free herself. 'I felt,' said
she, 'that I must make the sacrifice to God; and that
if I should refuse He would deprive me of my husband
and children both in this world and the next. Of this
I felt the strongest conviction, that in case of refusal,
one or the other of us would die and our children be

left orphans.' At length, unable to endure her agony
of mind, she imparted her thoughts to my father, who
tried to soothe her by saying that God did not require
such a thing of them, and that she must not permit it
to distress her. He told her that in penning those
lines, he had not meant them in the sense she had
taken, but only as expressive of his predilection for
the ministry, feeling himself bound to his family by
the laws of God and man. This would quiet her for
a while; but in spite of his assurance her trouble would
return, and at times with such violence that she was
obliged to call him from his school-room to give her
comfort. 'Then,' said she, 'he would take me in his
arms, wipe away my tears, and talk to me until my
fears were almost dissipated. Yet while he lavished
upon me all this tenderness, there was deep down in
my heart a whisper that said: 'This is not God. This
is not what He demands of you.' Neither was my
father without similar impressions, although he concealed them from her, deeming it his duty to do so
until better assured of the will of God. But when
this became manifest, he encouraged her to prefer
eternity to time and to look forward to their happy reunion in a better world. They were not long in taking their decision, for it was impossible for them to
remain in such a violent state of feeling for any great
length of time. Yet between its first suggestion and
final accomplishment some months must necessarily in-
tervene; and these were to my parents months of
agony. 'A thousand times,' said my mother, 'would

I willingly have had a dagger plunged into my breast, and have found it a relief; for not only did my heart ache with the sentiment of grief; but it ached physically—the very flesh ached, just as your head aches. Put your hand here; you cannot feel it beat; it is not in its natural place; it is sunk in back.' And truly enough, I could not feel the slightest pulsation; but on applying the hand to a spot between the shoulders, found the palpitations strong. I need not say I was much astonished at it, and wondered at the moral and physical strength with which God must have endued her to sustain an assault of mental suffering so long. My father, also, at times nearly gave way under the trial. 'When he was in depression of mind,' said she, 'he always wanted me to talk to him; and, as docile as a child, would, at my bidding, kneel and recite with me the Collect for Peace, as also that to the Choir of Thrones, which, I think, never failed to tranquilize him. Yet I did not immediately surrender myself to grace. I resisted as long as I could, and as long as I dared, striving to turn a deaf ear to it, and to persuade myself God did not demand such a course from me. But in vain. I was compelled to yield.' I once asked her how she had been able to accomplish such a sacrifice. 'I did not do it,' she answered. 'It was not I; I could not have done it. God did it for me. He took me up and carried me through it.'"

The heart of every man must thrill at that story of sacrifice, of the fight between the love for man and the love for God. Jerusha Barber rose to the occasion,

She was as heroic as her husband. If God wanted him
to be a priest, she would not stand in the way, and so
she assured him that to help his plan she would become a religious if the Church would sanction their
separation. They wrote to Father Fenwick about their
trouble of conscience. He hardly knew, considering
the difficulties of the case, how to advise them, but he
answered that there was no objection to their plan if
both with mutual consent consecrated their lives to
God, and if proper provision were made for the children. His answer was a relief to them, yet there was
a difficulty apparently insurmountable in providing for
the little ones, one of them a mere infant at its mother's
breast. They had nothing of this world's goods. Virgil had bought some land near Utica, which he had
not entirely paid for, but after his conversion he had
been forced to sell it at a sacrifice, so great was the
bitterness against him for his defection from Episco-
palianism. They had nothing now, but they did not
lose their confidence in God. They knew that He
would clear the way if He wanted them to lead the
religious life.

Again God used Father Fenwick. This good
priest went to Archbishop Neale of Baltimore, and
laid the case before him. It touched the Archbishop
to see such great faith, and he arranged to have Mrs.
Barber and her three daughters enter the Visitation
Convent at Georgetown, the three girls to be received
as boarders and the mother as a teacher with a view
to her entering the community.

Father Fenwick's mother was living in a large mansion near the college, and she consented to take the baby and care for it, while Mr. Barber and the boy Samuel were to go to Georgetown College. As soon as all was arranged in this way the family left New York and went to Georgetown, where, after a few days, the husband and wife were invited to the college chapel, and there, in the presence of many priests and lay people, after both had given their full consent, the Archbishop pronounced the dissolution of their union. It was like a scene from the ages of faith. What a great love of God it was that induced a loving husband and wife to sacrifice all their love, to part from each other, and even to break up their home and scatter their children! The ages of faith never showed anything more inspiring. It was a family upon which God poured His choicest blessings. Every one of them, husband, wife, and all the children, entered the religious life. Virgil and his son Samuel became Jesuits; Mrs. Barber and the baby Josephine, afterwards Sister Josephine, entered the Visitation Order, and the other three girls, Mary, Abby, and Susan, who had come to board with their mother at the Visitation convent, later on became Ursulines, Mary, the oldest, entering the Ursuline convent at Charlestown and being there at the time it was burned by the Know-nothing mob in 1834. She afterwards wrote the account of that happening. Abby joined the Ursulines at Quebec, and was a sister there for more than fifty years. Susan died with the Ursulines at Three Rivers, at the age of twenty-four, an example of great holiness. The son Samuel was a noble, self-sacrificing missionary priest, and died, in 1864, at the age of fifty.

But we are anticipating. Soon after his admission to Georgetown, Virgil was sent to Rome to make his studies. His wife meanwhile was deep in her new work in the convent. She was a fervent novice. So great had been her wish to become a nun, that she had even made a habit for herself before her admission. She was an excellent teacher, and for that reason a great acquisition to the Order. She was soon made a directress, and then a trainer of the novices in teaching. But three months after she had entered it was deemed advisable for her to return to the world for a time, and she went to live in a boarding-house at Baltimore. One day there came to this house a sea-captain named Baker, who, while relating the story of his recent voyage to Europe, told of one of the passengers, a Mr. Barber, who was so grief-stricken that they all feared he would die. The Captain, of course, did not know who Mr. Barber was, and that he was speaking to his wife. But as he told the story, as she listened to the description of the agony of the man who had been her husband, her heart sank. Was she right? was he right? she asked herself. Had they been mistaken in making the sacrifice? It was one of her great trials, but she fought against it, conquered the feeling in her heart, and went back to Georgetown to follow the will of God wherever it led. She was then twenty-eight years old.

At the end of that year she took her vows in the chapel. Her husband, who had but recently returned from Rome, was present, together with their five children. Who knows what feelings came to the hearts of them all? Was it not, after all, a way of the Cross? For this woman who had set foot upon her heart it was not a life of calm. From a natural point of view, it was a humiliating life. She realized that she and her children were dependents, inasmuch as Virgil was not able to support them. They were subjects for charity, she felt, even while she gave good service to the community. But the trial of poverty for her loved ones was a real one. She had the heart of a mother. She was not an unnatural mother. She loved her children. As she herself once said, "I could have put myself under the feet of any one who was kind to my children." One day Mrs. Fenwick brought the baby Josephine to see her. The child did not know her. It broke the mother's heart. "My God!" she cried, "my own child does not know me."

Meanwhile Virgil, soon after his return from Rome, made a visit to his father and mother at Claremont. That was in 1818, and he was accompanied by the Rev. Dr. Ffrench, an English Dominican, a convert. Daniel Barber was still minister of the Episcopal Church, but on the following Sunday Mass was said in his house by Father Ffrench. Daniel assisted at it before he went to conduct the services in his own church. On the ensuing Sunday he even invited the priest to say Mass and preach in the Episcopalian church, an invitation that was not accepted.

Evidently Virgil knew that his family was ready to come into the Church, and for that reason had brought the priest with him. No doubt all had been influenced by the Catholic books which Daniel was circulating, as also by the sacrifices made by Virgil and his wife.

The visit of the priest was as powerful an influence as the reading of the books. As a result of it, Mrs. Daniel Barber decided to become a Catholic. Her husband says of this decision: "My wife, who was one of the first in making an open profession of the Catholic faith, was a woman who possessed a strength of mind and resolution which qualified her for so important an investigation, and by which she set at naught the fear of man and the voice of the multitude. She improved the first opportunity of separating herself, and embracing the standard of the Cross, from which she never separated till death." She was an ardent Catholic, and died at the age of seventy-nine, after having received the sacraments from her son Virgil, who was then a priest.

In that week of Father Ffrench's visit, Mrs. Daniel Barber and her daughter, and also Daniel's sister, Mrs. Noah Tyler, and her daughter Rosette, were received into the Catholic Church. Later on Mrs. Tyler's husband and all her children—seven—became converts. One son became the Vicar-General of Boston, and then the first Bishop of Hartford. Four of the daughters became Sisters of Charity at Emmittsburg. One loves to think of the sturdy Nabby Tyler and her great family. Surely there were giants in those days!

So passed the summer. Virgil and Father Ffrench had returned to Georgetown. Daniel Barber was thinking, studying, praying, and in November he made his farewell to the people of whom he had been pastor for nearly twenty-five years, telling them that to follow his conscience he must resign. Who knows what it cost him to snap all the ties of years? In his conversion, no doubt, his wife played a great part. After his resignation he went south to visit some friends in Washington and Maryland, desirous of knowing more about the Church before entering it. During that absence he embraced the faith at Georgetown, and wrote letters to friends on the Catholic Church—letters that were afterwards published in a pamphlet entitled *Catholic Worship,* in which he gave his reasons for his change of faith.

After the death of his beloved wife he determined to go south again. He wrote to his children on this occasion. His heart ached on leaving the scenes of so much happiness. "I look back again," he wrote, "to the pleasant scenes of early life. Here is one object ever presenting itself to my recollection: it is she who once, and for many years, was the kind associate of all my cares, my hopes and wishes. Yes, for many a year we traveled the rugged path of life together; and at a time, too, when the looks and smiles of our helpless little children, dependent on us for their comfort and protection, called into exercise every principle of care and activity. Our anxious desires for the future happiness and prosperity of these gave a pleasure to our toils, our labors and sufferings; our hearts comforting us, at the same time, with the fullest assurance that these same little ones, at a future time, would add greatly to our happiness by supplying our wants if needy, consoling our declining years, and wiping away from us the tears of sorrow and old age."

Later on he took minor orders and sometimes preached in the Cathedral at Boston. When Virgil was ordained and sent to Claremont it was an edifying sight to see the old man who had made so many sacrifices for his faith serving his son's Mass. Later he used to go from one Jesuit house to another, and visit different Catholic families. He died in 1834, at the age of seventy-eight, and was buried in the cemetery of the Jesuit mission at St. Inigoes, Maryland.

Virgil Barber, on his return to Georgetown, settled down to his theological studies. After four years he was ordained in Boston by Bishop Cheverus on the feast of St. Francis Xavier in 1822. That Christmas he assisted as one of the officers at the Pontifical High Mass in the Boston Cathedral. From Boston he was sent to Claremont, where he was given charge of the Catholics, and where he labored zealously to make the faith known and loved. By his zeal many converts were made, entire families coming into the Church. In the winter of 1824 he visited Canada to

collect for the building of a church at Claremont, and
there he was received kindly and helped, so that he
was able to build a little church, the upper part of
which served as an academy, where he himself taught,
and where he had among his pupils such men as Fathers Wiley, Fitton, and Tyler, who later served the
Church so well. Virgil was assisted in the academy
by his father. So passed the happy days there. Mrs.
Daniel Barber was very happy to have her own son
as her pastor. She was the first to be buried in the
graveyard near the little Catholic church.

In that same fall Father Fenwick was chosen Bishop
of Boston, and Father Barber, full of joy at this honor
to his dear friend and benefactor, was present at his
consecration in the Cathedral at Baltimore. On that
occasion he went to Georgetown and visited the Convent of the Visitation to pay a farewell visit to his
wife and children. It was the last time he saw them
all together. "It was a tearful and sorrowful parting," his daughter wrote. The next day he set out for
Boston with Bishop Fenwick and Bishop England,
and on the Sunday following their arrival there Bishop
Fenwick was installed, and Father Barber was deacon
of the Mass.

Father Barber then returned to his beloved parish at
Claremont. It was composed of about one hundred
and fifty persons, and most of them were converts.
In the following May, Bishop Fenwick visited him
there and administered the sacrament of Confirmation, the church being crowded, mostly with Protes-

tants from the church on the opposite side of the village, which, the Bishop naïvely remarks in his diary, "they have completely deserted, to the very great dissatisfaction of the minister there attending." The following November Father Barber was called to Boston, and at the wish of the Bishop visited different places in New Hampshire and Maine. He was everywhere received with great welcome by the scattered Catholics, who rejoiced to see a priest. Even among the Indians he found great piety, and regretted that there was no priest among them. Shortly after his return from this missionary journey he was recalled to Georgetown by his superiors, and a few weeks later the church at Claremont was closed. In later years, once in 1829 and again in 1830, he made brief visits to his old home. His last days were spent at Georgetown, and there he died in 1847.

One cannot think of this man and the sacrifices made by him without being thrilled. It is like a page from the life of a great saint. There is a letter which Father Fitton, one of his pupils, who afterwards labored in East Boston, wrote to Sister Josephine, the baby in arms when the conversion of her parents took place. "I have still a vivid recollection," he wrote, "of your grandfather Daniel, his aged wife, son Israel, and daughter Rachel. Mrs. Tyler also, with her husband, sons, and daughters (Sisters of Charity), not omitting my sainted school-fellow, the late Bishop of Hartford. Many a little anecdote I could tell of the early days of Catholicity at Claremont, not forgetting Cornish, the house of Captain Chase and sister, especially, whom, previous to their receiving the grace of faith, I was accustomed to regard as the corner-stone of Calvinism! And there were the Marbles, and the Holdens, etc., all related to the Church by the footprints and untiring zeal of your own sainted Rev. Father, even of whom I must tell a secret. When his seminary was in full progress and the house adjoining was occupied by students, my curiosity was to know, if he ever slept, where did he sleep? And behold! I found his bed to be a strip of narrow carpet on the floor, which was privately rolled up by day and hid in the closet."

The Captain Chase and his family mentioned were faithful to the end. His sister Sarah joined the Ursulines at Boston, and was known as Sister Ursula. After the burning of the convent, she, with Sister Mary Joseph Barber, went to the convent at Three Rivers, Quebec, where she died at the age of eighty-eight.

Sister Mary Joseph visited the Chase family in 1830, and thus describes them: "The family was a saintly one; they said morning and night prayers; also the Rosary aloud every day, adding to the latter a sixth decade, 'For Father Barber.' On Sundays they recited the whole catechism through, and sang the Kyrie, Gloria, Credo, and Sanctus of the High Mass, Captain Chase and his wife presiding, and his eldest son accompanying on the flageolet. Their family formed the choir, and they chanted the Mass not only through devotion, but in order to retain what they had learned, and to teach their children the same; for there was then no priest in Claremont, but one from Burlington visited the station every three months, lodging at Captain Chase's, where an apartment was always kept in reserve for him."

While Father Barber was doing his great missionary work, his wife, as Sister Mary Augustine, was doing hers in the convent. After the days of trial in the novitiate, during which human nature, love of her husband, and love of her children fought against grace, there had come the peace of Christ. Her perseverance and her faith in God had triumphed. Her trials brought their reward. She saw all her children embrace the religious life, the greatest consolation that could be given to the heart of any mother. Hers was a life hidden with Christ in God. It was the life of a Sister, with few events to be recorded. She was nineteen years at Georgetown, and then in 1836 went to aid in founding a house of the Order at Kaskaskia. There she remained eight years, and thence went to St. Louis, and then in 1848 to Mobile. Most of her life as a sister was spent in the work in which she excelled, that of training teachers. After an illness in which she edified all by her great patience, she died January 1, 1860, thirteen years after her husband.

What a story of faith and courage it is! And to the woman how much of it is due! How she might have pleaded against the call of God, that she had five little ones depending on her; how she might have opposed the vocation of her husband on the plea that he belonged to her, that she loved him, that he was

necessary for her and her children. But she made
all the sacrifices,—and hard sacrifices they were, the
way before her many a time being dark,—and made
them because she felt that God required them of her.
If there is any woman who can be held up as an
example of utmost trust in God, it is Jerusha Barber.
Surely she deserves a high place in the roll of the
Church's great wives and mothers.

MARY O'CONNELL, WIFE OF THE LIBERATOR

(1775-1836)

THE Irish mother! One speaks her name reverently. It is synonymous with all that is pure and sweet in life. A good mother is one of those things taken for granted in Ireland, such a truism that it begets little wonderment. It has rarely occupied the attention even of the poets. Search for mother-poems among the innumerable Irish ballads, and you will marvel at their scarcity. Just so, because no one thinks it extraordinary that all Irish mothers should be holy and motherly.

And that expression—holy and motherly—well describes the typical Irish mother. Holiness and motherliness are her inheritance of the ages, her share of the world. No one so much as she has guided the destinies of Erin. The history of Ireland has been the struggle of truth against error, light against darkness, sanctity against sin. And there never could be any doubt about the outcome. All else must be sacrificed rather than the faith. And in keeping that inviolate, what a share the Irish mother had! In the world, she never has been of it. Her eyes are

[320]

forever set on the Kingdom of God. She has sought no worldly advancement. Let others have that if they are foolish enough to want it. The one thing that has counted with her is God.

Some one has said that the position of woman in any age is proportionate to that age's devotion to the Mother of God. That, more than anything else, explains the character of the Irish mother. She is ever the friend of Mary. Mary is her exemplar, her adviser. Small wonder, then, that from centuries of looking to this model, she is pure, and holy, and dutiful, and humble.

The Irish mother is a philosopher, even when unlettered; a poet, though untrained; wise with that wisdom which she knows how to get out of her Rosary. She is, indeed, the handmaid of the Lord. Very often hers is a life's portion of labor, of bearing and rearing children, of struggle against poverty; yet her eyes never lose their gentleness and their wistfulness. Hers is a world where fairies mingle with men, but, more than all, a world where the eyes behold the finger of God directing the most trivial things.

The will of God! That is the secret of her philosophy. Come famine, come exile, come misery, it is all bearable because of the will of God shining through. And when prosperity comes, it does not change her. Simplicity of soul is her birthright. She desires no greater glory than to be queen of her home, the mother of men.

Rich or poor, of high or humble station, the Irish

mother is always the same. Ireland has her mother-saints among her gentlewomen as among her peas‑ants. She has glorified wifehood and motherhood, she has kept marriage a holy thing, and that is not the least of the proofs that the faith of St. Patrick has not failed. Canon Sheehan says somewhere in *My New Curate*:

"Married life in Ireland has been up to now the most splendid refutation of all that the world and its gospel, the novel, preach about marriage, and the most splendid and complete justification of the super-naturalism of the Church's dogmas and practices."

There is one great Irish wife and mother that we choose as a type. There have been many as great as she. Indeed, she would be the last one to lay claim to any greatness. She was, to her own mind, just an ordinary, happy wife and mother, looking after the comforts of her husband, answering the calls of her seven children.

But Mary O'Connell is especially appealing to the Irish Catholic from the fact that she was the wife of him to whom Ireland and the faith owe so much—the immortal Liberator.

To read the life of Daniel O'Connell even to-day is to be thrilled. No man ever had such influence with his followers. Greville well says: "History will speak of him as one of the most remarkable men who ever existed; he will fill a great space in its pages. His position was unique; there never was before, and there never will be again, anything at all resembling it." And Fagan, one of his biographers, does not hesitate to declare that he was "the greatest man this [Ireland] or any other country ever produced."

Where was the secret of that power? In his great character, of course, a character that was, first and foremost, formed by religion. Yet hand in hand with that influence went another—that of the wife he idolized. As he said once at a banquet in Edinburgh, when responding to a toast to the health of his wife: "A man cannot battle and struggle with the malignant enemies of his country unless his nest at home is warm and comfortable." It is said that at all the banquets in his honor there was sure to be a toast to "the health of Mrs. O'Connell, the pattern of mothers, the pattern of wives—a lady whose charitable and exemplary conduct sheds lustre upon her sex and station." On one occasion he replied to this toast with these words:

"To the lady whose health you have drunk I owe most of the happiness of my life. The home made delightful by my family is, after the cares and agitation of professional and public life, a most blessed retreat. I am, indeed, happy in that home, happy in a dear wife, happy in children into whose minds a fond mother early and carefully instilled a reverence for religion, the love of God and the love of country."

On another occasion he said: "There are some topics of so sacred and sweet a nature that they may be comprehended by those who are happy, but cannot possibly be described by any human being. All that I shall do is to thank you in the name of her who was the disinterested choice of my youth, and who was the ever-cheerful companion of my manly years."

Surely it was no small service for a woman to have been the inspiration of one who served his God and his country so whole-heartedly. And that alone would entitle Mary O'Connell to a high place on the honor-roll of the great women of all time. The debt to O'Connell for his work for Catholic Emancipation cannot be fully paid without a tribute to his wife, the idol of his heart.

O'Connell was, indeed, blessed in all his women-folk. A loving and dutiful son, he pays a noble tribute to his mother, to whom he ascribes much of his success. She was a pious, sensible and affectionate woman, a typical Irish mother. The only picture we have of her shows a face far from beautiful, yet with roguish eyes and a delightfully humorous smile. Her maiden name was Kate O'Mullane, and she was thoroughly Irish. In 1841 O'Connell wrote of her:

"I am the son of a sainted mother, who watched over my childhood with the most faithful care. She was of a high order of intellect, and what little I possess was bequeathed me by her. I may in fact say without vanity that the superior situation in which I am placed by my countrymen has been owing to her. Her last breath was passed, I thank Heaven, in calling down blessings on my head. And I have valued her blessing since. In the perils and dangers to which

I have been exposed through life, I have regarded her blessing as an angel's shield over me; and as it has been my protection in this life, I look forward to it also as one of the means of obtaining hereafter a happiness greater than any this world can give."

One would like to know more of this mother of ten children, who merited from her famous son such a tender tribute.

His grandmother, too—his father's mother—was a notable woman,—"remarkable," all the biographers call her. Indeed, she was remarkable alone from the fact that she had twenty-two children. But she had also great intellectual talent. When her son, the future Count O'Connell, the "last Colonel of the Irish Brigade," then aged sixteen, left his native land to enter the service of France in 1761, taking with him eighteen Irish recruits, four of them his cousins, she showed that she was a true poet in the lament she composed in Irish on that occasion. The mother of twenty-two children, yet writing poetry—surely that is possible only among the Irish!

O'Connell was twenty-seven years old when he married his cousin, Mary O'Connell. He was at that time a rising young lawyer who had met with success on the circuit, and who had already made his first political speech against the proposed Union.

She was the daughter of a Dr. O'Connell of Tralee, a man highly respected for his professional skill, but with very little of the goods of this world. He was, indeed, unable to provide his daughter with a dowry.

Maurice O'Connell, Daniel's uncle, who had adopted him and was likely to make him his heir to the property at Derrynane, was not in favor of the match on account of the lack of money. Exercising his rights over his adopted nephew, he had already selected a wife for Daniel, and the chosen lady was a spinster who was well endowed with money if not with youth and beauty. But poor Mary Ann Healy, rich as she was, was not the woman to win the heart of a romantic young lawyer. Daniel was aware that in following the dictates of his heart instead of the wishes of his uncle he was likely to be disinherited, but that gave him little worry about his decision. He was in love with Mary O'Connell and, after all, that was the only thing that counted. "I never," said he to his secretary in 1843, long after the death of his wife, "proposed marriage to any woman but one—my Mary. I said to her, 'Are you engaged, Miss O'Connell?' She answered, 'I am not.' 'Then,' said I, 'will you engage yourself to me?' 'I will,' was her reply. And I said I would devote my life to make her happy. She deserved that I should. I thought my uncle would disinherit me, but I did not care. I was richly rewarded by subsequent happiness. She gave me thirty-four years of the purest happiness that man ever enjoyed."

It was a marriage of true love, and O'Connell and his wife were always supremely happy. But it did not take place without opposition. All the kinsmen of Daniel, worrying, perhaps, about Derrynane and

Uncle Maurice, were set against the marriage. Letter after letter was written to dissuade him, but to no avail. The marriage was privately celebrated at the home of Mary's brother-in-law, James Connor, in Dublin, on the twenty-third of June, 1802.

They kept it quiet for several months. But at last it was known to all. Old Maurice was especially indignant, and he never quite forgave Dan, even though he did not disinherit him. Two years after the marriage we find Count O'Connell writing to Maurice in behalf of the criminal. "His fate," pleaded the Count, "must be truly deplorable if you irrevocably cast him off. The bare perquisites of his profession are probably very inadequate to the support of a wife and family, besides his personal expenses." In due time the old man relented.

Mary O'Connell was not a woman of remarkable intellect, but she understood her husband and sympathized with him in all his work. Who knows how much of what he accomplished was due to that sympathy? She was his helpmate and his companion. She gave him a quiet home, and while he was away corresponded with him. She was a quiet source of strength, a gentle, sweet creature, who had, as her husband testifies, "the sweetest, the most heavenly temper." He tells this little incident to show his wife's character. Speaking, one day, of Mary's old aunt, with whom she used to live, he said: "It was my delight to quiz the old lady by pretending to complain of Mary's want of temper. 'Madam,' said I, 'Mary would do very well, only she is so cross.' 'Cross, sir? My Mary cross? Sir, you must have provoked her very much! You must yourself be quite in fault! My little girl was always the gentlest, sweetest creature born.'"

How O'Connell idolized his wife is seen from his letters. One of his biographers says: "In thorough contrast to his wrathful tone on public questions are the tender letters to his wife and daughter."

O'Connell declared himself "the very worst letter-writer in the world." But he could write to Mary. Here is a letter written shortly after their marriage. It is dated from Dublin, November 25, 1802, when Mary was, very likely, still living with her aunt.

"Darling," he says, "I can write but a few lines, as it is grown so late and my time is small. I was finishing some law business which I had solemnly promised to dispose of this night. You will know, my heart's dearest treasure, that whether I write few or many words, there certainly is not in the world a man who more fondly dotes on, or who so anxiously longs for the arms of his wife. Day and night you are continually present to my fond thoughts, and you always increase my happiness or lessen my cares. With you I could live with pleasure in the prison or the desert. You are my all of company, and if I can but preserve your love I shall have in it more of true delight than can be imagined by any one but he who sincerely loves.

"Sweet Mary, I rave of you! I think only of you!

I sigh for you, I weep for you! I almost pray to you! Darling, I do not—indeed, I do not—exaggerate. If there be more of vehemence in my expressions, believe me that vehemence has its justification in my heart—a heart that is devoted to the most enticing of her sex. Indeed, you are a dear, charming little woman. Your last letter I have read again and again. It is in every respect a most pleasing letter to me, not only from the heart-flowing strain of tenderness in which it is written, but the saucy gaiety of some of the passages show me how much recovered my love is. . . .

"Mary, how fondly I shall cherish the little stranger coming! I hope it may be a daughter, and as like you as possible. O God, how I then will love her! How sincerely will I express my affection to the mother in the caresses I bestow on the child! Dearest, sweetest wife, I can thus hope to be able to prove to you the pleasing affection with which my whole soul dotes on you.

"Dearest, I am writing this with great rapidity, but still my thoughts run much faster than my pen. I could praise you a thousand times faster than I write, as I love you a thousand times more than I can tell. I shall soon see you, dearest darling. Love to dear mother.

"Ever your devoted husband,

"DANIEL O'CONNELL.

"In a week we shall be able to fix the time of our departure. Happy, happy moment that gives me my sweet wife again!"

As the years went by and the children came, their love seemed to increase. In 1812 he writes to her:

"MY DEAREST MARY:

"I was a little impertinent in my letter of yesterday, and the reason was because I found myself decidedly in more business than any other individual here; and so, dear heart, I avenged myself upon you, which was poor spite. I, however, now *forgive* you, darling, because you promised me so faithfully to take care of yourself and grow fat in my absence. Seriously, love, I am quite in a temper to indulge vanity, but in nothing more so than in you and my sweet, sweet babes. Darling, you have no idea of the time I take in thinking of you and them, and in doting upon both. Kiss them a thousand times for their father, and tell them he will not be happy until he has his three little girls on his knees and his three boys looking at him there. . . . Tell each and every one of the babes how I love them. Ask John if he ever intends to get a tooth. . . ."

She was his idol, and he was hers. Fifteen years after their marriage she could write:

"MY OWN DARLING DAN:

"I assure you, my darling, you are our continual subject. When a kind husband or father is spoken of, Ellen or Kate will exclaim, 'Mamma, sure he is not so good a husband or father as our father is.' You may guess, darling, what my reply is. You know

what you deserve, and you are aware that in existence I don't think there is such a husband and father
as you are and always have been. Indeed, I think
it quite impossible there could; and if the truest and
tenderest affection can repay you, believe me that I
feel and bear it for you. In truth, my own Dan, I
am always at a loss for words to convey to you how
I love you and dote on you. Many and many a time
I exclaim to myself, 'What a happy creature am I!
How grateful I should be to Providence for bestowing on me such a husband!' And so, indeed, I am.
We will, Love, shortly be fifteen years married, and
I can answer that I never have had cause to repent
it. I have, darling, experienced all the happiness of
the married state without feeling any of its cares,
thanks to a fond and indulgent husband. . . ."

What a solicitous love she had for him is evident
from this practical letter, written about the same time,
when he was at the Cork assizes:

"MY DEAREST LOVE:
"I wish to God you could contrive to get out of
court for a quarter of an hour during the middle
of the day to take a bowl of soup or a snack of some
kind. Surely, though you may not be able to spare
time to go to a tavern, could not James get anything
you wished for from the Bar mess at your lodgings,
which is merely a step from the court-house? Do,
my heart, **try** to accomplish this; for, really, I am

quite unhappy to have you fasting from an early hour in the morning until nine or ten o'clock at night. I wish I were with you to make you take care of yourself."

It was always that practical devotion she had towards him. No wonder he could write to her: "You sweetest, know how miserable it makes me to be kept away from you, when all my happiness in this world rests in my family. . . . Lay it to your heart, darling, that there never was a woman so loved." Truly, marriage among the Irish is a great sacrament!

Nearly twenty years after their marriage O'Connell writes:

"MY HEART'S DARLING:

"I got your affectionate letter of Wednesday, and felt the extreme happiness of having so tender a partner of every care and every joy. I could write something like poetry to my own darling if I thought that it would express more strongly what I feel. I cannot tell you how my heart languishes to be with you, or express that kind of seething of the heart which I feel at being so long absent from you, but I will indeed hasten to meet you. . . ."

And after nearly a quarter of a century, he could write as if of "love's young dream":

"MY OWN AND ONLY LOVE:

"It was Kate wrote me the letter I got this morning, and I do most tenderly love Kate. Yet, sweetest

Mary, I could have wished to see one line also in that handwriting which gives me recollections of the happiest hours of my life, and still blesses me with inexpressible sweetness and comfort when we, darling, are separated. All the romance of my mind envelops you, and I am as romantic in my love this day as I was twenty-three years ago, when you dropped your not unwilling hand into mine. Darling, will you smile at the love-letters of your old husband? Oh, no; my Mary—my own Mary will remember that she had the fond and faithful affection of my youth, and that, if years have rolled over us, they have given us no cause to respect or love each other less than we did early in life. At least, darling, so think I. Do not smile, either, at the mere circumstance of not getting a letter making me somewhat melancholy. It is so cheering to my heart to hear from you—it is so delicious to me to read what you write, that indeed I cannot but feel lonely when I do not read your words."

It was a happy life they lived at Derrynane on the Kerry coast. O'Connell lived among his tenants like a feudal chief. His home was at all times filled with guests. There was always hospitality, and always the spirit of religion. The Chaplain occupied the place of honor. There was the family chapel, and there all the members of the household met in daily prayer. Through it all was infused the spirit of Mary O'Connell. She was the head of the family, the guide even of the great Liberator himself. Her heart was fixed on her husband and her children. It was from watching her that O'Connell knew what influence a good mother has. On one occasion his son-in-law, Charles Bianconi, asked his advice about sending his daughter away to school. "Oh, no, no, no," answered O'Connell; "never take her from her mother. Get a governess to assist her mother in little Kate's education, but never take the child from the mother's care. The tender affection of the mother educates the daughter's heart."

But Mary O'Connell was more than a guide to her children. She was her husband's strength in times of difficulty. In 1830, when he refused a peerage, she wrote him this letter:

"MY DEAREST LOVE:

"Thank God you have acted like yourself, and your wife and children have more reason to be proud of you than they ever were. Had you acted differently from what you have done, it would have broken my heart. You can't abandon the people, who have always stood by you, and for whom you have sacrificed so much. You will, darling, be rewarded for all; you will have the prayers and blessings of your country to cheer and console you for what you have given up. Had you been betrayed into acceptance of the terms offered by the government, you would die of a broken heart before six months expired.

"You now stand firmly in the affections and in the love of your countrymen, and when that country is aware of the splendid sacrifice you have now made for them, depend upon it, they will strain every nerve to reward you. I shall hold up my head higher than ever I did. I sha'n't be afraid to look at the people, as I certainly should if you were a titled prisoner of the government.

"I sha'n't say a word, as they give you their sentiments, their respective signatures attached. I never saw anything like the pleasure that danced in their eyes when assured of your refusal. May God bless you, my own love. Words are inadequate to tell you how much I love and respect you for this late act, so like and so worthy of yourself. My heart overflows with gratitude and pride for being the wife of such a man and the mother of such grateful children.

"The report through town yesterday and to-day is that you are to be the new Master of the Rolls. You may rely on our discretion, though we long to have the great news public. What a welcome you will get from the people of Ireland! May God bless and protect you. You will carry the Repeal of the Union without bloodshed, as you did the Emancipation. I put my trust in that God who sees and knows the purity of your heart. I can't write more here, there are so many in and out. With love from your children, believe me, always with truth,

"Your fondest and most grateful

"MARY O'CONNELL."

[335]

No wonder O'Connell was proud of her, a wife who could rejoice to see him refuse a peerage! No wonder that he dreaded to lose this great prop. When she was lying on her bed of death he wrote to his friend, Richard Barrett:

"God help me! My beloved is in a state of much suffering, and daily losing ground. I do most potently fear she cannot recover. She may linger. One week may— O God, help me! The purest spirit that ever dwelt in a human breast. She did not believe in the existence of evil. I am incompetent or too womanish and too weak to do my public duty, and that is what she would condemn. But I think I can rally. She would advise me to devote my energies, even in misery, to Ireland. I need not smile, for that would resemble a crime; but what am I writing! Only, after all, my great consolation will be a dogged and determined activity in the cause of Ireland."

After she died, in October, 1836, he wrote: "I can never again know happiness, and every day convinces me more and more of that fact." At that time he said at a temperance meeting in Belfast: "I am a father, and I know what it is to respect as well as love those whom, in paternal language, I call my angel daughters. They have never given breath to a word of offence against me; they have always been dutiful and kind to me; their affection soothes every harsher moment of my life; and whatever storms I may be engaged in abroad, when I return home I have, as it were, attendant angels waiting about me and cheering me on to renewed exertion. But that subject brings me back to a being of whom I dare not speak in the profanation of words. No, I will not mention that name. The man who is happiest in his domestic circle may have some idea of what my happiness was. Yes, I was her husband then— Did I say was? Oh, yes, I am her husband still. The grave may separate us for a time, but we shall meet again beyond it, never, I trust, to be separated more."

No wonder that, after her death, he seemed like a different man. She had been the only being to whom he could unbosom himself, and her death was a shock from which he never recovered. He often adverted to her memory. Towards the end his fits of despondency were frequent, and death was welcome.

The year after her death he wrote: "I never had so much reason to remain in this country as long as I can, save 'the aching void left craving at my heart.' I can never again know happiness, and every day convinces me more and more of that fact." Later on he said of her:

"She sleeps in an abbey ruin which rears its mouldering head above the ever-dashing billows of the Atlantic—a wild but sublime resting-place, typical alike of the past and present fortunes of Ireland, once resounding to the choral hymn of praise, now crumbling and desolate. Swept by the storms and deluged by the spray of the wintry ocean, which bathes its rocky foundations, it bids defiance to time, preserves the memory of the past, the relics of ages of piety, and the ashes of the faithful repose within those desolate but consecrated walls. *Requiescat in pace!*"

So she passed, that great wife and mother, with a blessing of love to him, her idol, a blessing which he called "an angel's shield." One of their daughters wrote:

"My mother was exactly the wife to suit my father in every way. She was devotedly attached to him, and she sympathized with him as thoroughly in his public as in his private life. She knew that it was necessary for the success of affairs, both of law and politics, with which his mind was occupied continually, that he should never be troubled with household affairs; and she therefore, while regulating her family with the greatest exactness, took care never to harass him with any of her domestic troubles, as so many unthinking women are in the habit of doing. On the contrary, she endeavored to arrange matters so that he should never find anything but peace and repose at his own fireside."

Mary O'Connell was, indeed, a tower of strength to the great Liberator. And surely, in being that, she rendered an invaluable service, not only to him, but to Ireland and the faith. Father Ventura, in his famous eulogy of O'Connell, a eulogy that took four hours to deliver, mentioned the share which the Irish women had in what he accomplished.

"Not a little singular, too," said he, "was the enthusiasm, the fidelity, and the affection with which, by his disinterestedness, his charity, and his zeal on behalf of liberty and religion, he had succeeded in inspiring the women of Ireland. This feminine enthusiasm contributed not a little to that great moral force by which he controlled his countrymen. Let those learn this truth, who, devoid of foresight, mentally blind, and with hearts steeled to every softer feeling, consider themselves alone qualified to govern mankind, of whose nature they are ignorant. Let them learn that when an idea, whether political or religious, conceived by the intellect of man, once finds its way into the heart of woman and there becomes a sentiment, its power increases so prodigiously that no resistance to it will avail.

"The women of Ireland, then, were on the side of O'Connell, whom they looked on as the sole supporter and vindicator of their common country and religion. They it was who maintained in vigor that affection towards him which existed in the hearts of the fathers, husbands, and sons, and which strengthened and encouraged them cheerfully to submit to every sacrifice for the sake of their common Liberator."

Of that glorious tribute to Irish womanhood, Mary O'Connell should have the greatest part, for without her the O'Connell that we know would have been impossible.

After the winning of Emancipation the Liberator was called "the Uncrowned King of Ireland." If so, surely she deserved to be called the Queen, that humble mother who hid herself from the world and found her dearest throne in the hearts of her husband and her children. Surely she was a great wife and mother, such as that other of whom Holy Scripture says: "The heart of her husband trusteth in her, and he shall have no need of spoils. She will render him good, and not evil, all the days of her life. . . . Her children rose up, and called her blessed; her husband, and he praised her."

LADY GEORGIANA FULLERTON

(1812-1885)

CARDINAL NEWMAN had very little association, either personally or in writing, with Lady
Georgiana Fullerton; yet in a few words he has left
one of the best tributes ever paid to her. When Mrs.
Craven, that other great Catholic who with her pen
so well served her religion, was writing the life
of her dear friend, Lady Fullerton, he wrote to her
that since he had become a Catholic he had looked
upon Lady Fullerton "with reverence and admiration for her saintly life." That was a great deal,
coming from the saintly Newman. And then he
wrote what may be considered a suitable epitaph for
her, calling her "a fit representative of those ladies
of rank and position in society who, during the last
half-century, have thought it little to become Catholics by halves, and who have devoted their lives and
all they were to our Lord's service."

Their lives and all they were to God's service! To
no one can these words be better applied than to
Lady Fullerton, "one of the simplest and humblest
souls ever seen, perhaps, outside the walls of a cloister." Born of a family in which gentility had been

[341]

for centuries an inheritance, having an assured social position in the most exclusive set, a woman of extraordinary literary talent, an admirable musician, a linguist,—a woman, in short, of the most exquisite culture, she was, in spite of all that, the humblest and most grateful of Catholics, using social position, literary talent, her life and all she was to glorify God and to help her neighbor.

Lady Fullerton raised an enduring monument to her own fame in the many books she wrote. She is not read to-day perhaps as much as she should be by the Catholics to whom she gave all her talents; nevertheless, we believe that much of her work will live on account of its real beauty and its honesty of sentiment.

But we are not making here a literary study of this great woman. Rather do we wish to review her life as an example of the saintly wife and mother, a mother that suffered the greatest affliction a mother can suffer, yet used even her sorrow to bring her soul nearer to God. All cannot be great writers, but all can imitate her humility, her immolation of self, her life of prayer and penance, her charity to the poor, her zeal for God's Church—in a word, her complete submission to the will of God.

Her maiden name was Georgiana Charlotte Leveson-Gower. Her father was Lord Granville Leveson-Gower, the youngest son of the first Marquis of Stafford. He was created Viscount Granville in 1815, and Earl Granville in 1833. Her mother was Lady

Harriet Cavendish, an excellent woman, daughter of
the fifth Duke of Devonshire. When the little Georgiana was born in 1812, she came to a family that was
allied to the finest English aristocracy, with an ancestry on both sides that had been of importance in the
service of their country. Among her near relatives
were the Dukes of Norfolk, of Beaufort, of Suther-
land, of Westminster, of Argyll, and of Leinster, and
the Earls of Carlisle, of Harrowby, and of Ellesmere.
It was in every way an excellent family, not in rank
only, but in the real things of life,—in honor, in virtue, in affectionate and sacred family life. With all
this nobility and fortune, there was no nonsense in
that family. Georgiana's mother, the Countess Granville, was a great lady, a woman of fine culture, a
woman of society, but also of a great sense of responsibility in the bringing up of her children. Her chief
care was not for their social advancement, but for
their education as good men and women and practical
Christians. She had a fine reverence for the things of
religion. She placed the two girls, Georgiana and
Susan, under the care of an excellent governess, who
did not scruple to make them endure what even poor
children would consider hardship.

"I used to be kept awake by the iciness of my feet
in bed," wrote Georgiana later; "but as I was the
strongest of girls, I was ashamed to complain of it.
Our food, too, was of a very austere description, and
we had not very much of it."

Even in those days the character of the woman who

later on sought to be a saint was being formed. But she was far from being pious. She was having a good time, and religion had no special attraction for her. The family was, of course, Protestant, and their religion was mostly an external thing that had little appeal to the affections. They went to church on Sundays, had their morning and evening prayers, and read their Bible daily. Religion was not that gripping thing which it is to the Catholic. Yet even in those childhood days the little Georgiana, in the midst of her dances and her other good times in a luxurious home, was troubled with a sense of sin, so much so that she was scrupulous over the smallest faults.

When she was eleven years old, her father, Viscount Granville, was sent as ambassador to the Hague. But he remained there only a short time, being transferred as ambassador to France. There he remained for four years, and it may be seen that the association of Georgiana with the religion of France in those impressionable years from twelve to sixteen must have had an influence upon her life, even though she little suspected it. It was a pleasant life for a young girl, being introduced to royalty, and seeing all the fine people that came to her father's house.

When she was sixteen her father returned with his family to England, and there they remained three years, during which time the young girls made their début in English society. In 1831 Lord Granville was reappointed ambassador to France. Georgiana was now nineteen, and spent in Paris the next ten years of her life. It was a position to turn the head of a girl, admitted as she was to the best society, welcomed at court, and soon an intimate friend of Queen Marie Amélie and her family. The life at the embassy was brilliant; there were always the best people there, the leading men of the day, and Georgiana loved the excitement. It was good to be alive in those days. "Georgy likes going out," said her mother of her. No wonder! Any girl in her position would have enjoyed to the full such a life. And yet it did not spoil her. Better than the social whirl did she love the family circle, loved to be with her mother, sewing and talking, loved to welcome home to the embassy her brothers when they came on a visit, and preferred to ride with them rather than go to the most brilliant reception in the gay capital.

In 1833 her sister Susan married Lord Rivers, and the parting of the two sisters who had been inseparable, and who had loved each other tenderly, was the first break in what had been a life of calm. But the separation was made endurable from the fact that Georgiana, too, was at that time looking forward to her own marriage. She was in love with Alexander George Fullerton, and he with her. He was then an officer in the Guards, and was heir to his father's estates in England and Ireland. But Lord Granville wanted the marriage postponed indefinitely, as he did not think young Fullerton had enough income to support his daughter in the style to which she had been accustomed. Georgiana, though she felt keenly the disappointment, did not oppose her father's decision. She agreed to wait. She did not have to wait long, however, for her uncle, the Duke of Devonshire, took a hand in the matter, and out of his love for the young people helped to arrange things so that it was decided that young Fullerton should resign from the army and live with his wife at the embassy, where they would be of great service in helping in the affairs of the Ambassador.

So they were married in July, 1833. It was a marriage of the greatest happiness. They were devoted to each other then, and as devoted at the end, after a life of more than fifty years together in joy and sorrow. We get a glimpse of Georgiana's happiness in those days when, a few months after her marriage, she wrote:

"I am in truth the happiest person in the world in every way. I suppose my husband is not perfect, for no one is in this world, but he is certainly very nearly so. His unutterable gentleness is joined to great firmness and the gaiety of a child. He loves application, and has need of occupation which does not let him be a moment idle. If, with such a teacher as he is, I do not acquire a love for occupation, I shall certainly be incorrigible. I don't think there is happiness on earth equal to mine. I love him in a way which makes me tremble, for he is all I have in the world."

It was surely one of the marriages made in heaven. Under God, Lady Fullerton owed all that she became to the excellent man who for more than half a century was her companion, her strength, and her leader into the Catholic Church.

Her cup of joy, already full, was overflowing with the birth of her son, a year after her marriage. Her husband and her baby gave Georgiana a new view of life. She began to think more of the things of eternity, now that her life was settled, and the gay social times made less of an appeal to her. No doubt this beginning of serious thought was due in a great measure to the serious thought of her husband. Indeed, it was a time when religion was being revived in England. The year before her marriage the Oxford movement had begun. The spirit of Newman and his great associates was putting life into the dead body of the Anglican Church. The cultured people were reading the *Tracts for the Times* and listening to those sermons of Newman that struck a strange note; and it is not surprising that Lady Georgiana and her husband were among the most interested. Religion became for them a serious matter. Added to this influence was a visit which she made with her husband to Genoa and Turin, where she was edified by Catholic society, and where for the first time in her life she came upon a Catholic book. It was the *Introduction to a Devout Life* of St. Francis de Sales. All these things were preparing her soul for the great grace of conversion, which did not come, however, for some years. But her increased devotion to the religion of the church in which she had been baptized turned her attention to the poor. And even as a Protestant she began that work of charity to which, in one form or another, her whole life was to be devoted. She found plenty of opportunity among the poor of Paris, and she did not spare herself.

"My child," said her mother to her one day as the young wife came home looking worn out, "you work yourself too hard."

"Mamma," said Georgiana, "we can never work too hard for God."

That might be taken as the motto of her life as a Catholic.

When Lord Granville resigned the ambassadorship in 1841, the family went to travel on the Continent. It was on this journey that the first suffering came into the life of Lady Fullerton, in the illness of the child she so adored.

"I do not know," she wrote, "how I could bear the anxiety about a child so fearfully precious, without the deep conviction I have in the goodness of God and of His boundless power, if He wills, to spare the life of my only child, as He often raises up children for whom we have never trembled."

God did spare the life of the child then, but only to make the cross heavier a few years later, when by his death the very heart of the mother was crushed forever.

One sees the hand of God in the journey made at that time. The family spent the winter at Rome, and the sight of the Eternal City made a lasting impression upon Lady Fullerton. But the visit was of

greater importance to her husband. He had been looking into the doctrines of the Catholic Church, but even
his wife did not know of his investigations. He did
not trouble her with his doubts. He was attending
to the affairs of his own soul.

One thing that made a deep impression upon him
during this visit to Rome was the conversion of Alphonse Ratisbonne.

Ratisbonne was a bigoted Jew. One day he entered the Church of S. Andrea delle Fratte with a
friend who was showing him about Rome. The
Comte de la Ferronnays, the father of Countess
Craven, who was later to be such a friend of Lady
Fullerton and also her biographer, was to be buried
from that church the following day, and the friend of
Ratisbonne went to speak to some of the priests in
regard to the funeral. While he was absent, our Lady
appeared to Ratisbonne. He was converted immediately, and the incident created a sensation in Rome.
This story, when told to Fullerton, had a great effect
on him, and no doubt hastened his conversion. When
his wife and her family left Rome in the middle of
April, he remained behind, and was received into the
Catholic Church at the Gesu. He then rejoined the
travelers, and told his wife the story of his conversion.
Needless to say, she was shocked at the news, since
she had not even suspected that he was under instruction. They had ever been of one mind in everything,
and now came the separation. There was something

to stand between them and their love, even though that something was religion.

Would Lady Fullerton ever have become a Catholic if her husband had not shown the way? It is hard to say. But even then her soul was torn with doubt. It was a great deal for a Protestant of her position to think of becoming a Catholic. It was against all the traditions of her family and the society of which she was an intimate. She longed for the truth, yet when it came to the decision she almost prayed to find the Catholic faith false. "Great was the struggle, fierce the fight," she writes in describing her search for truth.

And during this struggle she began her first novel. The chief motive she had in writing was to get money for her poor. Indeed, writing was never really a pleasure for her. It was a task. Later on she wanted to lay down her pen to avoid the temptation of pride, but she was prevailed upon to continue it as a duty, so that she was never moved by the mere desire of literary glory.

Her first work was *Ellen Middleton,* a book which, strangely for a Protestant writer, preached the necessity of confession and the crying need of the soul for absolution from sin. The novel created a furore at once. Georgiana Fullerton awoke one day to find herself famous. Gladstone reviewed it at length and gave it unlimited praise. He was enthusiastic about the new writer, but afterwards, when she became a Catholic, he almost cut her. All the great critics were em-

phatic in their commendation of the book; even Miss
Martineau praised it. In fact, everybody spoke well
of it, so much so that it went through many editions
and was translated into foreign languages. It did for
the people what the scholarly men of the Oxford
movement did for the learned: it gave them a longing for the Catholic life, which the author, even while
she was a Protestant, had delineated in her book.
And no doubt it brought many souls into the Catholic
Church.

The writer of this book was evidently on her way
into the Church; yet her conversion did not take place
until two years afterwards. The book had appeared
in 1844; in the October of the next year Newman was
received into the Catholic Church. His conversion
had disturbed many minds. It was the time of great
converts—Newman, Faber, Hope, Manning, Wilber-
force, the Duchess of Norfolk, the Duchess of Buc-
cleuch, the Marchioness of Lothian, the Marchioness
of Londonderry; from the universities, from society
they came to follow the light of their conscience. No
doubt the conversion of Newman helped to disturb the
mind of Lady Fullerton also. The family knew
whither she was tending, and her mother dreaded the
step because Lord Granville was in failing health, and
it was feared that if Georgiana became a Catholic it
would be a great shock to him. Not that even her love
for her father would have deterred Lady Fullerton,
once she saw her duty. She would have followed the
direction of God even though it meant a shock that

would kill her father. But the grace did not come until two months after his death. She finally saw the light, and was received into the Catholic Church on Passion Sunday, 1846. She was then not quite thirty-four years of age, and had been married nearly thirteen years.

It had been a hard trial for her to make up her mind. Her family had tried to dissuade her, especially Lady Rivers, the sister she so loved. But there was nothing mean in their opposition. They merely could not understand. Once the step was taken, there were no reproaches; and her relations with her family continued as intimate as ever, for they all loved her. But in her own heart she knew her gain. If anybody ever appreciated the gift of faith, it was she. One can imagine the joy of her husband when she whom he so loved was one in faith with him. Together they could now devote themselves to the education of their son. They were united more closely than ever, bonded together by religion. Their interests were now the same in everything.

Fullerton was a man of living faith, of practical charity, and of great service to the Church. He was greatly instrumental in bringing about the establishment of the Oratory in London in 1859, and also helped much in the establishment of the English branch of the Society for the Propagation of the Faith. His wife was heart and soul with him in all his pious projects, and even from the beginning went about the work of sanctifying her soul, going to confession twice a week, having a great devotion to that sacrament, for which she had longed even as a child outside the faith.

Georgiana now saw that her talent at writing was to be used for the faith. After her first literary venture, and while still a Protestant, she had wanted to write the life of St. Elizabeth of Hungary. But her mother had opposed it quietly, thinking that Georgiana was becoming too Catholic. The year following her conversion, she brought out her first novel as a Catholic, *Grantley Manor,* which, though absolutely Catholic, was greatly admired by her Protestant readers. It made its special appeal, however, to the Catholics, who rejoiced in this new writer of theirs, striking the Catholic note in a literature which, as Newman said, had become Protestant. Even the French Queen wrote that she thought it one of the most charming books she had ever read. Lady Fullerton was an untiring writer. The next year she gave to the world another book, *Ladybird,* also animated by the Catholic faith.

During those years of her first fervor there was little of interest outside her literary work and her devotion to religion. She was happy in her husband, happy in her young son growing to manhood, and happier still in the blessings of the faith. The only incident worthy of particular note is the visit which she, with her husband and son, made to Rome in 1851. She had been there eight years before, but the circumstances were entirely different now. She was a Catholic coming to the centre of the Catholic faith, and she enjoyed all that the city could offer to her deeply religious soul. The Catacombs, the shrines, the relics, the numberless wonderful churches, lifted her soul to Heaven. She herself describes it somewhat in her *Life of St. Francis of Rome,* which she wrote later on.

"To pass along the street, so often trod by holy feet in former and in latter days, and seek the church appointed for that day's station; to approach some time-worn basilica, or ancient sanctuary, without the city walls maybe, and, passing on the threshold, give one look at the glorious works of Almighty God in the natural world,—at the wide Campagna, that land-sea, so beautiful in its broad expanse and its desolate grandeur, at the purple hills and their golden lights and their deep-blue shadows, and the arched sky telling so vividly the glory of its Maker; and then slowly lifting the heavy curtain that stands between that vision of earthly beauty and the shrine where countless generations have come to worship; to tread under foot the green boughs, the sweet-smelling leaves, the scattered flowers, that morning strewn upon the uneven, time-trodden, time-honored pavement; bowing in admiration before the Lord in His tabernacle, to thank Him for the wonders that He has worked in His saints, for the beauty of the world of grace, of which that of the visible world is but the type and the shadow; and then move from one shrine to the other, wherever the lights upon the altars point the way, and invoke the assistance, the prayers of the saints whose relics are there displayed;—all this is one of those rare enjoyments which at once feed the soul and awake the imagination, and which the devout Christian can find in no place but Rome."

The visit strengthened her soul in its faith. And the time was coming when she would need all that faith.

Her son Granville, her only child, was now twenty years of age, a bright, intelligent youth and a favorite with everybody. He had been delicate in his young years, but apparently now had overcome all weakness, so much so that he entered the army and was waiting for his commission in the Grenadier Guards. As his grandmother, Lady Granville, wrote to Lady Fullerton about him: "He is full of gaiety, without being boisterous; his manner to me and to all is charming; every one loves him and speaks of his goodness and amiability." When he was so popular with all, no wonder his father and mother doted on him.

It was in 1855 that all their hopes were shattered. He had wanted to go to the Crimea, but the doctor had forbidden it, and the parents were delighted that they were to keep him. One day he went to pay a visit to his aunt, Lady Rivers. He was the life of the big country house, full of his cousins and friends of his own age. One evening he walked with one of his cousins, and was telling her of the plans he was making, of what his father was to do for him when he came of age, and how soon that would be, as he was so near twenty-one. The next day he died suddenly. Lady Rivers telegraphed to Cardinal (then Doctor) Manning, who lived close to the home of Lady Fuller-

ton. It was he who broke the news to the Fullertons.
It broke their hearts. The mother never spoke her
son's name again. No one ever uttered his name in
her presence. It was a grief that remained with her
all her life. His picture, even, was covered with a
veil; and when she was on her death-bed, an old
woman, she said, looking toward it, "I wish I had
the courage to draw it aside and look at him." It
was a grief buried deep in her heart, but she never
rebelled against God. "Thy will be done," was her
prayer and the prayer of her husband. Their resignation was perfect. Her son's death closed entirely the
heart of Lady Fullerton to the things of earth, and
drew her closer to Heaven.

When Father Faber, who had been her great consolation in those trying days, published his *Foot of
the Cross* in 1857, he dedicated it to her,—"To the
Lady Georgiana Fullerton this volume is inscribed in
affectionate remembrance of a season of darkness
which God consecrated for Himself by a more than
common sorrow." In her son's babyhood she had
given him the pet-name of "Dieu-donné," or "God-
given."

"Even to-day, in the midst of my grief," she wrote
shortly after his death, "I call thee still my child Dieu-
donné; God has taken back His treasure."

On the night before he had left her for the last time
she had gone with him to visit Father Faber at the
Oratory. A year afterwards she wrote to the priest a
letter which shows how she had sanctified her grief.

"DEAR FATHER FABER:

"My husband is deeply touched by your most kind and affectionate letter, and, from my heart, I thank you for it. The eve of St. Philip's day! the eve of the day when I saw my boy for the last time! It seems as if I had no leisure for grief now, and those with whom I labour are strangers for the most part to my former existence, in which joy and anguish are so strangely blent. I never hear his name, never speak of him now. I sometimes scarcely feel as if I were the same person I used to be, so absorbed has my life been by a wholly new direction, so dedicated to a special line of work and thought. But it is lying there in my heart, only buried deeper, the love, the grief, the purpose, formed in those days of sorrow, when I leant upon you, my dear, dear Father Faber. I never can forget what you did for me then. How wonderfully I see now God's fatherly hand in the removal of my child! What fearful dangers stood in his way, had he been left on earth! What fearful suffering it would have been to see him falter, if not fall, like others, in these days of trial! God has been very good to me. Pray for me, that I may not always be the 'whited sepulchre' which I feel myself to be, that I may not be unworthy of the teachings and example I am constantly receiving. Give me your blessing, and believe me ever gratefully and affectionately yours,

"GEORGIANA FULLERTON."

[357]

She sought to conquer her grief, to console and comfort her husband, who had been as stricken as herself, and now more than ever she devoted herself to the poor. Hers was not the character to indulge in selfish grief. Her martyrdom was known only to God.

How greatly she strove towards sanctity is evident in the spiritual diary she kept from time to time. Two years after the death of her son, we find her and her husband in Rome, where they both joined the Third Order of St. Francis. She wrote in her diary as follows:

Rome, May 4, 1857.

"Behold, now is the accepted time; behold, now is the day of salvation. To-morrow morning, the anniversary of my beloved child's last Communion, I am to be admitted into the Third Order of St. Francis, and I firmly purpose and intend, by God's grace, that it be the beginning of a new life, strictly dedicated to God and His service. In the first place, I renew the vow I made, with Father Faber's consent, nineteen months ago. Secondly, I make a firm resolution to practise poverty in every way in my power in everything, using such things as are poorest and oldest and cheapest, within the limits of discretion and what is due others; to consider my money as not belonging to myself, but to God and the poor; only to take for myself what is strictly necessary for dress and those things I have to pay for. Not to spend anything that is not directly or indirectly for the glory of God, lit-

tle presents of affection and kindness being, as I consider, included in the latter class. If I feel any doubt
on any question of that kind, to refer it to my confessor. To try not to allow in myself anything that
I am not obliged to that would be unbecoming in a
religious: over-excitement in conversation, complaint
at want of comforts, negligent and self-indulgent pos-
tures. To try, as much as possible in my position and
without neglecting any duty, to lead a religious life.
To do nothing from fancy or impulse, remembering
that 'patience is to seculars what the rule is to religious.' I will try, as the rule directs, to keep to two
meals a day. If I take anything else, to let it be only
a bit of dry bread. This I may be obliged to change
at times, but at present I will at all events keep to it.
To make a careful and attentive study of my rule,
observing every point of it, keeping to the spirit, if I
cannot to the letter, examining myself upon it, and noting down my transgressions. I will make my meditation to-morrow on the Five Wounds of Our Lord,
with ardent prayers to St. Francis to obtain for me
the five virtues of humility, obedience, mortification,
love of poverty and patience."

In this simple baring of her soul and its desires for
the things of God, we get a glimpse of the woman's
true greatness. And all the while she was using her
pen, producing those novels which in her time did so
much in furthering the cause of the Catholic Church.
She had a literary talent of a high order, and she
might have attained a higher rank in English literature

had she been content with merely a secular literary career. But that was so unworthy of her that she did not even give it a thought. Her writing was for God. She even turned her talent to writing in French, for she wrote that language as well and as easily as her mother-tongue. So we have from her pen such books as *Too Strange to Be True, A Stormy Life,* and *Mrs. Gerald's Niece,* a book which the Marquis of Ripon, who was cabinet minister in Gladstone's administration, said had finally convinced him of the truth of the Catholic faith. She also wrote *A Will and a Way* and *Rose Le Blanc* and *La Comtesse de Bonneval* in French, which she then translated into English. She also translated many other works. Her last novel was *Constance Sherwood,* a story of the persecutions under Elizabeth, and one of the most accurate historical novels in the language. Besides her novels, she wrote the *Life of St. Francis of Rome,* to which she added sketches of Blessed Lucy of Narni, Blessed Dominica of Paradiso, and Anne de Montmorency; also the *Life of Luisa de Carvajal,* the *Life of Father Henry Young,* and other books which there is no need of mentioning. It is a great list, and is well worth reading even to-day.

One sees from that long list what a busy woman Lady Fullerton was. And yet her writing did not occupy all her time. She always found time for works of charity, and, above all, time to give to the worship of God in her prayer and meditation. She was in everything thoroughly Catholic, wondering at the goodness of God in giving her the Catholic faith. When Lady Herbert of Lea came into the Church, Lady Fullerton wrote to her: "I have now been just nineteen years a Catholic, and never ceased to wonder with an adoring heart at the infinite mercy of God in bestowing on one so unworthy as myself that blessed gift of faith not vouchsafed to so many who would make a better use of it."

Her humility is seen in that statement. She wished ever to keep in the background. Even after she had begun her works of charity she would retire and let some one else take the glory of them. All she cared about was to do the work. And so we find her going out among the poor, bringing them not only gifts of money, but even sweeping their rooms, making the beds, happy to do the most menial tasks for the glory of God. She would go on foot to save a few cents' cab-fare, in order that she might have more for her poor. Every penny she got hold of went to the poor, and when she had none of her own she would go out begging from her friends so that she might not have to turn anybody away. She was not a rich woman, and even though her husband was wealthy, she did not often beg from him, for she knew that he had his own charities to care for, and, moreover, she wished to live the life of a poor woman.

Her whole life may be summed up in the statement that she wished to serve others. After her son died, she retired almost absolutely from the world. Society had no charm for her when her boy was gone. It had

less charm for her now, after all the years spent in
religious exercises, in visits to the poor, in writing
her many books. But her spiritual director suggested
to her that it was her duty to go out into society in
order to work for the faith among the people of her
own social position. She had no inclination for re-
newing social life, yet she did it, and tried to take
an interest in passing things, in current literature, in
visits, all for the purpose of being able to do something to bring others nearer the Church. She never
denied herself to others. Even in the midst of her
writing, if some one came to see her, even if a beggar
called, she was always willing to put aside what she
was doing in order to attend to what she considered
a greater charity.

One little incident shows her perpetual desire to
serve others. She was an excellent musician and had
studied under Liszt, becoming so talented that her
brothers would keep her playing the piano for hours
at a time. When her son died, she closed the piano.
But years afterwards she took up her music again,
solely that she might give pleasure to others.

It is not strange that a woman with such consideration for others even in these simple things should
be active in what may be called great works of charity—institutional charities, as distinguished from her
personal visits and gifts to the poor. Lady Fullerton
really loved the poor, and reverenced them. Her
mother had been very charitable and was always
working for the poor. So no one ever heard Lady

Fullerton finding fault with them and blaming them for their condition; rather did she consider the great temptations that assailed them. But a charity that appealed to her more than all others was the care of the orphans. She was the life of the charity that took the little ones and prevented them being brought up Protestants. There was one little orphan asylum humbly founded by two poor working girls who had taken some orphan children into a couple of rooms. The girls worked for the support of these orphans; sometimes they did not have a cent. Yet God came to their help, and among the friends He sent them was Lady Fullerton, who not only gave of her money, but also gave her personal help and even wrote a booklet giving an account of this humble charity.

A sample of her charity is given in a letter written by a gentleman to Mr. Fullerton after the death of Lady Georgiana. It came from Mentone, where she used to spend the winter.

"Every year," he wrote, "the venerated Lady Georgiana passed about three months in this town, and during that time her every thought and every occupation turned upon works of charity. There were very few poor in those days who were not benefited by her. She set an example of true humility, and none who saw her, always plainly dressed, carrying relief and comforts to the poor and sick in the dark and narrow alleys of the town, would have believed that one so simple and unassuming belonged to one of the first families of the English nobility."

But all these charities may be called side issues with her; for she desired to establish some charity that would live after her. And it was due principally to her efforts that the Community of the Poor Servants of the Mother of God was established. She worked for this in season and out, and even parted with her most cherished jewels to keep the work going. If she had done nothing else, her name would be worthy of remembrance. Yet she did not seek to be honored as the founder; she was content to be known as the inspirer of it. The woman who was associated in this work with her was Mother Mary Magdalen Taylor, the daughter of an Anglican minister, who had been a nurse in the Crimean war under Florence Nightingale. She had been so edified by the Catholic soldiers in the practice of their faith, that when she returned to England she entered the Catholic Church. Her intimacy with Lady Fullerton in charitable work in London finally led to the establishment of the community, of which she became the Superior-General. There are many houses now of that community in England and Ireland, every one of them a jewel in the crown of Lady Fullerton.

It would take a large book to describe all the charities of this great woman. Every moment of the day she was thinking of somebody else. Even as early as 1850 she had opened a school for poor Catholic children, the beginning of many such schools. When she came to settle in London she went to the priests and learned from them the needs of the poor in the neighborhood and began at once to visit them. If she could not go herself to them, she would send some one to take her place. And this led to her work, with other ladies, in bringing to London from Paris the Sisters of St. Vincent de Paul. She was always particularly fond of children. A friend of hers used to say, "Lady Georgiana goes only to the three S's—the sick, the sorrowful, the sinful." Even on her deathbed her thoughts were of the poor that needed help.

Her last illness was a long one. From May to January she lay in bed, and then finally the summons came, and she passed away without a sigh on the nineteenth of January, 1885.

The sorrow at the death of Lady Fullerton was universal. She had lived a long life, her name was a household word through her books and her charities. Everybody loved her, and it was felt by all that she never could be replaced. In the many letters that came to the faithful and loving husband after her death there breathes nothing but love and sorrow that the world had lost one of its saints.

And surely, as we read the journal she kept in her retreats, as we read her diary, even if we had no knowledge of her outward life of devotion to the service of the Church and the poor, we come to the conclusion that Lady Fullerton was a saintly woman. Her one great prayer to God was: "Make me a saint." To this end her life was ordered. Her prayers and meditations, her spiritual readings, her visits to the Blessed Sacrament—all seem more the works of a nun in her convent than of a woman of the world. It was a life of penance as well as of prayer. She used the discipline on herself, denied her appetite, sought occasions to mortify herself. She lived for God alone. Hers was a life of personal sacrifice. There was no one to whom the world held out more. She was a woman of great talent, of fine family, to whom a high position in society was assured. Yet she put it all aside to lead, as far as she could, the life hidden with Christ in God.

God demanded a great deal of her. He took away her first-born son, whom she loved devotedly, yet she submitted to His will, and only drew nearer to the hand that had struck her. A devoted wife of fifty years, a loving mother, who saw God's mercy even in the death of her son, what an example of love and faith is she to the wives and mothers of all time!

MARGARET HAUGHERY

(1814–1882)

A S we read the story of the great women who
have merited a place of honor in the history
of the Church, we discover one attribute that is common to them all—charity. No matter what the position they occupied in the world, whether of high or
low degree, the epitaph of every one of them could
be this: "She was kind to the poor." They loved
God with all their hearts; hence, too, they loved their
neighbor. "Religion clean and undefiled before God
and the Father," says St. James (Epistle i, 27), "is
this: to visit the fatherless and widows in their tribulation, and to keep one's self unspotted from this
world."

Practical charity has ever been a characteristic of
our women. They do not talk much about social
service, and uplift, and philanthropy. With them
charity is a part of "religion clean and undefiled."
When there is work to be done, they say nothing, but
at once put their hand to it. It is not a condescension
on their part. They are the honored ones, not the
poor who furnish them with this means of sanctifi-

cation. Nothing is menial if it be for the glory of God.

In an old chronicle of the eleventh century we read that when a certain church was building, Bertha, the mother of St. Eberhard, who had been archbishop of Salzburg, carried stones on her shoulders, walking barefoot half a mile. And again, in those same ages of faith, we read that once, when an abbey in England was burned, everybody helped in the reconstruction. "Nor must we forget," says the monk who tells the story, "among so many benefactors, Juliana, a poor old woman of holy memory at Weston, who out of her poverty gave us all her living, namely, some yarn and spinning thread to make vestments for the brethren of our monastery."

Poor old Juliana! How little she thought that with her gift of thread and yarn she was purchasing immortality! Somehow, God never forgets the widow's mite.

But this sacrifice of self was not alone a virtue of the middle ages. It is of all ages, as long as we have the poor with us; and that is always. There are many manifestations of it. Mrs. Craven interested her friends in private theatricals to raise money for the poor. Mrs. Taigi, herself poor, went out begging for those more destitute than herself. Lady Fullerton wrote her books so that she might have more to bestow upon the needy. She would even walk long distances to save the cab-fare for them. Orphans particularly appealed to her. One asylum in which she

was especially interested was a very humble one founded by two poor working girls. They had nothing
themselves, and worked hard for a living. But they
saw the needy orphans about them, and, having a
couple of rooms, they took as many children as they
could, and supported them out of what was scarcely
enough to maintain themselves. What a lesson in
charity from these two poor working girls! What
humble instruments God sometimes uses to do His
work! One realizes, then, that it is not the human
effort, but the grace of God, which accomplishes the
task. God gives the increase!

In this respect there is nothing more striking than
the story of Margaret Haughery of New Orleans,—
"Our Margaret," as a grateful community loved to
call her. It is a simple story, yet a thrilling one, an
inspiration for every woman, rich or poor, to the life
of charity which God has made the condition of eternal happiness.

Margaret's maiden name was Gaffney, and she was
born in the County Cavan, Ireland, in 1814. Her parents, Charles and Margaret (O'Rourke) Gaffney, like
so many of the Irish people, determined to seek their
fortune in the New World. They were young and
strong and ambitious, and so they bade farewell to
their native land, and with little Margaret, their only
child, set sail for America. But the voyage that looked
so promising ended disastrously. Both of the immigrants were stricken with the terrible yellow fever,
then of frequent occurrence, and died soon after in

Baltimore in 1822, leaving behind the little orphaned Margaret, who in the years to come was to be known as the "Mother of Orphans."

But she was far from giving promise then of ever being a notable character. A homeless child of little more than seven years, her outlook on life was not a rosy one. It was a sad condition, one she never forgot, a memory that was the inspiration of her life.

On the same boat that had brought the Gaffneys to America there was a Welsh couple with whom they became very friendly. When the stricken parents knew that their end was near, they begged their new friends to be good to the little girl, soon to be left alone in the world. The kind-hearted couple, though different in religion—they were Baptists—promised to take the orphan, and thus little Margaret found a home with truly charitable people. The character of this good man and woman may be judged from the fact that they were faithful to their trust, and brought up Margaret in the Catholic faith. They did the best they could for her, and she was ever faithful to their memory; but they were poor and struggling themselves, and while they fed and clothed her and sheltered her from public charity, they were unable to give her an education. Very early in life she was thrown on her own resources, and never learned even to read or write, a fact that makes her great success in business all the more remarkable.

It was in 1835 that she married Charles Haughery. It was not a brilliant match. He was a poor, hard-

working man. But it must have seemed to the orphan
girl like the ending of all her troubles. In fact, however, they had only begun. The young husband began
to fail in health, and, thinking that a warmer climate
would benefit him, they left Baltimore and went to
New Orleans. But even with the change his health
did not improve. As a last resort he was advised to
take an ocean voyage, and so, leaving Margaret and
her young baby, he set sail for Ireland. She never
saw him again. He died in the Old Country, and she
was left again to struggle alone in the world. Another sorrow soon came in the death of her baby; and
now, a widow and childless, scarcely over twenty, she
faced life again with only the memory of a few
months' happiness.

But she was not the kind to sit and moan over her
sorrows. There was always a masculine energy in
her character, together with the womanly gentleness.
In one of the hotels of New Orleans she found employment as a laundress. It goes without saying that
her wages were small, scarcely enough to support herself. Under these trying conditions what chance had
she to do charity? Rather was she deserving of charity herself, a poor young widow, washing and iron-
ing for a bare livelihood. Yet in the midst of her
poverty she found pity for others. She thought of
the days when she herself was a helpless orphan dependent on charity. She thought, perhaps, of the baby
hands that had twined about her own heart. God
had taken her baby, but there were numberless other

babies in the world crying for a mother's love. She had the heart of a mother, and the orphans won it to their cause.

In those days, when the yellow fever was so prevalent, the city had more than its share of orphans. Epidemic followed epidemic, often taking both father and mother and throwing the children on the mercy of the world. The good Sisters of Charity, eager as they were to care for every homeless child, were hard pushed for accommodations and for the means to feed and clothe their charges. To Margaret Haughery, over her wash-tub and her ironing-board, there came from time to time the sad news that the Sisters of the orphan asylum were in hard straits. It was more than her big Irish heart could stand. If she could help, not one child should be turned away. If the asylum were too small, then a larger one should be built. And so, poor laboring woman that she was, she came to the Sisters and said to them, "I will do what I can to help you."

What could she do, indeed? It almost seemed ridiculous. But the good Sisters gladly accepted her proffered help. They little knew what wonderful things she was going to accomplish. In her spare hours, after her hard work in the hotel, she helped in the work of the orphan asylum. But that was not enough. To her sorrow, she saw that many of the children did not have enough to eat. But she did not waste any time in useless lamentation. She was too practical for that. She began to work for them, that they might have enough. Day after day she made the round of the hotels, and collected the discarded scraps of food. She brought them home and made them into palatable dishes for the orphans. Many a time, if it had not been for this, they would have gone to bed hungry. Besides that, she went out on the street to beg for them, and would carry the food and clothing she obtained in a wheelbarrow to the asylum.

But Margaret was not content with the small returns of begging. She had a business instinct and she turned it to account. Out of the few dollars which she had saved from her meagre wages she bought two cows and established a dairy on a small scale. She delivered the milk herself. No matter what the weather, she could be seen driving her wagon, dressed in her calico dress, a little shawl on her shoulders, and on her head the sunbonnet that was always characteristic of her. It was a humble beginning, but the prayers of the orphans brought a blessing upon the work.

By her interest in the asylum Margaret had won the love and admiration of the Superior of the Sisters of Charity, Sister Francis Regis Barret, who soon saw in the young widow an angel of mercy. Together they planned for a larger asylum. It was a big undertaking, but nothing is too big for those who have confidence in God. The larger asylum was built, and in ten years, thanks chiefly to Margaret and her dairy business, always increasing, it was freed from debt.

Margaret's business still increased. Money was made, and this money went to the orphans. The dairy was enlarged, and as the business increased, Margaret's charity also increased. Not content with the building of the orphan asylum, an infant asylum, which she called her "baby house," was erected, and then a training asylum for larger girls. And in all this work Margaret Haughery was the prime mover, the chief supporter.

Yet, in spite of all these charities, the thrifty widow found that from the proceeds of her dairy she had money to invest. Her widow's cruse seemed never to run dry, no matter how lavish she was with its contents. One of her creditors, to whom she had loaned money, failed. He was a baker, and Margaret was obliged to accept his bakery business in payment of the debt. It did not look promising, but nevertheless she determined to continue the business. She gave up the dairy and devoted all her energy to the bakery. It was as big a success as the dairy had been. She was soon a familiar figure driving the baker's cart.

Margaret's new business was a godsend to the asylums. She supplied them at a trifle, and, besides that, gave away countless loaves of bread to the poor all over the city. Not an efficient way to do business, apparently; yet somehow the bakery prospered marvelously. The more she gave away, the more she had. In a true sense, she cast her bread upon the waters and it returned to her. Soon she was obliged to increase her output. The bakery was enlarged to a factory run by steam, and was noted as the first steam-bakery in New Orleans.

Her bakery and herself became inseparable. There, in the doorway, she would sit and hold her court. She was filled with a sense of Irish humor and she loved to talk. No one passed her door without a word with her. From the bootblack to the banker, all found it worth while to talk with "Margaret," to consult her about their business, and to benefit from the wise advice she knew so well how to give. To all of them she was "Margaret." Some of them never knew what her other name was. She was just "Margaret," and they called her that with love and admiration. "Margaret, the Orphans' Friend"—that was the title which drew to her the affection of a grateful city. All saw in her a charity which had no bounds. Black or white, Jew or Gentile, Protestant or Catholic, all were her children if they needed help. "They are all orphans alike," she would say. She remembered that when she herself was a needy orphan it was a Protestant family that had kept her from public charity.

And not only did she help the orphan. Wherever there was need, there was she. Besides her aid in the building of the asylums for the orphan children, she gave her means and her wisdom also to the founding of a home for the aged and infirm. And more than that, St. Teresa's Church was virtually built by her and Sister Francis Regis. Indeed, there was no good work that appealed to her in vain.

And with her charity there went a genuine patriotism. During the dread days of the Civil War she fed many a hungry soldier. Confederate prisoners espe-

cially were objects of her solicitude. She gave them
her constant care. All the children that were left orphans by the death of their parents during those terrible days found in her a loving protector. Once she
went so far as to brave General Butler, and carried a
cargo of flour across the lines so that her orphans
might not be hungry.

It was the same spirit which she had shown during
the yellow fever epidemic of the fifties, a scourge she
had reason to remember, since, long before, it had
deprived her of father and mother. She did not fear
it, however. She went from house to house, bringing
comfort to the sick. Many a dying mother she con-
soled by promising that she would care for the children soon to be motherless. She was everywhere
when she was needed. During those days the periodi-
cal floods of the Mississippi brought desolation. After
the destruction came want. And Margaret, fearless,
with that masculine energy which went hand in hand
with gentleness, visited the submerged districts in a
boat loaded with bread to save the people from starvation.

So passed this simple yet heroic life. It had only
one inspiration—to do good to others. But, simple
as it was,—the life of a woman who could not read
or write; who, when signing her will, could only use
her mark,—it was such a life as to bring her universal
love and fame.

When she died, in 1882, the event was regarded as
a public calamity. All the papers in the city were

bordered with black in mourning for her. It seemed as if the whole city turned out to attend her funeral. The Archbishop, the Governor, the Mayor, the rich and the poor, all came to do honor to this noble, simple soul. It was a time of universal sorrow. No one could get used to the thought of her death. She was a very part of the city. It seemed strange that its life could go on without Margaret sitting there in her doorway.

The orphans especially had reason to mourn their friend. At her funeral there were hundreds of these little ones, coming from the eleven different asylums which had shared in her bounty. But they were not alone. Merchants, lawyers, judges, public officials, all considered it an honor to pay this last tribute to the unlettered woman who had been such an inspiration to their city and to the world.

She was buried in the same grave with Sister Francis Regis Barret, the Sister of Charity who had died in 1862, and who in the early days had been her co-worker for the poor.

When Margaret Haughery's will was read—the will which she had signed with her mark—it was found that all her money had been left to the poor. The asylums, no matter to what creed they belonged, were remembered; for, as she had said, "They are all orphans alike."

The admiration of the city of New Orleans was not a momentary one. So great was its esteem for Margaret, that the whole community resolved she should not be forgotten, and it was decided to erect a statue to her memory. The strange thing about it was that no subscription paper was passed. No one had to be asked. The money flowed in so fast that soon the committee had to give notice that there was more than sufficient for the purpose.

In a little more than two years after her death the statue was unveiled. It was a memorable occasion. There were congregated all the dignitaries of the city, and, more than all, the orphans whom she loved so well. One of the orphans pulled the cord that unveiled the statue. When the little ones beheld the friend they had known so well sitting there,—the familiar short, stout, good-faced woman, always so gentle and kind, sitting as she was accustomed to sit in the doorway of her bakery, in her simple calico dress and shawl, her arm about an orphan girl,—they shouted with joy, a cry that was taken up by the crowd that filled the streets. It was their "Margaret" back with them once more! That was the only name on the monument—just "Margaret"—but it told a story eloquent with sacrifice and love.

The speaker at the dedication thus summed up her work. "To those who look with concern upon the moral situation of the hour," said he in part, "and fear that human action finds its sole motive to-day in selfishness and greed, who imagine that the world no longer yields homage save to fortune and to power, this scene affords comfort and cheer. When we see the people of this great city meet, without distinction of age, rank, or creed, with one heart to pay their tribute of love and respect to the humble woman who passed her quiet life among us under the simple name of 'Margaret,' we come fully to know, to feel, and to appreciate the matchless power of a well-spent life. The substance of her life was charity; the spirit of it, truth; the strength of it, religion; the end, peace;— then fame and immortality."

The story of Margaret Haughery is one of the sweetest ever told. Her life is a lesson of love in charity which this age needs to learn. While philanthropists and social workers vainly talk about problems, she solved them; for she met those problems with the wisdom that came from the love of her big Irish heart. In her simple life we read again the lesson that there is but one way to become great in the Kingdom of God. And because she found that way, Margaret Haughery, the "Mother of the Orphans," is entitled to a high place among the great wives and mothers who have brought glory to the Catholic Church.

PAULINE CRAVEN

(1808-1891)

O F the numerous biographies by which the private records of society illustrate the century,"
says one of the biographers of Mrs. Craven, "few
so well prove that it is possible to live in the world
and yet be not of it."

One feels the truth of that remark in the story of
the lives of some of our great Catholic literary
women. Lady Fullerton, with her well-established
position in the innermost circles of London society,
with all her varied activities, with her interest in people and the affairs of the different countries in which
she lived, was at heart a Sister of Charity. It was the
same with Madame Swetchine. "Mother, sister,
friend, she was all to me," says Mrs. Craven of her
whose salon was ever open, who was a guide of such
men as Lacordaire in a critical time in the history
of Catholic France, yet who, amid all her work, was
a cloistered spirit. So with Vittoria Colonna, who
took an interest in all the big things of her day, who
was one of the leading characters in the Renaissance,
yet used all these things to sanctify her soul. To all

of these good and great women could be applied these words: "The kingdom of God is within you."

But to none are they more applicable than to the woman to whom Catholic society and Catholic literature, and in truth all true womanhood, owe so much— Mrs. Augustus Craven. Madame Swetchine, Lady Fullerton, Lady Herbert of Lea, and Mrs. Craven were contemporaries, and, more than that, there was a personal bond between them. They all had some kind of association with one another, so much so that in thinking of one, one thinks of all the others. Yet it is not the mere association of friendship that links their names together; it is the bond of the true faith, that faith for which all of them worked and for which they made so many sacrifices.

Of the four, Mrs. Craven was the only one that was born to the faith. She was also born to the best society of the world. She was welcomed by the finest people everywhere, in England, in France, in Italy. She had been referred to by her friends as a perfectly accomplished woman of the world, a finished actress in drawing-room comedy, a woman of shrewd political instincts, a singularly well read and cosmopolitan lady, and, as one man of the world remarked, the cleverest woman he ever met. Yet, more than all that, she was known as a woman of great faith, a woman to whom the only thing worth striving for was the glory of God.

She was born in London in 1808, the child of French parents who had emigrated from France at

the time of the Revolution and who during their exile
had more than their share of poverty and sacrifice.
Her father was the Comte Auguste Marie de la Ferronnays, who looked back to a noble line of ancestors,
and her mother, too, who was perhaps more remarkable in character than any of her wonderful children,
was of an historic family and more than noble blood,
a perfect wife and mother, who had been taught in the
school of sacrifice, and hence knew how to inculcate
religion and sacrifice in the hearts of her many children.   Eleven children were born to the de la Ferronnays, four of whom died in infancy.   In more
senses than one the Countess may be considered a great
mother.

After the long period of exile, brighter prospects
came with the Restoration.   The Count, who had always been a loyal friend of the Duc de Berri, returned
with him to France as his aide-de-camp, and his wife
was given a position of honor at the court.   All looked
bright until the Count resented an insult at the hands
of his friend the Duke, and immediately, being an
independent soul, left the Tuileries, never to return.
He had no money, no prospects, but he kept his honor.
The Duke made amends later on by having his old
friend appointed ambassador to St. Petersburg, a position he held for eight years.   The subject of our
memoir, then Pauline de la Ferronnays, was seventeen
years old at the time, a very attractive girl, who became at once popular at the Russian court.   The
family returned to Paris in 1827, when the Count was

made Minister of Foreign Affairs by special request of Charles X.

Pauline was nineteen when she took her place in the brilliant Paris society of that day. She was then a remarkably intelligent girl, whose head could not be turned, since she had known too well what hardship was and how uncertain is the favor of princes; a girl who had been reared in piety, and who found in her own family that love and devotion which have rarely been equaled in any family. Brilliant as society was then, with its fine writers, its Lamartines, its Châteaubriands, there was nothing that could replace for her the delights of her family circle. She was beautiful, vivacious, able to converse on every topic, and with a voice that was called by her friends golden. She was recognized as one of the best conversationalists of her day, and was, through her sojourn in different countries, a remarkably fine linguist.

So happy was she at home that she was in no hurry to choose a husband. But when she did, it was not to make what the world would call a fine match, but to choose according to her heart. In 1828 her father had a slight stroke, and on that account resigned his ministry. After traveling in northern Italy he was nominated as ambassador at Rome, and thither his family accompanied him. To Pauline that was a great incident in her life, perhaps the greatest, since it turned her heart in a special way to God.

She describes her first visit to the Catacombs: "My soul overflowed with thoughts. I could not resist the satisfaction of kissing those sacred stones before I returned to the church. When again in it, I knelt down and longed to remain there. I had felt emotions never before experienced by me. I owed them to the religion in which, happily, I was born. I felt the need of thanksgiving and of prayer to God that all my life should be an expression of my gratitude and of my love towards Him."

Sacrifice was again demanded of the family. When the "Revolution of the Three Days" broke out, the Count resigned his position, although he knew not how he was going to provide for his family. But the family was so used to changes through politics that they were not cast down, and they found their true happiness in the society of one another. Besides that, the Count had many good friends who helped him in tiding over the bad places. So that when they settled down in Naples for a time, it was to the full enjoyment of life. Naples must ever have been a dear place to Pauline, for it was here that her beloved brother Albert obtained his wife, the charming Alexandrine, who later became a Catholic and gave such evidence of a holy life that in many respects she is even more remarkable than her famous sister-in-law, and it was here, too, that Pauline herself met her fate in the person of Augustus Craven.

Augustus Craven was born in 1806, the son of Keppel Craven, whose mother, Lady Craven, later married to the Margrave of Anspach, had at her death left several estates to her son. Keppel Craven had occupied the position of adviser to Queen Caroline, the wife of George IV. His son, Augustus, had served in the army, and after that was attached to the British legation at Naples. He was at once attracted to Pauline de la Ferronnays, and she to him. He was handsome and accomplished and his tastes were similar to hers. But he was a Protestant, and his father, who was bitterly anti-Catholic, did not approve of the marriage, and even threatened to disinherit Augustus if he married the Catholic girl. But Augustus was just as determined, and the father finally had to withdraw his opposition. They were married in the summer of 1834, and went to Rome, where Augustus was at once received into the Catholic Church. He had waited until after his marriage to make his submission, so that his motives in becoming a Catholic would not be misunderstood. He became a Catholic from sincere conviction.

In 1836 the Cravens returned to England, and Pauline took her place in the most select English society. For her own sake as well as for that of her husband, she was interested in all social affairs, yet all the while her heart was with her own people. And no wonder. It was a family that would attract any one, even though not connected with it by ties of blood. It was Pauline's labor of love to make her family known in the *Sister's Story,* which she wrote later on. Religion dominated all, yet the family was one of the happiest and most talented. One could write a book about the brother Albert, who died from tuberculosis soon

after his marriage, so wrapt was his soul in spiritual
things; about his charming wife, Alexandrine, who
sacrificed great prospects to marry a poor young man.
It was one of the happiest marriages, even while it was
overshadowed by death from the very beginning.
Alexandrine had been a Protestant prejudiced against
the Church, but the prayers of her husband and his
earnest devotion finally converted her before his
death. Her short widowhood, for she died young,
was filled with prayer and charity. Reading the *Sister's Story,* one lingers over that model wife and husband; and also over the other two sisters of Pauline—
Eugenie, who died soon after her marriage, and the
sweet Olga, who died in the bloom of her youth.

Soon after the conversion of Alexandrine, Pauline
was summoned to Paris, where Albert was dying. It
was the first time she had come in contact with sorrow and death, and it had a chastening effect on her
whole life. It brought her nearer to God. The death
of Albert in his prime was a terrible loss, not only to
the young wife, but to all the members of the family.
It was an abiding sorrow, and was all the harder for
Pauline to bear in that her husband was made attaché
at Lisbon, and she had to go with him away from her
family when they most needed her consoling presence.
The Cravens remained in Lisbon eighteen months,
broken only by a short visit on her part to France
for the marriage of her sister Eugenie to Comte
Albert de Mun.

But that marriage, too, was not of long happiness.

The beloved Eugenie died soon after the birth of her second child, who was famous later as the Comte Albert de Mun. Shortly before that affliction her father had died in Rome, in 1842, an event famous in Catholic annals inasmuch as it was the occasion of the conversion of the bigoted Jew, Alphonse Ratisbonne, who attributed his conversion to the prayers of a man he had never known. Five months later her sister Olga died. Albert, Eugenie and Olga all died of consumption. A few months more, and to the list of the dead were added Albert's widow, the saintly Alexandrine, and finally Madame de la Ferronnays, the great mother of a great family. One after another, Pauline saw her beloved ones pass away. She was heart-broken over all these losses, but she did not become moody. With her strong faith, the dead became even nearer to her than they were in life. They served but to draw her nearer to God, so sweet was the memory of the sanctity which had animated all of them.

During the succeeding years in England she took an ardent interest in the Catholic revival, as she had also done in the Tractarian movement, which had brought so many great ones into the Church. She was always interested in politics, but the thing that interested her more than all else was the Church; for, like all her family, she was first and foremost a Catholic. And it was a practical interest she took. When the anti-Catholics in the House of Commons made an attack on the Church on the occasion of the restoration of conventual life in England, she sat down and wrote a pamphlet in which she showed the utter injustice of these men. The pamphlet created a sensation among her friends, who had always regarded her merely as a charming woman of the world, a devout but not a militant Catholic.

On the death of his father, Augustus Craven came into the possession of quite a fortune. He was a man of great accomplishments, and it was thought advisable for him to seek to be elected to Parliament. He gave up his diplomatic position, and he and his wife threw themselves into the work of electioneering. But it was a time of No-Popery agitation, and it did not help matters that Craven was a convert and his wife a militant Catholic; and so he was badly defeated, and with the loss of so much money that it virtually crippled them for the rest of their lives. England became distasteful to them because of this manifestation of bigotry, and they went to live at Naples. On the way Mrs. Craven renewed her associations with the great Madame Swetchine, an intimacy that continued till the death of the woman who had done so much for the faith to which she had been converted.

The Casa Craven at Naples soon became famous. Diplomatists of every nation, French friends, all were eager to belong to the charming society which gathered there. As Lady Drogheda once wrote: "I used to hear of Mrs. Craven's acting and her great social talents, and her virtues and admirable qualities, until I grew to believe that there was no one like her. The following year I learned to know and love her, and to look on her almost as a saint. It is all gone now, that brilliant and beloved society. There was no one like Pauline Craven; I think of her with tenderness no words can describe."

In Naples at that time there was much charity to the poor, and Mrs. Craven naturally became interested in the good work. As has been said, she had a great talent for dramatics, and so had her husband. They turned their house into a theatre, had a stage erected, and with the help of some very fine amateur actors and actresses among their friends produced many plays and even operas. It was an event long remembered, a great social success; but, more than that, it accomplished what it was intended for—the helping of the poor.

But the apparent frivolity of the theatricals did not take her mind from serious thoughts. Religion, after all, was the principal thing in her life, and it is no surprise to find her at this time enthusing over the spirit of faith in Rome, and to see her making spiritual retreats, withdrawing for a time from the world to give herself wholly to thoughts about eternity. Hers was a great soul that could act in a comedy one moment, and then retire to prayer. She loved the *Imitation of Christ,* and even ascetic and mystical theology. It was this spirit of faith that made her such a dear friend of Lady Fullerton, who was in so many ways like Mrs. Craven. Their ideals were the same, and it was a delight for Mrs. Craven to visit the woman whose life she afterwards wrote so well.

So we find her writing in her journal, one day, after reading a certain book: "I know not what will come of all this. Nothing, perhaps. Nothing! Great God, that is impossible! I shall have seen and heard and tasted all this, and make no further steps along the path Thy grace has shown me? It may be so, for so it has been a thousand times with me. Ah! that, indeed, is to be feared, and grieves me, and there is naught else in the world that can be feared. I should never again feel sorrow or alarm if I could be, and know that I was, faithful. But such as I am, it is no wonder that I am trembling and troubled, and that I live uneasily between earth's delights, which no longer please me, or are not for me, and that heavenly peace which I have not known how to attain."

It was the cry of a soul dissatisfied with itself. It was more so when she again came in contact with Madame Swetchine, and saw the deep religion of that great woman. But it stirred up Mrs. Craven to new and practical efforts after perfection. She is not content with general aspirations, but comes down to particulars, and makes the practical resolution to get up early, a thing that had always been hard for her to do. It is such little things as this that show her wish to correct her life.

We find her at this time writing out her meditations, a practice she continued for years.

It would be an endless task to follow her through

all her journal, quoting her references to the state of her soul. As in all spiritual journals, there must be a similarity, for it is the same old striving day after day. But the thing that does not appear in her journal is the good that she did to others. Her example, her spirit of faith, must have had a lasting effect upon the many friends she met. She was so proud of her faith, so grateful to God for the gift.

And with that there went a great charity. With one of the priests she had planned the establishment in Naples of an infant asylum in each quarter of the city, to be managed by the Sisters of Charity, but the plan fell through, as the city was afraid of being considered too clerical if it accepted the services of the Sisters; and so, at her own expense, she established a crèche, which proved so efficient that after a time the city withdrew its objections and the other asylums were established. Not only did she give her money to charity, but she gave what was of greater value— her energy and her intelligence. When, in 1861, many of the monasteries were suppressed, she used her influence to have some of them exempted.

All the while she was working at her writing. She had been laboring at her famous *Sister's Story* for many years, ever since the death of those loved ones whose biography it is; and finally it was published in 1865. In a few months it went through nine editions, creating a furore. As one critic wrote of it, "Never was there a more human book." It was the story of great Catholic hearts written by a great

Catholic heart. No greater tribute could be paid to it than the fact that it was crowned by the French Academy.

But it was not for literary fame she had toiled over it. Her introductory words show that. "O my God," she writes, "Thy Name is the first written as I begin this book. I desire that it may move men to love those remembered in it; but far more earnestly I desire that it may enkindle love for Thee."

With great literary fame there also came a season of trouble. Her brother Charles died that year, her husband met with great financial losses, and they had to part with their home in Naples, where they had been so happy. And so they removed to Paris.

She soon published her novel, *Anne Severin,* which went through many editions on account of the furore which the *Sister's Story* had created. And then appeared, after short intervals, *Fleurange* and *Le Mot d'Enigme.* We need not enter into a discussion of the literature produced by Mrs. Craven. Her works were artistic, and were always sure of their audience, in France, in England, in Italy, in America. She had the highest purpose in writing them. To see the amount of literary work she accomplished is to marvel, especially when one remembers her as the *grande dame* of the world, the lady of the salon, the woman who was interested in politics, charity, everything; and, above all, the woman who was at heart a recluse. It was no easy task for her, especially when one sees the financial difficulties she faced, and when one

knows that she had even to sell her diamonds at a big
sacrifice so that she should avoid being in debt. The
more we read about her the more we admire the religion that created such a woman. As the years went
on, and the income from her writings was not sufficient, she had to part with her pictures and with many
other objects of art. And yet she did not worry about
it. Her heart, after all, was not attached to the things
of earth.

As Fanny Kemble wrote after the death of Mrs.
Craven, "She was a most sincere, devout Roman
Catholic. Her books were written under a strong religious feeling, and with the desire of influencing persons who thought differently from her on religious
questions. The beauties and support of her belief
were so real to her that her great wish was to make
others see and feel them as she did."

It was that same spirit of faith that made her accept her trials. She wrote in 1880, when she was
seventy-two: "To-day my renunciation of the world
is at once voluntary and imperative. I only reappear
in it when it is a duty, and I always undergo in it a
sense of humiliation, and I have for a long time given
up going to the theatre, which is so far different from
other pleasures that one can enjoy a play at every age.
Who knows if I might not have kept up these worldly
habits if there had been no change in my fate? When
I think of this, I bless our ruin and all the suffering
and trouble which followed and which yet accompany it. It is certain that it helped me to break my

last ties with the world, as without our losses I know not if I should have had the courage to do so. It was good for me to be crushed by the cruelest impressions—impressions calculated to crucify my self-love; good for me that my futile tastes, not less than my pride, have been continuously and usefully mortified."

In 1884 Mr. Craven died. It was the last link with the world. They had been married for more than fifty years, a tenderly devoted couple. Nothing is more affecting than her description of his last illness and death. When he was laid away it was with difficulty she took up the thread of her life again.

But hers was not a nature to pause until the final rest. She went at life again. She still wrote, still kept up her correspondence with her friends, still was interested in all that concerned the welfare of the Church she so loved. So it went on till the end.

She was eighty-three years old when the summons came. But it was only through the greatest suffering that she passed to her reward. She was stricken, and lay helpless, not being able even to speak for a year. She died on April 1, 1891.

"When she was told that she was about to receive the last sacraments," writes one of her biographers, "those around her heard, in token of her acquiescence, her soft murmur, which was habitual, change to a sudden cry of joy. When the sacred Host was brought to her, her body, which had been almost entirely inert, sought to rise, and her eyes lightened with a last flame. After that, all for her was finished. A few hours later, peacefully and without struggle, she re-joined in the bosom of God those good and delightful souls of whom she had told the story and immortalized the memory. During her long career she had lived the life of the world, the life of letters, and the Christian life, and in each of these three very differing lives she had equally excelled. Hers is a rare and perhaps an inimitable example of the supernatural harmony which can blend in one perfection the beauty of natural gifts, of the intellectual powers and of the spiritual being."

The year after her death the Abbé Mugnier said of her in a lecture to his students: "When in after times the Christian apologists of the day are counted, it will doubtless be found that it was a simple woman, without pretensions to theological learning, who best knew how to raise an imperishable monument to her faith, and hers were the passing and delicate materials of smiles, of kisses, and of tears."

Pauline Craven surely is a great model. She was a noble wife through fifty years. Never blessed with children of her own, she was, nevertheless, truly a mother of souls, a guide to the throne of God.

SOME LITERARY WIVES AND MOTHERS

THERE are many ways of serving God. Every one has his special talent to be employed in sanctifying his own soul and in helping to build the Kingdom of Christ on earth. One has one vocation; another has another. Not all are called to enter the cloister. There have been queens whose vocation it was to be queens, who used their royal position to further the interests of the Church.

And so in the history of Catholic womanhood we find a wonderful variety of service. There have been women who were raised up to do great works of charity, like Fabiola, who established the first hospital in the history of the world; to give womanhood and motherhood an example of loyalty to the faith even unto death, like Margaret Clitherow; to establish religious communities, like St. Jane Frances de Chantal; to be an example of sanctity in the humble home, like Anna Maria Taigi. In every department the wife and mother has been chosen by God to help in His work.

Not the least among the wives and mothers who devoted themselves to the service of the true faith are the women who used their literary talent for the cause. Many of them deserve particular notice. There is, indeed, nothing new in this kind of serv-

ice. Almost from the beginning of the Church, we
find Catholic women interested in the pursuit of learning and in the cultivation of letters as means to spread
the faith. The great intellectual giant, St. Augustine,
did not think it a condescension to discuss philosophical matters with his mother, or to write to Proba. St.
Jerome was not above allowing the widow Paula to
help him in his scriptural studies. It may be said that
Paula established the first women's college. When St.
Jerome came to Rome, it was in her house he found
lodgings, to which she begged him to come in order
that she and her family might be under his spiritual
direction. In her house the Roman ladies used to
meet in order to listen to St. Jerome read from the
Scriptures, and so earnest did they become that he
tells us that some of them wrote in Hebrew as perfectly as in Greek and Latin.

It was so, too, with the wealthy widow Proba, who
was our first Catholic woman poet. Even before her
conversion to the faith, she had written an epic cele-
brating the wars between Constantine and Maxentius,
a poem now lost. After her conversion she wrote a
long sacred poem dealing with the chief events of the
Old Testament, and with the life of Christ according
to the Gospels. The poem is of interest now only as
a literary curiosity, yet it served its purpose at the
time in bringing the knowledge of the Gospel to
others who otherwise might never have known it.
Even as late as the middle ages it enjoyed popularity;
but whatever its merit, we owe a tribute to the woman

who wrote it, the woman of fabulous fortune, of highest social position, who used her literary talent and all that she had to glorify God.

So has it been through all the ages. If we were dealing with the history of woman in education, we would see what a great part she played in the institutions of learning. Sometimes we hear about the modern educational advantages of women; but these advantages are not modern, not new. Hand in hand with religion there has always been science. Woman has enjoyed these advantages. We have instances of women holding the most learned chairs in the great universities. Not only that: even women in the home, while they considered literature and learning as but their secondary duties, were eager to cultivate their minds. We recall the admiration of the learned Erasmus for the literary attainments of Margaret Roper, daughter of Sir Thomas More. Her knowledge of Latin astounded him. She and her sisters enjoyed a European reputation, and yet they were but simple, home-loving, pious Catholic women. So learned were they that once, in the royal presence of Henry VIII, they held a public philosophical disputation.

But the list of professional writers, as we may call them, among our Catholic wives and mothers may be said to begin with the Italian poet, Vittoria Colonna, the most celebrated woman poet of Italy (1490-1547).

She lived at the time of the Renaissance, and was one of its brightest jewels. It was a time famous for its women, as for everything else. "They come before us," says a certain writer, "adorned with that wonderful fifteenth-century teaching of which we, in these days when education is our most popular fetish, have no adequate conception, because we do not choose to cast our eyes back on the nobler past and see what it has to teach us. It is pitiful to hear women exult in the liberal training now provided for them, and yet to know that the curriculum of the high school, chiefly directed to the passing of examinations, would have been absolute intellectual starvation to the women of five centuries ago." Women in those days were highly educated, highly cultured, accomplished in many ways. To know what society was learning in those days, and then to listen to assertions about the glorious educational advantages of the Reformation, is to laugh.

A great representative of the womanhood of her time is Vittoria Colonna. She had beauty, birth, talent, culture, piety; and she holds a prominent place in the history, the art, the religion, and the literature of her day.

She was a daughter of one of the great Roman houses, the Colonna, a family celebrated and powerful, which had given a pope and many cardinals to the Church, and many famous generals, statesmen, and scholars to the world. Her father was Fabrizio Colonna, high constable of Naples, a man who played an important part in his day, and her mother was the younger daughter of the Duke of Urbino. She was born in the castle of the Colonnas at Marino.

We know very little about her early years. It was a time of political struggle and warfare. At the age of four she was betrothed to a boy of the same age, Fernando d'Avalos, son of the Marchese de Pescara, descendant of the noblest Spanish and Neapolitan families. The marriage took place in 1509, when they were both nineteen years of age. In those days they were very happy together; life looked bright, they had intellectual tastes in common, and they were young and rich. Great rejoicings were held in their honor at Naples, and they settled down in a villa on Monte Sant' Ermo.

Vittoria enjoyed two years of happiness, but after that her life was like a widowhood, for from that time till her husband's death in 1525 they were hardly ever together, owing to the fact that the Marchese was a soldier, and by the necessity of the warlike times was in the camp rather than at home. Vittoria's father was second in command of the Spanish army in Italy assisting the Pope against the French, and the Marchese went to join him as commander of the light-armed cavalry. He was a brave soldier, occupied high posts, and was popular with the army. Happy to serve her country, Vittoria willingly allowed him to depart, and remained at home herself, where, having no children of her own, she spent her time in looking after the education of her husband's young orphaned cousin, who became like her own child.

The spirit of this woman is shown in her loyalty to her husband's honor. After one of the great battles in which he was victor, he became involved in a conspiracy, and was offered the crown of Naples if he turned against the Emperor. But she dissuaded him from his treason, preferring to sacrifice a crown rather than gain it by dishonor. There was no Lady Macbeth ambition in her. She declared that she preferred to die the wife of a most brave marquis and a most upright general than to live the consort of a king dishonored with any stain of infamy. It was a decision that did honor to the heart of a great Catholic woman.

The Marchese was finally wounded seriously at the battle of Pavia. He sent for his wife, but died before she could reach him, while yet a young man, only thirty-six. When she heard of his death, she fell from her horse and remained in a state of unconsciousness for two hours. So great was her sorrow that she begged to be taken to a convent and given a nun's habit. She lay on the ground and could not be induced to eat. Her brother came to her assistance, and brought her to Rome, and there she went to live in the Convent of San Silvestro, where an ancestor of hers, the Blessed Margherita Colonna, was buried. She was grief-stricken over the loss of the man she so loved. It was, indeed, her grief that turned her attention to literature, since most of her poetry was written as a tribute to his memory. In her writing she found a solace for her woes. At that time her one idea was to enter the religious life, for religion was the very key-note of her life. But God had other work for her to do. The glory of the life of the world was gone for her, buried in the grave with her husband. She might have lived the life of a great lady on her estates, she might have married again, and married well, but none of these things had any attraction for her. Henceforth she lived in convent after convent, leading a life of almost monastic simplicity, her food and her dress of the simplest. With that simplicity went a great love for the poor. Indeed, she became as one of the poor herself.

Yet at the same time she kept up her association with the world, and was interested in things spiritual and intellectual. She was blessed in her friends, and they in her. Who knows what her influence was in those trying days for the Church! Among her friends were Pietro Bembo, Michelangelo, and other great men of the age, with whom she labored for the reformation of the evils that had fallen on the Church. One of her greatest friends in her last years was Cardinal Pole, to whom she declared that she owed the salvation of her soul, since he guided her at the time she was almost led astray by the new doctrines of the Reformation.

She was adored by her own relations. It has been said of her: "She was indeed a woman to be proud of, untouched by scandal, unspoiled by praise, incapable of any ungenerous action, unconvicted of one uncharitable word. Living in the midst of such religious and political dissension as divided and uprooted families, she yet preserved in all relations of life that jewel of perfect loyalty which does not ask to be justified."

It was this sentiment of loyalty, no doubt, that drew from her heart her first poems in memory of her husband, which were the means of drawing to her the great friends that made her so famous, and which showed what a true woman she was. The history of her friends is the history of the Renaissance. Any woman who could inspire the friendship of such men as Michelangelo and Cardinal Pole must have been a great woman. The one thing that explains it is the deep religion of them all; that was the bond, more than talent and art. When she died, Michelangelo was for a long time overcome with grief.

Her later poetry was almost entirely religious. In it she showed her great spirit of faith, especially in her chief poem, the *Triumph of Christ*. This was because her life was full of faith and piety. She even wore herself to a shadow by her mortifications.

Vittoria was a great religious poet because she followed the life of the Cross. Her faith is seen in one of the prayers she composed: "Grant, I beseech Thee, O Lord, that I may always adore Thee with that abasement of soul which befits my humbleness, and with that exaltation of mind which Thy Majesty demands, and let me ever live in the fear which Thy justice inspires and in the hope which Thy mercy allows, and submit to Thee as Almighty, yield myself to Thee as All-wise, and turn to Thee as to supreme Perfection and Goodness. I beseech Thee, most tender Father, that Thy most loving fire may purify me, that Thy most clear light may illumine me, and that Thy most pure love may so avail me that, without let or hindrance of mortal things, I may return to Thee in happiness and security."

When she was about to die—Michelangelo was with her at the time—she made a will giving a large sum to charity, and requesting that she be buried among the nuns. She died in 1547.

Whatever may be thought of her poetry, it is certain that Vittoria Colonna will endure as an example of true Christian virtue, a type of the Christian widow who devoted all she had, all she was, to the service of God and the help of souls.

A woman who occupies a high place in the world of letters on account of her correspondence, which is but an expression of her maternal devotion, is Madame de Sévigné. Lamartine, on account of her devotion to her daughter, has placed her among the great civilizers of the world. Yet, classic as her mother-letters have become, it is rather as a woman of virtue amid examples of vice that she makes her greatest appeal to us. Madame de Sévigné would be of interest if only for the fact that she was the granddaughter of the famous St. Jane Frances de Chantal.

We recall that when St. Jane was leaving her home, in order to take up the work to which God called her, her son, then a mere boy, threw himself across the threshold and weepingly implored her to remain with him; but not even that appeal of affection could turn her from the call of God. This boy grew up into a handsome, reckless, accomplished, but devout man, afraid of nothing. He became the Baron de Chantal, and married Marie de Coulanges, a pious and gentle girl, who was very wealthy. He died in battle at the age of thirty-one, leaving his heart-broken widow and an only child, who afterwards became the celebrated Madame de Sévigné. The young widow died shortly afterwards, and the little girl was placed under the care of her uncle, her mother's brother, the Abbé de Coulanges, whom the child grew to love and with whom she was associated for more than fifty years. The Abbé returned her love, and saw to it that she received a fine education. Besides her native French, she knew Latin, Italian, and Spanish. The Abbé was a man of piety and learning, so one can imagine the kind of instruction he gave his niece.

When she was fifteen (she was born in 1626), she was introduced to Parisian society. Learned and modest, wealthy and beautiful, she created a real sensation. She had many fine offers, but set them all aside in order to marry the young Marquis de Sévigné, handsome, dashing, courageous, the kind that appeals to a romantic girl. He was selfish and sensual, but she loved him devotedly even though he was not really in love with her. He had a good position at court. It was a brilliant, dazzling world at the time, and the handsome young couple found an immediate welcome into it. Bossuet, Corneille, and other famous men belonged to the society of her day. Everywhere there were wits, orators, writers. And everywhere, too, there was vice. She found herself in a society composed of pedants—it was the time of the *précieuses,* or "blue-stockings"—and gay livers.

Yet in spite of the surrounding vice, nothing ever sullied her fair name. She was deeply in love with her husband, even though he was unworthy of that love. But her heart soon began to be heavy, for she discovered that the man she loved was faithless to her; he even told her openly that he could not love her, adding insult to injury. In order to reclaim him she persuaded him to retire with her to their estate in Brittany. It was a sacrifice for her to leave the gay world of Paris and bury herself among rustics, but she made it gladly in the hope of winning his love. She was twenty, and he twenty-four. There they passed three years, and there her two children, a son and a daughter, were born.

When the civil war of the Fronde broke out, the Marquis was recalled to Paris. It meant new slights, new insults for her on the part of the inconstant husband. He dissipated his fortune, and at last she was driven to get a separation from him, and went into retirement, a disillusioned woman.

Here she received the news that he had been killed

in a duel over an unworthy love affair. She was now a widow at twenty-three, grief-stricken after the husband she had always loved in spite of his wickedness and his squandering of her fortune. These years she devoted to the education of her children, and finally, after an absence of four or five years, as beautiful as ever, she returned to Paris society. It was the age of Corneille, Racine, Molière, La Fontaine, and Boileau, and it was a tribute to her that she was sought by everybody for her learning, her wit, her beauty, and her common sense. She was soon besieged by many suitors, some of them of princely rank, but she refused them all. She lived at court and numbered the highest ladies as her friends, but her heart was centered in her children, and especially in her daughter, who was soon famous as "the prettiest girl in France." The daughter was finally married to the Comte de Grignan, a man of good reputation and fine family. It was this marriage that was the occasion of the letters which have made Madame de Sévigné a classic in French literature.

The Comte de Grignan was obliged to live in the south of France, and this meant the separation of the mother and daughter. The mother idolized her daughter; she could not become accustomed to the separation, and bore it only because she had to. One cannot help contrasting this kind of affection with that of her grandmother, St. Jane, who could even step over the prostrate body of her son in order to enter religion.

Madame de Sévigné wrote to her daughter three
or four times a week, sometimes twice a day, for
twenty-seven years. She actually lived for her child
with a love that has rarely been paralleled. It filled
her life in place of many unworthy things that might
have come to a grand lady of the salon whose house
was the center of a gay world. Nor is it surprising
to know that while she was always a pious woman, she
became particularly devout in her later years, a worthy
descendant of a great saint.

When her beloved daughter was taken ill, Madame
de Sévigné went to Provence to nurse her. She
was then, 1696, nearly seventy years of age, and it
was winter. Night and day for three months she
tended her, and then she herself was seized with the
smallpox and died. Her letters are still regarded as
the most charming in existence, surely a tribute to
the mother-love that inspired them.

One biographer thus describes her: "A French woman with none of the vices and little of the frivolity
of French women, a true Louis-Quatorzienne without
the prejudices of that reign, a woman of society and
one of its leaders, yet a prodigy of domestic affection,
a frequenter of the court but a lover of the fields, a
wit without attempting it, and a great writer without
knowing it, Marie de Sévigné has justly won the admiration of every great man who appreciates wit
and honors virtue."

One always thinks kindly of the grand lady, the

afflicted wife, and the devoted mother, the grand-daughter of St. Jane Frances de Chantal.

The influence which Madame Swetchine had on her circle is similar to that which Vittoria Colonna had on hers.

She was born Anne Sophie Soymonoff, at Moscow, in 1782, where her father was then private secretary to the Empress Catherine II. Both her father and mother were of distinguished families, and their daughter may be said to have inherited her great talents. When Paul I came to the throne, the young Anne was appointed maid of honor to his Empress Marie, and thus grew up at court, where the family had an apartment in the imperial palace at St. Petersburg, and where she received all the advantages a young girl could receive. Her father was a grave and learned man, and, noting the talent of the child, gave her a fine education in everything but religion. She was taught music and drawing, and at fourteen she knew Russian, English, Italian, French, German, and, moreover, was studying Latin, Greek, and Hebrew—rather a big program for a girl of her age. Later on she developed a remarkable voice and used to accompany herself on the piano with great skill. She was evidently of extraordinary talent.

At that time politics were uncertain, and the country was in an unsettled condition; in order, therefore, that she might have a protector, the father arranged a marriage between her and General Swetchine. He was forty-two, and she seventeen. Soon after the marriage her father was dismissed from St. Petersburg and returned to Moscow, where he died suddenly. It was Madame Swetchine's first trial, and it drew from her her first real prayer.

General Swetchine was a man of fine character. It is told of him that once he was entrusted by the Emperor to execute a sentence which was barbarous and unjust upon a colonel of the Russian army. The General went to the square where the man was waiting and told him that he had been reprieved, gave him back his sword, and commanded him to leave Russia at once. Then he returned to Paul's apartment and said to him: "Sire, here is my head. I have not fulfilled your Majesty's command. Colonel —— is free. I have restored to him honor and life. Take mine instead." The Emperor was furious, but finally forgave the General. Later, however, he fell into disgrace, and retired to his country estates with his wife, where she read everything she could lay her hands on until she became one of the most educated and intellectual women of the age.

At her salon all the great men of international reputation could be found, for after the accession of Alexander she returned to St. Petersburg. During the sorrow she had experienced at the death of her father she had become very religious, even though she was still a member of the Greek Church. But in that brilliant society there were many French émigrés, some of whom had been given places of trust. Several of the eminent French clergy were there, with some Jesuits, all of whom were having a silent influence upon her. Her salon was the center of culture. Among those who had an influence upon her was the Comte de Maistre, whose strong Catholic faith appealed to her. In 1811 the General returned to active service against the French. All the while she kept up her studies, and at last she was led to a consideration of the claims of the Catholic Church. She retired to the country to think out the matter for herself. During all that autumn and winter she read history and dogma, going through great tomes that would have daunted another. She was sincere in her search for the truth, and copied out whole books, one might say libraries.

The Princess Galitzin had become a Catholic in the meantime, and was praying for the conversion of her friend Madame Swetchine. At last the light came, and she also made her submission to the Church. She was at the time thirty-three years of age. It was an act that required a great deal of courage, for it was a time when Catholics were suspected at court. But Madame Swetchine did not mince matters. She was a Catholic through and through, and openly professed her change of faith. The Jesuits were proscribed at that time, and this injustice made her so indignant that she came to their aid financially and even pleaded for them before the court. She had great influence with the Emperor, and this, as well as her conversion, aroused the resentment of the bigots against her. Finally things became so unbearable through the plots set on foot against the General that they decided to leave Russia. They went to Paris, where they remained for six months, and then returned to Russia for a year. But she found the prejudice so bitter against the Catholic Church that they finally left Russia for good and made their home in Paris.

Her home became one of the most attractive centers of Paris society. Here congregated all the learning and piety of the great capital. She was then, as always, a fascinating woman, and drew people to her by her boundless power of sympathy. Even the women idolized her. She liked studies of the heaviest kind, yet she also liked to have young and pretty women about her. The young girls used to come to her to show her their dresses on the way to the ball, and afterwards with their griefs to ask her advice. She knew how to advise, and could give ear to the griefs of others.

At the time of the Revolution of 1830 there arose the question of the relations of the Church to the new government. It was then that a group of young men arose to proclaim the entire freedom of the Church. It was the famous group of "L'Avenir." One of the leading spirits of the movement was the famous Father Lacordaire, who was introduced to Madame Swetchine by Montalembert. This great woman and fervent Catholic soon saw in him, says Montalembert, a son of predilection, and "concentrated on his head, already storm-beaten in spite of his youthfulness, all the force of tender solicitude and close sympathy which her noble, upright soul contained. For a quarter of a century she continued to be the guide, the counselor, and the healer of his struggling, agitated temperament, which grew calm and self-possessed beneath her softening influence. Nothing ever marred the blessed union of those two hearts, of that mother and son, who were so worthy of each other; a union so characteristically defined by Lacordaire when he said, 'I never met any one with such a thoroughly bold spirit of freedom confined within so solid a faith.' "

The great sermons which he preached in Notre Dame were due to her inspiration. She used to go there to listen to him, and sat behind a column, where she was pointed out by those who did not know her as his mother. Lacordaire says of her: "Madame Swetchine received me with a friendliness quite unlike the ordinary world's ways, and I soon grew accustomed to tell her all my troubles, my anxieties and plans. She used to enter into them as though I were her son, and her door was open to me even at those times when she rarely received her most intimate friends. What could have led her to devote her time and counsels to me? Doubtless some hidden sympathy moved her at first; but if I am not mistaken, she was confirmed in the course by the consciousness of having a mission to fulfil in me. She saw me surrounded by dangers, guided so far by my own inspirations, without worldly experience, without

other compass to steer by than my own pure inten-
tions, and she felt that in becoming a second Providence to me she was doing God's work. From that
day, in truth, I never made any decision without dis-
cussing it with her, and I owe it to her that I have
stood at the edge of many a precipice without falling
over." So great was her interest in the work he had
been raised up to accomplish that knowing how limited were his means, she tried to persuade him to
come and live at her house, an invitation which he,
however, declined.

And all the time she had her own share of trials.
Her adopted daughter, whom she so loved, had died,
an affliction soon followed by the death of her brother-
in-law. Then her sister, to whom she was so greatly
attached, settled in Moscow, a separation which came
hard to Madame Swetchine. But all these trials
brought her closer to God. Her life became even
austere.

Every day she went to Mass in the parish church,
and at other times found her chief refuge in her
chapel, where she spent her time almost continually
in meditation and prayer. With that devotion went
a great charity; she visited the poor in their homes,
cared for the children, and interested herself in the
institutions of charity, and all with an entire absence
of ostentation.

The General died suddenly at the age of ninety-
two. They had ever been a devoted, loving couple,
and she was heart-broken at the loss. But again

the sorrow only drew her nearer God. After his death she gradually grew weaker. In fact, she had been a sufferer for thirty years, enduring pain every day, scarcely ever sleeping through nights of agony. Yet that suffering never lessened her interest in those she could help. Even to the end she continued her self-examination. To one of her friends, who told her she was going to pray for her, she said: "Thank you, my good friend, thank you; but do not ask God for one day more or one pang less." "For many years," she once said, "my real and, I might almost say, my only trouble has been when I have not known or have failed to comprehend God's will in regard to me. However, I have all trust in His mercy; and in my present state trust seems my only means of glorifying Him."

When Lacordaire heard of her serious illness he hastened to her, and spent six days in constant attendance upon her. She was gradually growing weaker, but nothing interfered with her piety, daily Mass, frequent Communion, and meditation, sometimes of hours, in the chapel. He celebrated Mass several times for her and gave her Communion. He was not with her when she died, although many of her last thoughts and words were of him. It was like the friendship of Jerome and Paula, as Lacordaire himself said. After her death he wrote of her: "Hers was a first-rate intellect, and her heart was full of kindness, faith, devotion, and love."

And so died Madame Swetchine, one of the great-

est women that ever lived. Her fame is enduring,
even though she never had a thought for it. She
always sought to hide her private life from the world.
Yet in all her humility the influence exerted by her
was extraordinary, that on Lacordaire being but an
example among many. Who can estimate the good
she did in that salon of hers, where from three to
six, and again from nine to midnight, all the distinguished men of the day gathered, among them
Chateaubriand, Cuvier, Cousin, Tocqueville, and many
others. She was full of faith, almost a mystic, and
her spirit radiated holiness to all who came in contact with her. With her, all was the faith.

"My faith," she said, "is to me what Benjamin
was to Rachel, the child of my sorrow." Yet more
than that, the child of her joy. She was all that de
Maistre described her when, at the time she first came
to Paris, he wrote thus to one of his friends: "In
a short time you will see at Paris a Russian lady
whom I especially commend to you. Never will you
see such moral strength, wit, and learning joined to
such goodness.".

Hers was an influence that has been felt even by
those not of the faith for which she sacrificed so much.
The Protestant who wrote the preface of her *Life*,
written by her friend Falloux, pays her a glowing
tribute. "As a character," says he, "Madame
Swetchine must henceforth hold a front place among
the most powerful, original, pure, and fascinating re-
vealed in all history. The combination in her of

natural force, intense passion, acquired knowledge, resignation, and repose is truly wonderful. The picture of her steady progress from the perturbations of earthly and personal desires towards the perfection of saintly virtue and peace is charming in its portrayal and divine in its significance. . . . The character and life of Madame Swetchine, her lonely studies and aspirations, her sublime personal attainments, her philanthropic labors, her literary productions, her sweet social charm and vast influence, her thrice-royal friendships with kings and geniuses and saints, the sober raptures of her religious faith and fruition, form an example whose exciting and edifying interest and value are scarcely surpassed in the annals of her sex." Catholic womanhood may well be proud of having produced Madame Swetchine.

Coming down almost to our own day, we find in the life of Countess Ida Hahn-Hahn an instance of a wife and mother who nobly answered the call of God, and in doing it sacrificed much of that fame which the world holds so dear. Born in 1805, she was descended from a family that was at one time the wealthiest and the most illustrious of the Mecklenburg nobility. Her father had squandered his fortune upon the theater, for which he had a passion, and finally had to be placed under a guardian. Her parents were both Protestants, and she was brought up in a slipshod manner, receiving very little education. At twenty-one she married her cousin, Count von Hahn. It was an unhappy marriage. There was no love between them, and after three years the marriage ended in the divorce court, leaving her with an only child, mentally and physically deformed, and hence a constant source of anxiety to her. After the divorce she went to live with her mother, but soon left home and traveled nearly all over the world. Those twenty years of her life from 1829 to 1849 were far from edifying, and her reputation was not above suspicion. But one day the grace of God filled her. She opened her Bible at random and read the words in Isaias lx, 1: "Arise, be enlightened, O Jerusalem, for thy light is come, and the glory of the Lord is risen upon thee." She took that as the voice of God to her soul, communed with herself and prayed, and after several months determined to become a Catholic. On account of her previous reputation she was made to undergo a severe test before being admitted to the Church, but at length was baptized by Bishop von Ketteler in 1850. She then went to live with the Sisters of the Good Shepherd at Mainz, where she had helped in the establishment of a convent almost at her own expense.

It was one of the most notable conversions of the time, for the Countess Hahn-Hahn had already acquired a position as a writer. But of that fame she made little. She even condemned her previous books, an act which required more courage than one can suppose. It was the destruction of the labor of years, and only a hero could submit to such a sacrifice. But the act was only in keeping with her faith. To her the faith she had received was everything. To that she now devoted her talent, and for the last thirty years of her life, filled as they were with great piety, she wrote nothing but books with a high purpose, trying in that way to help the cause of the Church and to atone for what she considered the sins of her pen before she had seen the light.

It would be an endless task to give even the names of the books written by her. She was a tireless worker, and her output was enormous. It is a marvel how she accomplished so much, for she was often a great sufferer. The only explanation of her accomplishments is her zeal for the faith. She died in 1880, at the age of seventy-five, a wife and mother who was above all a loyal Catholic to whom no sacrifice was too great if it could help to sanctify her soul.

In previous papers we have studied the character and work of Mrs. Craven and Lady Georgiana Fullerton, and there is no need to review their lives here. One of their contemporaries was Lady Herbert of Lea, a convert, who gave her great literary talent to the service of the Church. When she was received into the Church, Lady Fullerton wrote to her as follows:

"MY DEAR LADY HERBERT:

"As you sent me a kind message by Lady Londonderry, I venture to write and tell you with what sincere joy and gratitude to God I heard of your being actually received into His Church, to which you have long been in heart devoted. I have now been just nineteen years a Catholic, and have never ceased to wonder with an adoring heart at the infinite mercy of God in bestowing on one so unworthy as myself that blessed gift of faith not vouchsafed to so many who would make a better use of it. You have a great part of life before you, and He who has called you into His Church will, I trust, give you many years to work for Him and to bring many others to the faith. It gave me great pleasure to hear that you were affiliated to the Sisters of St. Vincent de Paul. So have I been for the last three years, and I am happy to think we shall have a common object of interest. I suppose you have to look to many trials and many heartaches in consequence of your conversion, but I doubt not that strength and courage will be given you to bear whatever cross it may please our Blessed Lord to lay upon you. May such crosses be lightened and sweetened by heavenly consolations! Believe me, I may venture to say so now, when, although we have not very often met, we are linked by the same faith."

With these women it was always the faith! Lady Fullerton's prophecy was fulfilled. Lady Herbert did have a great many years before her in which to work for the faith she loved so well. She was born, in 1822, Elizabeth A'Court, the daughter of General A'Court, a soldier and member of Parliament. This,

together with the fact that she was the niece of Lord
Heytesbury, British ambassador at St. Petersburg,
gave her a firm place in early Victorian society. At
the age of twenty-four she married Sidney Herbert,
a brilliant young politician, the second son of the
Earl of Pembroke. She was deeply interested in all
his work, especially when he was made Secretary of
War during the Crimean campaign. She became
noted at that time for her help to Florence Nightingale. Her husband, who had been created Baron
Herbert of Lea, died in 1861, leaving her with four
sons and three daughters.

Cardinal Manning had been a friend of her husband, and it was through his influence that in 1866
she became a Catholic. She was not a half-hearted
convert. Gratitude for the gift of faith made her
a militant Catholic and in spite of her many home
duties she interested herself in all that affected the
Church. Gifted with fine ability as a writer, she gave
that talent wholly to religion, and produced numerous books, most of which were popular at the time
of their publication and are still widely read. There
is always something human in a book of Lady Herbert of Lea. Many of those books will hold a permanent place in standard Catholic literature. She died
in 1911, at the age of eighty-nine, after forty-five
years of labor, from the time of her conversion, in
the service of the Catholic Church. She was a noble
wife and mother, and a fervent Catholic.

The great work done for Catholic letters by Mrs.

Craven in France and by Lady Fullerton in England was equaled and in many ways surpassed by Mrs. Sadlier in America. Her whole life was given to the cause of Catholic literature. The very magnitude of her work is astounding. From her pen came more than sixty volumes, besides all the journalistic work she did, and all of this was done with the highest purpose, not for literary fame, but to serve the Church at a time when it needed just such service as she could give.

The Catholic Church in the United States and Canada owes a great deal to this woman, who helped to preserve the faith in many at a time when they endured great temptations. To-day we cannot pick up an old book of hers without thinking of the Catholic immigrants who were made prouder of their faith by her stories. She was born Mary Anne Madden, in County Cavan, Ireland, in 1820. Her father was a merchant, and of the old Irish school of book-loving people. In the beginning it was his encouragement that kept her writing. Even as a girl she had some of her work published in a London magazine. When the father died in 1844 she went to Montreal, where, two years later, at the age of twenty-six, she married James Sadlier, of the celebrated firm of that name which has done so much for Catholic letters. For fourteen years she lived there, writing continually, until her name soon became a household word in Catholic families. After that the family came to New York City, where, besides the publishing business, they owned a weekly paper, *The Tablet,* for which she wrote editorials as well as stories. Her husband died nine years later, and a few years after that she returned to Montreal, where she lived until her death, in 1903, at the age of eighty-three.

It was an uneventful life as far as external events are concerned, but it was a life of labor, a life of service for others. Not only was she a woman of strong faith herself, but a woman who knew the need of helping others to keep their faith. One could not write the history of the glories of the Catholic Church in the United States without giving a high place to this great pioneer, Mrs. Sadlier.

Another woman in this country who gave herself unsparingly to the cause of Catholic letters was Mrs. Dorsey. She was born at Georgetown, D. C., in 1815, the daughter of a minister, the Rev. William McKenney, a chaplain in the navy. In 1837 she was married to Lorenzo Dorsey. Three years later she became a convert to the Church, and from that time on for more than fifty years she devoted her life to writing Catholic fiction. Her name is a classic in Catholic literature. God had evidently raised her up for the work in which she excelled. She had four children, a son who was killed in the Civil War, and three daughters who survived her. She died in 1896, at the age of eighty-one. Surely a great wife and mother. She had her family duties, yet she found time to serve the Church and her fellow-Catholics. Her name is a benediction among us.

The last in our list of famous wives and mothers who have served the Church by their pen is Mrs. Craigie, known in literature under her pen-name of "John Oliver Hobbes." She was born Pearl Richards in Quincy, Mass., in 1867, of an old family of Colonial descent. At the age of nineteen she married Reginald Walpole Craigie, an English gentleman of good family, but the marriage was unhappy and she soon obtained a divorce, or rather separation, with the custody of her child. In 1891 she published her first book, which created quite a sensation. All the while she had been studying the Catholic religion, and in 1892 was received into the Church. From that time on her work was noted for its deep religious strain. When she was at the height of her fame, with an assured place in English literature, she died suddenly of heart disease in 1906, at the age of thirty-nine.

It is a glorious line, these women who were apostles of the faith. One must marvel at them. They were wives, many of them mothers; they had their position in the world; they had talent which might have given them a high place in secular letters. But their one thought, even more than for family and fame, was the Church. They became mothers of souls, striving to bring others to God; and, surely, whatever fame they may have attained in this world is little in comparison with the undying glory they have acquired in the Kingdom of God, to which they gave their all.

ACKNOWLEDGMENT

The author does not deem it necessary to give a complete bibliography of the innumerable works consulted in the preparation of these popular papers. He wishes, however, to acknowledge his indebtedness for certain facts to the standard biographies, Butler's *Lives of the Saints,* various encyclopedias, and particularly the *Catholic Encyclopedia.*

Printed in the United States
58276LVS00001B/1-66

9 780977 616886